AMBASSADOR
TO HUMANITY

AMBASSADOR TO HUMANITY

A selection of testimonials and tributes to
'Abdu'l-Bahá

Compiled by Robert Weinberg

GEORGE RONALD
OXFORD

George Ronald, Publisher
Oxford
www.grbooks.com

A catalogue record for this book is available from the British Library

ISBN 978–0–85398–640-9

Cover design: René Steiner, Steinergraphics.com

CONTENTS

INTRODUCTION

In 1914, when the English divine Thomas Kelly Cheyne penned *The Reconciliation of Races and Religions*, he titled a section, 'Ambassador to Humanity', devoted to the life and work of 'Abdu'l-Bahá. While 'Abdu'l-Bahá had numerous appelations and honorifics bestowed upon Him – from His birth name, Abbás, through 'The Mystery of God' and 'the Master', to Sir 'Abdu'l-Bahá Abbás Effendi, KBE – 'Ambassador to Humanity' seems particularly apposite.

The word ambassador derives from the Latin *ambactus* meaning 'servant', a direct equivalent to the title He preferred for Himself – 'Abdu'l-Bahá is Arabic for 'Servant of Bahá [Glory]'. An ambassador, distinguished for their public service, is appointed by a country as its presence in another land. As Bahá'u'lláh's public-facing representative during His own lifetime, and then as His chosen successor, 'Abdu'l-Bahá's diplomatic mission was the entire planet. And just as an ambassador takes care of their nation's interests and citizens far from home, 'Abdu'l-Bahá proved Himself the friend, guide and confidant to all humanity, through His care for the poor and vulnerable in society, His participation in the discourses of the age, His Writings, and His promotion of the Bahá'í Teachings.

'Abdu'l-Bahá was born in Ṭihrán, Írán, on 23 May 1844, at the precise moment when a new era was commencing in the spiritual and social evolution of the world. 'It is significant indeed,' observed the scholar Adib Taherzadeh, 'that as the Declaration of the Báb, the Herald of Bahá'u'lláh, took place on that memorable evening, so did the birth of the Person who was destined to become the recipient of His great Revelation.'[1] Thus, a child was born Who would grow up to be the embodiment and exemplar of the new Revelation's highest aspirations for the emergence of a 'new race of men'.

Following the Ascension of Bahá'u'lláh in May 1892, 'Abdu'l-Bahá showed that He was much more than the temporal head of a religious community. Those who encountered Him recognized a character of matchless virtue, an all-embracing love and altruism, extraordinary spiritual acuity, and super-human knowledge. Indeed, His humble yet magisterial presence led some of His early Western devotees to declare Him – albeit erroneously – the human presence of Christ returned in the Glory of the Father. Quickly dispelling any notion that He was a Prophet or Divine Messenger, 'Abdu'l-Bahá emphasised that He was the representative of the Covenant of Bahá'u'lláh in their midst, tasked with preserving the unity of an emerging global religion. 'In Him and Him alone the Covenant found its expression',[2] wrote historian Hasan Balyuzí.

> No description can measure up to the theme of a life which transcended every barrier to its total fulfilment. It lies beyond the range of assessment because every event in the life of the Son of Bahá'u'lláh carries a major accent.[3]

Neither could any soul who had the honour of meeting 'Abdu'l-Bahá in life adequately convey their experience of Him or fully emulate His example, although, as this collection demonstrates, many at least tried. 'To study a man's life is to live in his presence', wrote Marzieh Gail, through his words and the words of those who saw him or who have thoughts about him; and especially it is to see him in the lives of those he has influenced. Now that His pen is stilled, His voice hushed, 'Abdu'l-Bahá's words are the Bahá'ís; they are His message to the world; His conversation with mankind; and they reflect, however tentatively at this early stage of apprenticeship in Bahá'í living, the life of 'Abdu'l-Bahá . . .[4]

Shoghi Effendi, 'Abdu'l-Bahá's grandson and Guardian of the Bahá'í Faith, explained that through the implementation of His Will and Testament, the forces released into the world by two Divine Manifestations were 'mustered and disciplined'[5] into 'institutions that will come to be regarded as the hall-mark and glory of the age we are called upon to establish and by our deeds immortalize'.[6] In our raising up and support of these institutions – and 'the extent to which our own inner life and private character mirror forth in their manifold aspects the splendour of those eternal principles proclaimed by Bahá'u'lláh'[7] – will 'Abdu'l-Bahá's desire for humanity to 'make this nether world the mirror image of Thy Paradise'[8] be realized.

As Bahá'ís and their friends around the world prepare to mark the centenary of the passing of 'Abdu'l-Bahá and the inception of the Formative Age of the Bahá'í Faith – and as the immaculate structure of His own Shrine rises on the plain between Haifa and 'Akká – it is hoped that this book will serve to increase devotion to 'Abdu'l-Bahá and aid reflection on the qualities to be emulated. It is divided into five sections.

Part I contains appreciations of 'Abdu'l-Bahá penned by Bahá'u'lláh, selections from *God Passes By* and *The Dispensation of Bahá'u'lláh* by Shoghi Effendi, and excerpts from letters of the Universal House of Justice, the elected, supreme governing authority for the Bahá'í World today. Recollections of

'Abdu'l-Bahá's life and work by His devoted sister Bahíyyih Khánum, the Greatest Holy Leaf, are also included along with 'Abdu'l-Bahá's pronouncements about His own life, His station as Centre of the Covenant, and His sufferings.

Part II brings together accounts about 'Abdu'l-Bahá during the lifetime of Bahá'u'lláh, penned by His wife and one of His daughters, as well as some early Bahá'ís and a small number of Westerners who met Him.

Part III traces the 29–year period of 'Abdu'l-Bahá's Ministry, when pilgrims from the Western world visited Him for the first time. It also encompasses the three-year period – following 'Abdu'l-Bahá's release from a lifetime of imprisonment – when He made His historic travels to Egypt and the West, His social action in Palestine during the First World War, and the activities of His final years.

Part IV presents accounts of the passing and funeral of 'Abdu'l-Bahá as well as appreciations of the importance of His Will and Testament. It also includes further tributes that assess His unique character, as well as paintings and photographs for which He sat.

Beyond the extracts from the Writings of Bahá'u'lláh, 'Abdu'l-Bahá and Bahíyyih Khánum, and the letters of Shoghi Effendi and the Universal House of Justice, most of the passages collected here are the recollections of pilgrims, writers and journalists – including those who were not believers – who came into His presence. They recorded their personal impressions of 'Abdu'l-Bahá, and their perceptions of His station, His statements, and the story of His life and the history of the Bahá'í Faith, as they heard or understood it. By their very nature, these accounts include individual opinions or speculation, employ poetic or journalistic licence, or contain factual inaccuracies. They are thus, by definition, unauthenticated remembrances, but it is hoped that readers will find value and inspiration in the rich variety of experiences these writers were able to capture. The spellings and transliterations of 'Abdu'l-Bahá and other names have been maintained from their original sources.

What it has not been possible to include in a collection of this size and scope has been an appreciation of the extraordinary range and variety of 'Abdu'l-Bahá's own Writings. These are available in other publications and online at www.library. bahai.org. Readers may feel moved to make their own personal study of His letters and treatises in which His role as the appointed interpreter of the Revelation of Bahá'u'lláh is more in evidence. To this end, study of Book 8 in the Ruhi Institute courses, *The Covenant of Bahá'u'lláh*, also offers an invaluable starting point.

This collection is not only a tribute to 'Abdu'l-Bahá. It is also a testimony to those individuals, from the humble to the celebrated – and those remembered and honoured by the Bahá'í community today yet unknown to the wider world – who were so affected by meeting the Master that their attitudes, habits and behaviours were, in so many cases, forever transformed. These souls possessed the generosity of spirit to record their experiences so that future generations of 'Abdu'l-Bahá's admirers might themselves gain an inspiring glimpse of the man, and the moments they spent in His presence. In their accounts are preserved the exemplary actions of that single soul out of all humankind, created by Bahá'u'lláh to provide the pattern of right living to all people, for all time.

This book is also an appreciation of the visionary enterprise of George Ronald Publisher – founded by David Hofman in 1943 – to provide the opportunity to Bahá'í authors to share their knowledge, their insights and their experiences. Volumes about the life and work of 'Abdu'l-Bahá have formed a significant part of George Ronald's catalogue for almost eight decades, from stories for children to scholarly and historical works. Indeed, its first two publications were David Hofman's own commentary on the *Will and Testament* of 'Abdu'l-Bahá and the memoir, *Portals to Freedom*, by Howard Colby Ives. From the exceptional literary abilities of Hands of the Cause of God Hasan Balyuzí, Horace Holley and George Townshend to marvellous writers such as Adib Taherzadeh and Marzieh Gail, George Ronald has established a priceless heritage that will, undoubtedly, educate and enlighten the minds of seekers after truth for years to come. It is an honour to offer this anthology as a humble contribution to such an enduring and important legacy.

Robert Weinberg
London, January 2021

I

TESTIMONIALS

'Abdu'l-Bahá in the Words of Bahá'u'lláh

O Thou Who art the apple of Mine eye! My glory, the ocean of My loving-kindness, the sun of My bounty, the heaven of My mercy rest upon Thee. We pray God to illumine the world through Thy knowledge and wisdom, to ordain for Thee that which will gladden Thine heart and impart consolation to Thine eyes.[1]

☙

The glory of God rest upon Thee and upon whosoever serveth Thee and circleth around Thee. Woe, great woe, betide him that opposeth and injureth Thee. Well is it with him that sweareth fealty to Thee; the fire of hell torment him who is Thine enemy.[2]

☙

We have made Thee a shelter for all mankind, a shield unto all who are in heaven and on earth, a stronghold for whosoever hath believed in God, the Incomparable, the All-Knowing. God grant that through Thee He may protect them, may enrich and sustain them, that He may inspire Thee with that which shall be a wellspring of wealth unto all created things, an ocean of bounty unto all men, and the dayspring of mercy unto all peoples.[3]

☙

Thou knowest, O my God, that I desire for Him naught except that which Thou didst desire, and have chosen Him for no purpose save that which Thou hadst intended for Him.

Render Him victorious, therefore, through Thy hosts of earth and heaven . . . Ordain, I beseech Thee, by the ardour of My love for Thee and My yearning to manifest Thy Cause, for Him, as well as for them that love Him, that which Thou hast destined for Thy Messengers and the Trustees of Thy Revelation. Verily, Thou art the Almighty, the All-Powerful.[4]

❧

From the Súriy-i-<u>Gh</u>uṣn [Súrih of the Branch] – *'a Tablet which may well be regarded as the harbinger of the rank which was to be bestowed upon Him, in the* Kitáb-i-Aqdas, *and which was to be later elucidated and confirmed in the Book of His Covenant.'*[5]

There hath branched from the Sadratu'l-Muntahá this sacred and glorious Being, this Branch of Holiness; well is it with him that hath sought His shelter and abideth beneath His shadow. Verily the Limb of the Law of God hath sprung forth from this Root which God hath firmly implanted in the Ground of His Will, and Whose Branch hath been so uplifted as to encompass the whole of creation. Magnified be He, therefore, for this sublime, this blessed, this mighty, this exalted Handiwork! Draw nigh unto Him, O people, and taste the fruits of wisdom and knowledge that have proceeded from Him Who is the Almighty, the All-Knowing. Whoso hath failed to taste thereof is deprived of God's bounty, though he partake of all that the earth can produce, could ye but perceive it! [6]

❧

Render thanks unto God, O people, for His appearance; for verily He is the most great Favour unto you, the most perfect bounty upon you; and through Him every mouldering bone is quickened. Whoso turneth towards Him hath turned towards God, and whoso turneth away from Him hath turned away from My Beauty, hath repudiated My Proof, and transgressed against Me. He is the Trust of God amongst you, His charge within you, His manifestation unto you and His appearance among His favoured servants.[7]

❧

We have sent Him down in the form of a human temple. Blest and sanctified be God Who createth whatsoever He willeth through His inviolable, His infallible decree. They who deprive themselves of the shadow of the Branch are lost in the wilderness of error, are consumed by the heat of worldly desires, and are of those who will assuredly perish.[8]

❧

The Lawḥ-i-Arḍ-i-Bá [Tablet of the Land of Bá] *was revealed by Bahá'u'lláh on the occasion of 'Abdu'l-Bahá's visit to Beirut in 1879.*

Praise be to Him Who hath honoured the Land of Bá through the presence of Him round Whom all names revolve. All the atoms of the earth have announced unto all created things that from behind the gate of the Prison-city there hath appeared and above its horizon there hath shone forth the Orb of the beauty of the great, the Most Mighty Branch of God – His ancient and immutable Mystery – proceeding on its way to another land. Sorrow, thereby, hath enveloped this Prison-city, whilst another land rejoiceth. Exalted, immeasurably exalted is our Lord, the Fashioner of the heavens and the Creator of all things, He through Whose sovereignty the doors of the prison were opened, thereby causing what was promised aforetime in the Tablets to be fulfilled. He is verily potent over what He willeth, and in His grasp is the dominion of the entire creation. He is the All-Powerful, the All-Knowing, the All-Wise.

Blessed, doubly blessed, is the ground which His footsteps have trodden, the eye that hath been cheered by the beauty of His countenance, the ear that hath been honoured by hearkening to His call, the heart that hath tasted the sweetness of His love, the breast that hath dilated through His remembrance, the pen that hath voiced His praise, the scroll that hath borne the testimony of His writings. We beseech God – blessed and exalted be He – that He may honour us with meeting Him soon. He is, in truth, the All-Hearing, the All-Powerful, He Who is ready to answer.[9]

છ

From the Kitáb-i-Aqdas [The Most Holy Book]

When the ocean of My presence hath ebbed and the Book of My Revelation is ended, turn your faces towards Him Whom God hath purposed, Who hath branched from this Ancient Root.[10]

છ

O people of the world! When the Mystic Dove will have winged its flight from its Sanctuary of Praise and sought its far-off goal, its hidden habitation, refer ye whatsoever ye understand not in the Book to Him Who hath branched from this mighty Stock.[11]

From the Kitáb-i-'Ahd [Book of the Covenant]

The Will of the divine Testator is this: It is incumbent upon the Aghṣán, the Afnán and My kindred to turn, one and all, their faces towards the Most Mighty Branch ['Abdu'l-Bahá]. Consider that which We have revealed in Our Most Holy Book: 'When the ocean of My presence hath ebbed and the Book of My Revelation is ended, turn your faces towards Him Whom God hath purposed, Who hath branched from this Ancient Root.' The object of this sacred verse is none except the Most Mighty Branch. Thus have We graciously revealed unto you Our potent Will, and I am verily the Gracious, the All-Bountiful. Verily God hath ordained the station of the Greater Branch [Mírzá Muḥammad-'Alí] to be beneath that of the Most Great Branch ['Abdu'l-Bahá]. He is in truth the Ordainer, the All-Wise. We have chosen 'the Greater' after 'the Most Great', as decreed by Him Who is the All-Knowing, the All-Informed.[12]

Words attributed to Bahá'u'lláh

Ḥájí Mírzá Ḥaydar-'Ali *in his autobiography,* Bihjatu's-Sudúr [The Delight of Hearts], *records Bahá'u'lláh's description of the services and destiny of 'Abdu'l-Bahá:*

In Baghdad We Ourselves would go and take a seat in the coffee-house to meet the people – friends and acquaintances, strangers and inquirers alike. We brought those who were remote near to the Faith, and led many a soul into the fold of the Cause. Thus We served the Cause of God, gave victory to His Word and exalted His Name. The Most Great Branch undertook the same task and served in the same way, to a much greater degree, in Adrianople, and then to a far greater extent and with greater efficacy, in 'Akká. The same hardships and afflictions which were Ours in the early days befell Him. In Baghdád We were not prisoners, and the Cause of God had not obtained even a fraction of the fame which it has gained today. At that time the number of its opponents and adversaries and ill-wishers was far less than today. In the Land of Mystery [Adrianople] We used to meet with some and let them come into Our presence. But in the Most Great Prison We do not meet the people who are not within the fold of the Cause. We have closed the doors of social intercourse. It is the Master Who has taken every trouble upon Himself. For Our sake, in order that We may have ease and comfort, He faces the world and its peoples. For Us He has become a mighty stronghold, a mighty armour. At first He rented the Mansion of Mazra'ih. We were there for a while. Then he secured for Us this Mansion of Bahjí. He has arisen with all His power to serve the Faith, and confirmation crowns His effort. This work so occupies His days and nights that He is perforce kept away from Bahjí for weeks. We consort with the Friends and reveal His [God's] Word. He, the Master, is the target and bears all hardships.

A pleasing, kindly disposition and a display of tolerance towards the people are requisites of teaching the Cause. Whatever a person says, hollow and product of vain imaginings and a parrot-like repetition of somebody else's views though it be, one ought to let it pass. One should not engage in disputation leading to and ending with obstinate refusal and hostility, because the other person would consider himself worsted and defeated. Consequently further veils intervene between him and the Cause, and he becomes more negligent of it. One ought to say: right, admitted, but look at the matter in this other way, and judge for yourself whether it is true or false; of course it should be said with courtesy, with kindliness, with consideration. Then the other person will listen, will not seek to answer back and to marshal proofs in repudiation. He will agree, because he comes to realize that the purpose has not been to engage in verbal battle and to gain mastery over him. He sees that the purpose has been to impart the word of truth, to show humanity to bring forth heavenly qualities. His eyes and his ears are opened, his heart responds, his true nature unfolds and by the grace of God, he becomes a new creation . . . The Most Great Branch gives a willing ear to any manner of senseless talk, to such an extent that the other person says to himself: He is trying to learn from me. Then, gradually, by such means as the other person cannot perceive, He gives him insight and understanding.

The force of the utterance of the Most Great Branch and His powers are not as yet fully revealed. In the future it will be seen how He, alone and unaided, shall raise the banner of the Most Great Name in the midmost heart of the world, with power and authority and Divine effulgence. It will be seen how He shall gather together the peoples of the earth under the tent of peace and concord.[13]

❦

At stated periods souls are sent to earth by the Mighty God with what we call the Power of the Great Ether. And they who possess this power can do anything; they have all power . . . Jesus Christ had this power. People thought of Him as a poor young man Whom they had crucified; but He possessed the Power of the Great Ether. Therefore He could not remain underground. This ethereal Power arose and quickened the world. And now look to the Master, for this Power is His.[14]

'Abdu'l-Bahá in His own Words

The example of 'Abdu'l-Bahá

My name is 'Abdu'l-Bahá. My qualification is 'Abdu'l-Bahá. My reality is 'Abdu'l-Bahá. My praise is 'Abdu'l-Bahá. Thraldom to the Blessed Perfection is my glorious and refulgent diadem, and servitude to all the human race my perpetual religion . . . No name, no title, no mention, no commendation have I, nor will ever have, except 'Abdu'l-Bahá. This is my longing. This is my greatest yearning. This is my eternal life. This is my everlasting glory.[1]

ↄ

My name should be confined to 'Abdu'l-Bahá in all writings. This is the collective name which will gather all the people, and it is the strong fortress and protection of the Cause of God. The beloved ones must limit themselves to this. However, ye may mention me as the Light of the Love of God, the Flame of the Guidance of God and the Banner of Peace and Harmony.[2]

ↄ

Verily, I say unto thee, that I am indeed an humble, submissive and imploring servant of God; a servant of His Beloved; a messenger of the exaltation of His Word; a spreader of His Fragrances; an extoller of the banner of love and harmony; a promoter of the greatest peace among all nations and tribes; a kindler of the fire of the love of God in the hearts of the people; a runner to the place of martyrdom in the Cause of God; a yearner for every calamity in the love of God; a longer for suspension upon the cross for the love of the beloved; a herald of the Kingdom of God among the sects of all horizons. This is my station and condition; this is my blazing crown; this is my glorious throne; because my servitude to the Holy Threshold is my brilliant light, my shining star and my drawn sword; and beside this I have no other name.[3]

❧

Look at me: I am so feeble, yet I have had the strength given me to come amongst you: a poor servant of God, who has been enabled to give you this message! I shall not be with you long! One must never consider one's own feebleness, it is the strength of the Holy Spirit of Love, which gives the power to teach. The thought of our own weakness could only bring despair.[4]

❧

Never forget this; look at one another with the eyes of perfection; look at Me, follow Me, be as I am; take no thought for yourselves or your lives, whether ye eat or whether we sleep, whether we are comfortable, whether we are well or ill, whether ye are with friends or foes, whether ye receive praise or blame; for all of these things we must care not at all. Look at Me and be as I am; ye must die to yourselves and to the world, so shall ye be born again and enter the Kingdom of Heaven. Behold a candle and how it gives its light. It weeps its life away drop by drop in order to give forth its flame of light.[5]

❧

Do you know how I administer this Faith? . . . I pull the sails of the ship firmly and fasten the ropes tight. I locate my destination and then by the power of my will I hold the wheel and head out. No matter how strong the storm, no matter how dangerous the threat to the safety of the ship, I do not change course. I do not become agitated or disheartened; I persevere until I reach my goal. If I were to hesitate or change direction at the sight of every danger, the Ark of the Cause of God would surely fail to reach its destination.[6]

The Centre of the Covenant

In accordance with the explicit text of the Kitáb-i-Aqdas Bahá'u'lláh hath made the Centre of the Covenant the Interpreter of His Word – a Covenant so firm and mighty that from the beginning of time until the present day no religious Dispensation hath produced its like.[7]

❧

I affirm that the true meaning, the real significance, the innermost secret of these verses, of these very words, is my own servitude to the sacred Threshold of the Abhá Beauty, my complete self-effacement, my utter nothingness before Him. This is my resplendent crown, my most precious adorning. On this I pride myself in the kingdom of earth and heaven. Therein I glory among the company of the well-favoured!

. . . I am according to the explicit texts of the Kitáb-i-Aqdas and the Kitáb-i-'Ahd the manifest Interpreter of the Word of God . . . Whoso deviates from my interpretation is a victim of his own fancy.[8]

❧

The Blessed Beauty is the Sun of Truth, and His light the light of truth. The Báb is likewise the Sun of Truth, and His light the light of truth . . . My station is the station of servitude – a servitude which is complete, pure and real, firmly established, enduring, obvious, explicitly revealed and subject to no interpretation whatever . . . I am the Interpreter of the Word of God; such is my interpretation.[9]

&

If on some point or other a difference ariseth among two conflicting groups, let them refer to the Centre of the Covenant for a solution to the problem.[10]

&

The purpose of the Blessed Beauty in entering into this Covenant and Testament was to gather all existent beings around one point so that the thoughtless souls, who in every cycle and generation have been the cause of dissension, may not undermine the Cause. He hath, therefore, commanded that whatever emanateth from the Centre of the Covenant is right and is under His protection and favour, while all else is error.[11]

&

Inasmuch as there was no appointed explainer of the Book of Christ, everyone made the claim to authority, saying, 'This is the true pathway and others are not.' To ward off such dissensions as these and prevent any person from creating a division or sect the Blessed Perfection, Bahá'u'lláh, appointed a central authoritative Personage, declaring Him to be the expounder of the Book. This implies that the people in general do not understand the meanings of the Book, but this appointed One does understand. Therefore, Bahá'u'lláh said, 'He is the explainer of My Book and the Centre of My Testament.' In the last verses of the Book instructions are revealed, declaring that, 'After Me', you must turn toward a special Personage and 'whatsoever He says is correct'. In the Book of the Covenant Bahá'u'lláh declares that by these two verses this Personage is meant.[12]

℆

It is as though a king should appoint a governor-general. Whosoever obeys him, obeys the king. Whosoever violates and disobeys him, violates the king. Therefore, whosoever obeys the Centre of the Covenant appointed by Bahá'u'lláh has obeyed Bahá'u'lláh, and whosoever disobeys Him has disobeyed Bahá'u'lláh. It has nothing to do with Him ('Abdu'l-Bahá) at all – precisely as the governor-general appointed by the king – whosoever obeys the governor-general obeys the king; whosoever disobeys the governor-general disobeys the king.[13]

The sufferings of 'Abdu'l-Bahá

O ye my spiritual friends! For some time now the pressures have been severe, the restrictions as shackles of iron. This hapless wronged one was left single and alone, for all the ways were barred. Friends were forbidden access to me, the trusted were shut away, the foe compassed me about, the evil watchers were fierce and bold. At every instant, fresh affliction. At every breath, new anguish. Both kin and stranger on the attack; indeed, onetime lovers, faithless and unpitying, were worse than foes as they rose up to harass me. None was there to defend 'Abdu'l-Bahá, no helper, no protector, no ally, no champion. I was drowning in a shoreless sea, and ever beating upon my ears were the raven-croaking voices of the disloyal.

At every daybreak, triple darkness. At eventide, stone-hearted tyranny. And never a moment's peace, and never any balm for the spear's red wounds. From moment to moment, word would come of my exile to the Fezzan sands; from hour to hour, I was to be cast into the endless sea. Now they would say that these homeless wanderers were ruined at last; again that the cross would soon be put to use. This wasted frame of mine was to be made the target for bullet or arrow; or again, this failing body was to be cut to ribbons by the sword.

Our alien acquaintances could not contain themselves for joy, and our treacherous friends exulted. 'Praise be to God,' one would exclaim, 'Here is our dream come true.' And another, 'God be thanked, our spearhead found the heart.'

Affliction beat upon this captive like the heavy rains of spring, and the victories of the malevolent swept down in a relentless flood, and still 'Abdu'l-Bahá remained happy and serene, and relied on the grace of the All-Merciful. That pain, that anguish, was a paradise of all delights; those chains were the necklace of a king on a throne in heaven. Content with God's will, utterly resigned, my heart surrendered to what-ever fate had in store, I was happy. For a boon companion, I had great joy.

Finally a time came when the friends turned inconsolable, and abandoned all hope. It was then the morning dawned, and flooded all with unending light. The towering clouds were scattered, the dismal shadows fled. In that instant the fetters fell away, the chains were lifted off the neck of this homeless one and hung round the neck of the foe. Those dire straits were changed to ease, and on the horizon of God's bounties the sun of hope rose up. All this was out of God's grace and His bestowals.

And yet, from one point of view, this wanderer was saddened and despondent. For what pain, in the time to come, could I seek comfort? At the news of what granted wish could I rejoice? There was no more tyranny, no more affliction, no tragical events, no tribulations. My only joy in this swiftly passing world was to tread the stony path of God and to endure hard tests and all material griefs. For otherwise, this earthly life would prove barren and vain, and better would be death. The tree of being would produce no fruit; the sown field of this existence would yield no harvest. Thus it is my hope that once again some circumstance will make my cup of anguish to brim over, and that beauteous Love, that Slayer of souls, will dazzle the beholders again. Then will this heart be blissful, this soul be blessed.[14]

✧

All praise and thanksgiving be unto the Blessed Beauty, for calling into action the armies of His Abhá Kingdom, and sending forth to us His never-interrupted aid, dependable as the rising stars. In every region of the earth hath He supported this single, lonely servant, at every moment hath He made known to me the signs and tokens of His love . . . Meanwhile, by the power of His might, He hath made this broken-winged bird to rise up before all who dwell on earth. He hath shattered the serried ranks of the rebellious, and hath given the victory to the hosts of salvation, and breathed into the hearts of those who stand firm in the Covenant and Testament the breath of everlasting life.[15]

Know ye that 'Abdu'l-Bahá dwelleth in continual delight. To have been lodged in this faraway prison is for me exceeding joy. By the life of Bahá! This prison is my supernal paradise; it is my cherished goal, the comfort of my bosom, the bliss of my heart; it is my refuge, my shelter, my asylum, my safe haven, and within it do I exult amid the hosts of heaven and the Company on high.[16]

∻

This prison is sweeter to me and more to be desired than a garden of flowers; to me, this bondage is better than the freedom to go my way, and I find this narrow place more spacious than wide and open plains. Do not grieve over me. And should my Lord decree that I be blessed with sweet martyrdom's cup, this would but mean receiving what I long for most.

Fear not if this Branch be severed from this material world and cast aside its leaves; nay, the leaves thereof shall flourish, for this Branch will grow after it is cut off from this world below, it shall reach the loftiest pinnacles of glory, and it shall bear such fruits as will perfume the world with their fragrance.[17]

∻

For the dearest wish of this wronged one is that the friends be spiritual of heart and illumined of mind, and once this grace is granted me, calamity, however afflictive, is but bounty pouring down upon me, like copious rain.

O God, my God! Thou seest me plunged in an ocean of anguish, held fast to the fires of tyranny, and weeping in the darkness of the night. Sleepless I toss and turn upon my bed, mine eyes straining to behold the morning light of faithfulness and trust. I agonize even as a fish, its inward parts afire as it leapeth about in terror upon the sand, yet I ever look for Thy bestowals to appear from every side.[18]

૮৩

In the East people were asking me, 'Why do you undertake this long voyage? Your body cannot endure such hardships of travel.' When it is necessary, my body can endure everything. It has withstood forty years of imprisonment and can still undergo the utmost trials.[19]

૮৩

I love to be alone. I love to be in a meadow and lie down under the tree. Beneath the green branches. But God has destined otherwise. He commanded me to speak. We have not come here to be silent. Otherwise, I love silence.[20]

૮৩

Lord! My cup of woe runneth over, and from all sides blows are fiercely raging upon me. The darts of affliction have compassed me round and the arrows of distress have rained upon me. Thus tribulation overwhelmed me and my strength, because of the onslaught of the foemen, became weakness within me, while I stood alone and forsaken in the midst of my woes. Lord! Have mercy upon me, lift me up unto Thyself and make me to drink from the Chalice of Martyrdom, for the wide world with all its vastness can no longer contain me.[21]

૮৩

O God, my God! Thou seest this wronged servant of Thine, held fast in the talons of ferocious lions, of ravening wolves, of bloodthirsty beasts. Graciously assist me, through my love for Thee, that I may drink deep of the chalice that brimmeth over with faithfulness to Thee and is filled with Thy bountiful Grace; so that, fallen upon the dust, I may sink prostrate and senseless whilst my vesture is dyed crimson with my blood. This is my wish, my heart's desire, my hope, my pride, my glory. Grant, O Lord my God, and my Refuge, that in my last hour, my end, may even as musk shed its fragrance of glory! Is there a bounty greater than this? Nay, by Thy Glory! [22]

❧

I was happy in imprisonment. I was in the utmost elation because I was not a criminal. They had imprisoned me in the path of God. Every time I thought of this, that I was a prisoner in the pathway of God, the utmost elation over-came me . . . I was happy that – praise be to God! – I was a prisoner in the Cause of God, that my life was not wasted, that it was spent in the divine service. Nobody who saw me imagined that I was in prison. They beheld me in the utmost joy, complete thankfulness and health, paying no attention to the prison. [23]

❧

As to my drinking the cup of sacrifice: By the Lord of heaven, this is my utmost hope, the joy of my heart, the consolation of my soul and my final desire. Thou shouldst pray God that He may prepare this hope for me and ordain for me this mighty gift and that He may give me to quaff this cup which is over-flowing with the wine of faithfulness in the path of Bahá. [24]

Afflictions and hardships, ordeals or trials, do not make me weak or faint, nor do they in the slightest degree make me sad or unhappy.[25]

❧

I am the servant of the Blessed Perfection. In Baghdád I was a child. Then and there He announced to me the Word, and I believed in Him. As soon as He proclaimed to me the Word, I threw myself at His Holy Feet and implored and supplicated Him to accept my blood as a sacrifice in His Pathway. Sacrifice! How sweet I find that word! There is no greater Bounty for me than this! What greater glory can I conceive than to see this neck chained for His sake, these feet fettered for His love, this body mutilated or thrown into the depths of the sea for His Cause! If in reality we are His sincere lovers – if in reality I am His sincere servant, then I must sacrifice my life, my all at His Blessed Threshold.[26]

❧

While in Teheran I was seven years old. I became afflicted with consumption. All the physicians gave me up . . . The wisdom of this became apparent later on; because were I not sick I would not have been in Teheran. I would have been in Nour, Mazanderan. I could not be in Teheran when the Blessed Perfection was thrown into the prison. On account of that sickness I was kept in Teheran and later in company with Baha-ollah I was exiled to Bagdad. When all the doctors said that this young body is beyond the stage of recovery I suddenly got well. There was at that time an English Doctor in Teheran who pronounced my case as hopeless. The physicians were amazed at my sudden recovery. They could not believe that I have got completely well. Therefore, all the events of my life are shaped by divine hands. They are all based upon heavenly wisdom. I am ever controlled by the will of God . . .[27]

℃∕১

Look at Me! Thou dost not know a thousandth part of the difficulties and seemingly unsurmountable passes that rise daily before my eyes. I do not heed them; I am walking my chosen highway; I know the destination. Hundreds of storms and tempests may rage furiously around my head; hundreds of *Titanics* may sink to the bottom of the sea, the mad waves may rise to the roof of heaven; all these will not change my purpose, will not disturb me in the least; I will not look either to the right or to the left. I am looking ahead, far, far. Peering through the impenetrable darkness of the night, the howling winds, the raging storms, I see the glorious Light beckoning me forward, forward. The balmy weather is coming, and the voyager shall land safely.[28]

From the writings of Shoghi Effendi

From God Passes By

God Passes By – *written in 1944 to mark the completion of the first century of the Bahá'í Era – was described by Shoghi Effendi's wife, Rúhíyyih Rabbání, as 'one of the most concentrated and stupendous achievements'[1] of his life. Shoghi Effendi's unmatched devotion to his Grandfather 'Abdu'l-Bahá, his insightful appreciation of His self-sacrificing life and work, and His position as Centre of the Covenant of Bahá'u'lláh, are impeccably expressed in this 'most brilliant and wondrous tale of a century that has ever been told'.[2]*

Extolled by the writer of the Apocalypse as 'the Ark of His (God) Testament'; associated with the gathering beneath the *'Tree of Anísá'* (Tree of Life) mentioned by Bahá'u'lláh in the Hidden Words; glorified by Him, in other passages of His writings, as the *'Ark of Salvation'* and as *'the Cord stretched betwixt the earth and the Abhá Kingdom',* this Covenant has been bequeathed to posterity in a Will and Testament which, together with the Kitáb-i-Aqdas and several Tablets, in which the rank and station of 'Abdu'l-Bahá are unequivocally disclosed, constitute the chief buttresses designed by the Lord of the Covenant Himself to shield and support, after His ascension, the appointed Centre of His Faith and the Delineator of its future institutions.

In this weighty and incomparable Document its Author discloses the character of that *'excellent and priceless Heritage'* bequeathed by Him to His *'heirs'*; proclaims afresh the fundamental purpose of His Revelation; enjoins the *'peoples of the world'* to hold fast to that which will *'elevate'* their *'station'*; announces to them that *'God hath forgiven what is past'*; stresses the sublimity of man's station; discloses the primary aim of the Faith of God; directs the faithful to pray for the welfare of the kings of the earth, *'the manifestations of the power, and the daysprings of the might and riches, of God'*; invests them with the rulership of the earth; singles out as His special domain the hearts of men; forbids categorically strife and contention; commands His followers to aid those rulers who are *'adorned with the ornament of equity and justice'*; and directs, in particular, the Aghsan (His sons) to ponder the *'mighty force and the consummate power that lieth concealed in the world of being.'* He bids them, moreover, together with the Afnán (the Báb's kindred) and His own relatives, to *'turn, one and all, unto the Most Great Branch'* ('Abdu'l-Bahá); identifies Him with *'the One Whom God hath purposed', 'Who hath branched from this pre-existent Root'*, referred to in the Kitáb-i-Aqdas; ordains the station of the *'Greater Branch'* (Mírzá Muḥammad-'Alí) to be beneath that of the *'Most Great Branch'* ('Abdu'l-Bahá); exhorts the believers to treat the Ag̲h̲ṣan with consideration and affection; counsels them to respect His family and relatives, as well as the kindred of the Báb; denies His sons *'any right to the property of others'*; enjoins on them, on His kindred and on that of the Báb to *'fear God, to do that which is meet and seemly'* and to follow the things that will *'exalt'* their station; warns all men not to allow *'the means of order to be made the cause of confusion, and the instrument of union an occasion for discord'*; and concludes with an exhortation calling upon the faithful to *'serve all nations'*, and to strive for the *'betterment of the world'*.

That such a unique and sublime station should have been conferred upon 'Abdu'l-Bahá did not, and indeed could not, surprise those exiled companions who had for so long been privileged to observe His life and conduct, nor the pilgrims who had been brought, however fleetingly, into personal contact with Him, nor indeed the vast concourse of the faithful who, in distant lands, had grown to revere His name and to appreciate His labours, nor even the wide circle of His friends and acquaintances who, in the Holy Land and the adjoining countries, were already well familiar with the position He had occupied during the lifetime of His Father.

He it was Whose auspicious birth occurred on that never-to-be-forgotten night when the Báb laid bare the transcendental character of His Mission to His first disciple Mullá Ḥusayn. He it was Who, as a mere child, seated on the lap of Ṭáhirih, had registered the thrilling significance of the stirring challenge which that indomitable heroine had addressed to her fellow-disciple, the erudite and far-famed Vaḥíd. He it was Whose tender soul had been seared with the ineffaceable vision of a Father, haggard, dishevelled, freighted with chains, on the occasion of a visit, as a boy of nine, to the Síyáh-Chál of Ṭihrán. Against Him, in His early childhood, whilst His Father lay a prisoner in that dungeon, had been directed the malice of a mob of street urchins who pelted Him with stones, vilified Him and overwhelmed Him with ridicule. His had been the lot to share with His Father, soon after His release from imprisonment, the rigours and miseries of a cruel banishment from His native land, and the trials which culminated in His enforced withdrawal to the mountains of Kurdistán. He it was Who, in His inconsolable grief at His separation from an adored Father, had confided to Nabíl, as attested by him in his narrative, that He felt Himself to have grown old though still but a child of tender years. His had been the unique distinction of recognizing, while still in His childhood, the full glory of His Father's as yet unrevealed station, a recognition which had impelled Him to throw Himself at His feet and to spontaneously implore the privilege of laying down His life for His sake. From His pen, while still in His adolescence in Baghdád, had issued that superb commentary on a well-known Muḥammadan tradition, written at the suggestion of Bahá'u'lláh, in answer to a request made by 'Alí-Shawkat Páshá, which was so illuminating as to excite the unbounded admiration of its recipient. It was His discussions and discourses with the learned doctors with whom He came in contact in Baghdád that first aroused that general admiration for Him and for His knowledge which was steadily to increase as the circle of His acquaintances was widened, at a later date, first in Adrianople and then in 'Akká. It was to Him that the highly accomplished Khurshíd Páshá, the governor of Adrianople, had been moved to pay a public and glowing tribute when, in the presence of a number of distinguished divines of that city, his youthful Guest had, briefly and amazingly, resolved the intricacies of a problem that had baffled the minds of the assembled company – an achievement that affected so deeply the Páshá that from that time onwards he could hardly reconcile himself to that Youth's absence from such gatherings.

On Him Bahá'u'lláh, as the scope and influence of His Mission extended, had been led to place an ever greater degree of reliance, by appointing Him, on numerous occasions, as His deputy, by enabling Him to plead His Cause before the public, by assigning Him the task of transcribing His Tablets, by allowing Him to assume the responsibility of shielding Him from His enemies, and by investing Him with the function of watching over and promoting the interests of His fellow-exiles and companions. He it was Who had been commissioned to undertake, as soon as circumstances might permit, the delicate and all-important task of purchasing the site that was to serve as the permanent resting-place of the Báb, of insuring the safe transfer of His remains to the Holy Land, and of erecting for Him a befitting sepulcher on Mt Carmel. He it was Who had been chiefly instrumental in providing the necessary means for Bahá'u'lláh's release from His nine-year confinement within the city walls of 'Akká, and in enabling Him to enjoy, in the evening of His life, a measure of that peace and security from which He had so long been debarred. It was through His unremitting efforts that the illustrious Badí had been granted his memorable interviews with Bahá'u'lláh, that the hostility evinced by several governors of 'Akká towards the exiled community had been transmuted into esteem and admiration, that the purchase of properties adjoining the Sea of Galilee and the River Jordan had been effected, and that the ablest and most valuable presentation of the early history of the Faith and of its tenets had been transmitted to posterity. It was through the extraordinarily warm reception accorded Him during His visit to Beirut, through His contact with Midhat Páshá, a former Grand Vizir of Turkey, through His friendship with 'Azíz Páshá, whom He had previously known in Adrianople, and who had subsequently been promoted to the rank of Valí, and through His constant association with officials, notables and leading ecclesiastics who, in increasing number had besought His presence, during the final years of His Father's ministry, that He had succeeded in raising the prestige of the Cause He had championed to a level it had never previously attained.

He alone had been accorded the privilege of being called *'the Master'*, an honour from which His Father had strictly excluded all His other sons. Upon Him that loving and unerring Father had chosen to confer the unique title of *'Sirru'lláh'* (the Mystery of God), a designation so appropriate to One Who, though essentially human and holding a station radically and fundamentally different from that occupied by Bahá'u'lláh and His Forerunner, could still claim to be the perfect Exemplar of His Faith, to be endowed with super-human knowledge, and to be regarded as the stainless mirror reflecting His light. To Him, whilst in Adrianople, that same Father had, in the Súriy-i-Ghusn (Tablet of the Branch), referred as *'this sacred and glorious Being, this Branch of Holiness'*, as *'the Limb of the Law of God'*, as His *'most great favour'* unto men, as His *'most perfect bounty'* conferred upon them, as One through Whom *'every mouldering bone is quickened'*, declaring that *'whoso turneth towards Him hath turned towards God'*, and that *'they who deprive themselves of the shadow of the Branch are lost in the wilderness of error'*. To Him He, whilst still in that city, had alluded (in a Tablet addressed to Hájí Muhammad Ibráhím-i-Khalíl) as the one amongst His sons '*from Whose tongue God will cause the signs of His power to stream forth*', and as the one Whom '*God hath specially chosen for His Cause*'. On Him, at a later period, the Author of the Kitáb-i-Aqdas, in a celebrated passage, subsequently elucidated in the '*Book of My Covenant*', had bestowed the function of interpreting His Holy Writ, proclaiming Him, at the same time, to be the One '*Whom God hath purposed, Who hath branched from this Ancient Root*'. To Him in a Tablet, revealed during that same period and addressed to Mírzá Muḥammad Qulíy-i-Sabzivárí, He had referred as '*the Gulf that hath branched out of this Ocean that hath encompassed all created things*', and bidden His followers to turn their faces towards it. To Him, on the occasion of His visit to Beirut, His Father had, furthermore, in a communication which He dictated to His amanuensis, paid a glowing tribute, glorifying Him as the One '*round Whom all names revolve*', as '*the Most Mighty Branch of God*', and as '*His ancient and immutable Mystery*'. He it was Who, in several Tablets which Bahá'u'lláh Himself had penned, had been personally addressed as '*the Apple of Mine eye*', and been referred to as '*a shield unto all who are in heaven and on earth*', as '*a shelter for all mankind*' and '*a stronghold for whosoever hath believed in God*'. It was on His behalf that His Father, in a prayer revealed in His honour, had supplicated God to '*render Him victorious*', and to '*ordain . . . for Him, as well as for them that love Him*', the things destined by the Almighty for His '*Messengers*' and the '*Trustees*' of His Revelation. And finally in yet another Tablet these weighty words had been recorded: '*The glory of God rest upon Thee, and upon whosoever serveth Thee and circleth around Thee. Woe, great woe, betide him that opposeth and injureth Thee. Well is it with him that sweareth fealty to Thee; the fire of hell torment him who is Thy enemy.*'

33

And now to crown the inestimable honours, privileges and benefits showered upon Him, in ever increasing abundance, throughout the forty years of His Father's ministry in Baghdád, in Adrianople and in 'Akká, He had been elevated to the high office of Centre of Bahá'u'lláh's Covenant, and been made the successor of the Manifestation of God Himself – a position that was to empower Him to impart an extraordinary impetus to the international expansion of His Father's Faith, to amplify its doctrine, to beat down every barrier that would obstruct its march, and to call into being, and delineate the features of, its Administrative Order, the Child of the Covenant, and the Harbinger of that World Order whose establishment must needs signalize the advent of the Golden Age of the Bahá'í Dispensation.[3]

'Abdu'l-Bahá was at this time broken in health. He suffered from several maladies brought on by the strains and stresses of a tragic life spent almost wholly in exile and imprisonment. He was on the threshold of three-score years and ten. Yet as soon as He was released from His forty-year long captivity, as soon as He had laid the Báb's body in a safe and permanent resting-place, and His mind was free of grievous anxieties connected with the execution of that priceless Trust, He arose with sublime courage, confidence and resolution to consecrate what little strength remained to Him, in the evening of His life, to a service of such heroic proportions that no parallel to it is to be found in the annals of the first Bahá'í century.

Indeed His three years of travel, first to Egypt, then to Europe and later to America, mark, if we would correctly appraise their historic importance, a turning point of the utmost significance in the history of the century. For the first time since the inception of the Faith, sixty-six years previously, its Head and supreme Representative burst asunder the shackles which had throughout the ministries of both the Báb and Bahá'u'lláh so grievously fettered its freedom. Though repressive measures still continued to circumscribe the activities of the vast majority of its adherents in the land of its birth, its recognized Leader was now vouchsafed a freedom of action which, with the exception of a brief interval in the course of the War of 1914-18, He was to continue to enjoy to the end of His life, and which has never since been withdrawn from its institutions at its world centre.

So momentous a change in the fortunes of the Faith was the signal for such an outburst of activity on His part as to dumbfound His followers in East and West with admiration and wonder, and exercise an imperishable influence on the course of its future history. He Who, in His own words, had entered prison as a youth and left it an old man, Who never in His life had faced a public audience, had attended no school, had never moved in Western circles, and was unfamiliar with Western customs and language, had arisen not only to proclaim from pulpit and platform, in some of the chief capitals of Europe and in the leading cities of the North American continent, the distinctive verities enshrined in His Father's Faith, but to demonstrate as well the Divine origin of the Prophets gone before Him, and to disclose the nature of the tie binding them to that Faith.[4]

From *The Dispensation of Bahá'u'lláh*

In The Dispensation of Bahá'u'lláh, *written in 1934, Shoghi Effendi clarified the true and unique stations of the Central Figures of the Bahá'í Faith. In relation to the position of*

35

'Abdu'l-Bahá, Shoghi Effendi corrected the mistaken idea held by some early Western Bahá'ís that 'Abdu'l-Bahá was the return of Christ and that He and Bahá'u'lláh held the same station and reality. The Guardian himself described The Dispensation of Bahá'u'lláh *as an 'invaluable supplement'* [5] *to Bahá'u'lláh's* Kitáb-i-Ahd *and the* Will and Testament *of 'Abdu'l-Bahá.*

An attempt I strongly feel should now be made to clarify our minds regarding the station occupied by 'Abdu'l-Bahá and the significance of His position in this holy Dispensation. It would be indeed difficult for us, who stand so close to such a tremendous figure and are drawn by the mysterious power of so magnetic a personality, to obtain a clear and exact understanding of the rôle and character of One Who, not only in the Dispensation of Bahá'u'lláh but in the entire field of religious history, fulfils a unique function. Though moving in a sphere of His own and holding a rank radically different from that of the Author and the Forerunner of the Bahá'í Revelation, He, by virtue of the station ordained for Him through the Covenant of Bahá'u'lláh, forms together with them what may be termed the Three Central Figures of a Faith that stands unapproached in the world's spiritual history. He towers, in conjunction with them, above the destinies of this infant Faith of God from a level to which no individual or body ministering to its needs after Him, and for no less a period than a full thousand years, can ever hope to rise. To degrade His lofty rank by identifying His station with or by regarding it as roughly equivalent to, the position of those on whom the mantle of His authority has fallen would be an act of impiety as grave as the no less heretical belief that inclines to exalt Him to a state of absolute equality with either the central Figure or Forerunner of our Faith. For wide as is the gulf that separates 'Abdu'l-Bahá from Him Who is the Source of an independent Revelation, it can never be regarded as commensurate with the greater distance that stands between Him Who is the Centre of the Covenant and His ministers who are to carry on His work, whatever be their name, their rank, their functions or their future achievements. Let those who have known 'Abdu'l-Bahá, who through their contact with His magnetic personality have come to cherish for Him so fervent an admiration, reflect, in the light of this statement, on the greatness of One Who is so far above Him in station.

That 'Abdu'l-Bahá is not a Manifestation of God, that, though the successor of His Father, He does not occupy a cognate station, that no one else except the Báb and Bahá'u'lláh can ever lay claim to such a station before the expiration of a full thousand years – are verities which lie embedded in the specific utterances of both the Founder of our Faith and the Interpreter of His teachings.

'Whoso layeth claim to a Revelation direct from God,' is the express warning uttered in the Kitáb-i-Aqdas, 'ere the expiration of a full thousand years, such a man is assuredly a lying imposter. We pray God that He may graciously assist him to retract and repudiate such claim. Should he repent, God will no doubt forgive him. If, however, he persists in his error, God will assuredly send down one who will deal mercilessly with him. Terrible indeed is God in punishing!' 'Whosoever', He adds as a further emphasis, 'interpreteth this verse otherwise than its obvious meaning is deprived of the Spirit of God and of His mercy which encompasseth all created things.' 'Should a man appear', is yet another conclusive statement, 'ere the lapse of a full thousand years – each year consisting of twelve months according to the Qur'án, and of nineteen months of nineteen days each, according to the Bayán – and if such a man reveal to your eyes all the signs of God, unhesitatingly reject him!'

'Abdu'l-Bahá's own statements, in confirmation of this warning, are no less emphatic and binding: 'This is', He declares, 'my firm, my unshakable conviction, the essence of my unconcealed and explicit belief – a conviction and belief which the denizens of the Abhá Kingdom fully share: The Blessed Beauty is the Sun of Truth, and His light the light of truth. The Báb is likewise the Sun of Truth, and His light the light of truth . . . My station is the station of servitude – a servitude which is complete, pure and real, firmly established, enduring, obvious, explicitly revealed and subject to no interpretation whatever . . . I am the Interpreter of the Word of God; such is my interpretation.'

Does not 'Abdu'l-Bahá in His own Will – in a tone and language that might well confound the most inveterate among the breakers of His Father's Covenant – rob of their chief weapon those who so long and so persistently had striven to impute to Him the charge of having tacitly claimed a station equal, if not superior, to that of Bahá'u'lláh? 'The foundation of the belief of the people of Bahá is this', thus proclaims one of the weightiest passages of that last document left to voice in perpetuity the directions and wishes of a departed Master, 'His Holiness the Exalted One (the Báb) is the Manifestation of the unity and oneness of God and the Forerunner of the Ancient Beauty. His Holiness the Abhá Beauty (Bahá'u'lláh) (may my life be a sacrifice for His steadfast friends) is the supreme Manifestation of God and the Day-Spring of His most divine Essence. All others are servants unto Him and do His bidding.'

From such clear and formally laid down statements, incompatible as they are with any assertion of a claim to Prophethood, we should not by any means infer that 'Abdu'l-Bahá is merely one of the servants of the Blessed Beauty, or at best one whose function is to be confined to that of an authorized interpreter of His Father's teachings. Far be it from me to entertain such a notion or to wish to instill such sentiments. To regard Him in such a light is a manifest betrayal of the priceless heritage bequeathed by Bahá'u'lláh to mankind. Immeasurably exalted is the station conferred upon Him by the Supreme Pen above and beyond the implications of these, His own written statements. Whether in the Kitáb-i-Aqdas, the most weighty and sacred of all the works of Bahá'u'lláh, or in the Kitáb-i-'Ahd, the Book of His Covenant, or in the Súriy-i-<u>Gh</u>usn (Tablet of the Branch), such references as have been recorded by the pen of Bahá'u'lláh – references which the Tablets of His Father addressed to Him mightily reinforce – invest 'Abdu'l-Bahá with a power, and surround Him with a halo, which the present generation can never adequately appreciate.

He is, and should for all time be regarded, first and foremost, as the Centre and Pivot of Bahá'u'lláh's peerless and all-enfolding Covenant, His most exalted handiwork, the stainless Mirror of His light, the perfect Exemplar of His teachings, the unerring Interpreter of His Word, the embodiment of every Bahá'í ideal, the incarnation of every Bahá'í virtue, the Most Mighty Branch sprung from the Ancient Root, the Limb of the Law of God, the Being 'round Whom all names revolve', the Mainspring of the Oneness of Humanity, the Ensign of the Most Great Peace, the Moon of the Central Orb of this most holy Dispensation – styles and titles that are implicit and find their truest, their highest and fairest expression in the magic name 'Abdu'l-Bahá. He is, above and beyond these appellations, the 'Mystery of God' – an expression by which Bahá'u'lláh Himself has chosen to designate Him, and which, while it does not by any means justify us to assign to Him the station of Prophethood, indicates how in the person of 'Abdu'l-Bahá the incompatible characteristics of a human nature and superhuman knowledge and perfection have been blended and are completely harmonized . . .[5]

Exalted as is the rank of 'Abdu'l-Bahá, and however profuse the praises with which in these sacred Books and Tablets Bahá'u'lláh has glorified His son, so unique a distinction must never be construed as conferring upon its recipient a station identical with, or equivalent to, that of His Father, the Manifestation Himself. To give such an interpretation to any of these quoted passages would at once, and for obvious reasons, bring it into conflict with the no less clear and authentic assertions and warnings to which I have already referred. Indeed, as I have already stated, those who overestimate 'Abdu'l-Bahá's station are just as reprehensible and have done just as much harm as those who underestimate it. And this for no other reason except that by insisting upon an altogether unwarranted inference from Bahá'u'lláh's writings they are inadvertently justifying and continuously furnishing the enemy with proofs for his false accusations and misleading statements.

I feel it necessary, therefore, to state without any equivocation or hesitation that neither in the Kitáb-i-Aqdas nor in the Book of Bahá'u'lláh's Covenant, nor even in the Tablet of the Branch, nor in any other Tablet, whether revealed by Bahá'u'lláh or 'Abdu'l-Bahá, is there any authority whatever for the opinion that inclines to uphold the so-called 'mystic unity' of Bahá'u'lláh and 'Abdu'l-Bahá, or to establish the identity of the latter with His Father or with any preceding Manifestation. This erroneous conception may, in part, be ascribed to an altogether extravagant interpretation of certain terms and passages in the Tablet of the Branch, to the introduction into its English translation of certain words that are either non-existent, misleading, or ambiguous in their connotation. It is, no doubt, chiefly based upon an altogether unjustified inference from the opening passages of a Tablet of Bahá'u'lláh, extracts of which, as reproduced in the 'Bahá'í Scriptures', immediately precede, but form no part of, the said Tablet of the Branch.

It should be made clear to every one reading those extracts that by the phrase 'the Tongue of the Ancient' no one else is meant but God, and that the term 'the Greatest Name' is an obvious reference to Bahá'u'lláh, and that 'the Covenant' referred to is not the specific Covenant of which Bahá'u'lláh is the immediate Author and 'Abdu'l-Bahá the Centre but that general Covenant which, as inculcated by the Bahá'í teaching, God Himself invariably establishes with mankind when He inaugurates a new Dispensation. 'The Tongue' that 'gives', as stated in those extracts, the 'glad-tidings' is none other than the Voice of God referring to Bahá'u'lláh, and not Bahá'u'lláh referring to 'Abdu'l-Bahá.

Moreover, to maintain that the assertion 'He is Myself', instead of denoting the mystic unity of God and His Manifestations, as explained in the Kitáb-i-Íqán, establishes the identity of Bahá'u'lláh with 'Abdu'l-Bahá, would constitute a direct violation of the oft-repeated principle of the oneness of God's Manifestations – a principle which the Author of these same extracts is seeking by implication to emphasise.

It would also amount to a reversion to those irrational and superstitious beliefs which have insensibly crept, in the first century of the Christian era, into the teachings of Jesus Christ, and by crystallizing into accepted dogmas have impaired the effectiveness and obscured the purpose of the Christian Faith.

'*I affirm*', is 'Abdu'l-Bahá's own written comment on the Tablet of the Branch, '*that the true meaning, the real significance, the innermost secret of these verses, of these very words, is my own servitude to the sacred Threshold of the Abhá Beauty, my complete self-effacement, my utter nothingness before Him. This is my resplendent crown, my most precious adorning. On this I pride myself in the kingdom of earth and heaven. Therein I glory among the company of the well-favoured.*' '*No one is permitted*', He warns us in the passage which immediately follows, '*to give these verses any other interpretation.' 'I am', He, in this same connection, affirms, 'according to the explicit texts of the Kitáb-i-Aqdas and the Kitáb-i-'Ahd the manifest Interpreter of the Word of God . . . Whoso deviates from my interpretation is a victim of his own fancy.'

Furthermore, the inescapable inference from the belief in the identity of the Author of our Faith with Him Who is the Centre of His Covenant would be to place 'Abdu'l-Bahá in a position superior to that of the Báb, the reverse of which is the fundamental, though not as yet universally recognized, principle of this Revelation. It would also justify the charge with which, all throughout 'Abdu'l-Bahá's ministry, the Covenant-Breakers have striven to poison the minds and pervert the understanding of Bahá'u'lláh's loyal followers.

It would be more correct, and in consonance with the established principles of Bahá'u'lláh and the Báb, if instead of maintaining this fictitious identity with reference to 'Abdu'l-Bahá, we regard the Forerunner and the Founder of our Faith as identical in reality – a truth which the text of the Súratu'l-Haykal unmistakably affirms. 'Had the Primal Point (the Báb) been someone else beside Me as ye claim', is Bahá'u'lláh's explicit statement, 'and had attained My presence, verily He would have never allowed Himself to be separated from Me, but rather We would have had mutual delights with each other in My Days.' 'He Who now voiceth the Word of God', Bahá'u'lláh again affirms, 'is none other except the Primal Point Who hath once again been made manifest.' 'He is', He thus refers to Himself in a Tablet addressed to one of the Letters of the Living, 'the same as the One Who appeared in the year sixty (1260 A.H.). This verily is one of His mighty signs.' 'Who', He pleads in the Súriy-i-Damm, 'will arise to secure the triumph of the Primal Beauty (the Báb) revealed in the countenance of His succeeding Manifestation?' Referring to the Revelation proclaimed by the Báb He conversely characterizes it as '*My own previous Manifestation.*'

That 'Abdu'l-Bahá is not a Manifestation of God, that He gets His light, His inspiration and sustenance direct from the Fountain-head of the Bahá'í Revelation; that He reflects even as a clear and perfect Mirror the rays of Bahá'u'lláh's glory, and does not inherently possess that indefinable yet all-pervading reality the exclusive possession of which is the hallmark of Prophethood; that His words are not equal in rank, though they possess an equal validity with the utterances of Bahá'u'lláh; that He is not to be acclaimed as the return of Jesus Christ, the Son Who will come 'in the glory of the Father' – these truths find added justification, and are further reinforced, by the following statement of 'Abdu'l-Bahá, addressed to some believers in America, with which I may well conclude this section: '*You have written that there is a difference among the believers concerning the "Second Coming of Christ". Gracious God! Time and again this question hath arisen, and its answer hath emanated in a clear and irrefutable statement from the pen of 'Abdu'l-Bahá, that what is meant in the prophecies by the "Lord of Hosts" and the "Promised Christ" is the Blessed Perfection* (Bahá'u'lláh) *and His holiness the Exalted One* (the Báb). *My name is 'Abdu'l-Bahá. My qualification is 'Abdu'l-Bahá. My reality is 'Abdu'l-Bahá. My praise is 'Abdu'l-Bahá. Thraldom to the Blessed Perfection is my glorious and refulgent diadem, and servitude to all the human race my perpetual religion . . . No name, no title, no mention, no commendation have I, nor will ever have, except 'Abdu'l-Bahá. This is my longing. This is my greatest yearning. This is my eternal life. This is my everlasting glory.*'[6]

From the letters of the Universal House of Justice

Ever present in our contemplation . . . is the magnetic figure of 'Abdu'l-Bahá, the Centre of the Covenant, the Mystery of God, the perfect Exemplar, Whose unerring interpretation of the Holy Texts and luminous examples of their application to personal conduct shed light on a way of life we must strive diligently to follow.[1]

ଡ଼

In contemplating the Master's divine example we may well reflect that His life and deeds were not acted to a pattern of expediency, but were the inevitable and spontaneous expression of His inner self.[2]

ଡ଼

With the setting of the Sun of Bahá, the Moon of His Covenant rose in reflected glory, lifting the darkness of a night of despair, and lighting the path to the unity of all humankind. In the fullness of its radiance stands the magnetic Figure of 'Abdu'l-Bahá, the beloved Son Whom Bahá'u'lláh designated as the Interpreter of His Word and Executive of His authority, and Whom He appointed the Centre of His Covenant, an office without parallel in all religious history.

We acknowledge the mysterious power of His wisdom, the illuminating potency of His words, the immortal example and unific character of His deeds. By His untiring exertions the fame of the infant Cause was spread abroad, the design of its Administrative Order was completed, the World Centre of the Faith emerged into clear visibility, and the splendours of the Mountain of God, as alluded to in Bahá'u'lláh's Tablet

of Carmel, began to be manifested. With profound grati-
tude for such evident blessings we reaffirm our loyalty to the
Covenant of Bahá'u'lláh. And we exclaim: 'Glorified be the
All-Merciful, the Lord of Grace abounding!'[3]

❧

As the interpreter, 'Abdu'l-Bahá became the living mouth
of the Book, the expounder of the Word; as the Centre of
the Covenant, He became the incorruptible medium for
applying the Word to practical measures for the raising up
of a new civilization. The Covenant is, therefore, unique as
a divine phenomenon, in that Bahá'u'lláh, further to conferring upon 'Abdu'l-Bahá the necessary authority to fulfil the
requirements of His singular office, vested in Him the virtues
of perfection in personal and social behaviour, that humanity may have an enduring model to emulate. In no annals of
the past is there recorded such an arrangement for ensuring
the realization of the purpose of the Manifestation of God.[4]

❧

'Abdu'l-Bahá's position in the Faith is one for which we find
'no parallel' in past Dispensations. For example, Bahá'u'lláh,
in addition to His reference to the Centre of His Covenant
as the 'Mystery of God', states that 'Abdu'l-Bahá should be
regarded as God's 'exalted Handiwork' and 'a Word which
God hath adorned with the ornament of His Own Self, and
made it sovereign over the earth and all that there is therein'.
And from Shoghi Effendi we have the incontrovertible statement that the Guardian of the Faith while 'overshadowed' by
the 'protection' of Bahá'u'lláh and of the Báb, 'remains essentially human', whereas in respect of 'Abdu'l-Bahá Shoghi

Effendi categorically states that 'in the person of 'Abdu'l-Bahá the incompatible characteristics of a human nature and superhuman knowledge and perfection have been blended and are completely harmonized.'[5]

∾

The vehicle in this resplendent Age for the practical fulfilment of these duties is the Covenant of Bahá'u'lláh; it is, indeed, the potent instrument by which individual belief in Him is translated into constructive deeds. The Covenant comprises divinely conceived arrangements necessary to preserve the organic unity of the Cause. It therefore engenders a motivating power which, as the beloved Master tells us, 'like unto the artery, beats and pulsates in the body of the world'. 'It is indubitably clear', He asserts, 'that the pivot of the oneness of mankind is nothing else but the power of the Covenant.' Through it the meaning of the Word, both in theory and practice, is made evident in the life and work of 'Abdu'l-Bahá, the appointed Interpreter, the perfect Exemplar, the Centre of the Covenant. Through it the processes of the Administrative Order – 'this unique, this wondrous System' – are made to operate.[6]

∾

A century ago, the Faith was emerging from a period of severe crisis during which the incarceration of 'Abdu'l-Bahá by His inveterate antagonists in the Ottoman Empire had been renewed, a grievous assault on the unity of the Cause had been launched by the Covenant-breakers, and an upsurge in the persecution of the heroic Persian believers had produced a fresh wave of sacrifice. In the immediate future there lay dazzling victories. The strenuous and fate-laden journeys of 'Abdu'l-Bahá to the western world would release incalculable spiritual powers destined to give rise to unprecedented progress of the Faith in the American and European continents He visited. The Tablets of the Divine Plan would set in motion processes designed to bring about, in due course, the spiritual transformation of the planet. The Will and Testament of 'Abdu'l-Bahá would establish the basis for a future world order. [7]

☙

Tirelessly, He expounded the teachings in every social space: in homes and mission halls, churches and synagogues, parks and public squares, railway carriages and ocean liners, clubs and societies, schools and universities. Uncompromising in defence of the truth, yet infinitely gentle in manner, He brought the universal divine principles to bear on the exigencies of the age. To all without distinction – officials, scientists, workers, children, parents, exiles, activists, clerics, sceptics – He imparted love, wisdom, comfort, whatever the particular need. While elevating their souls, He challenged their assumptions, reoriented their perspectives, expanded their consciousness, and focused their energies. He demonstrated by word and deed such compassion and generosity that hearts were utterly transformed. No one was turned away. Our great hope is that frequent recollection, during this centennial period, of the Master's matchless record will inspire and fortify His sincere admirers. Set His example before your eyes and fix your gaze upon it; let it be your instinctive guide in your pursuit of the aim of the Plan. [8]

☙

In a talk delivered some days after He laid the cornerstone of the Mother Temple of the West, 'Abdu'l-Bahá stated that 'among the results of the manifestation of spiritual forces will be that the human world will adapt itself to a new social form', that 'the justice of God will become manifest throughout human affairs'. These, and countless other utterances of the Master to which the Bahá'í community is turning time and again in this centennial period, raise awareness of the distance that separates society as it is now arranged from the stupendous vision His Father gifted to the world.[9]

∾

We call upon all to reflect upon the significance of the endeavour in which the community of the Greatest Name is engaged, the purpose of which the Master strove to underline so often in the course of His travels, and to rededicate themselves to contribute their share to its outcome. 'Try with all your hearts', He urged one audience, 'to be willing channels for God's Bounty. For I say unto you that He has chosen you to be His messengers of love throughout the world, to be His bearers of spiritual gifts to man, to be the means of spreading unity and concord on the earth.' 'Perchance,' He remarked on another occasion, 'God willing, this terrestrial world may become as a celestial mirror upon which we may behold the imprint of the traces of Divinity, and the fundamental qualities of a new creation may be reflected from the reality of love shining in human hearts.' To this end do all your efforts tend . . . In our prayers at the Sacred Threshold, we will entreat the Almighty to sustain all those who would be a part of this immense undertaking, who prefer the true prosperity of others over their own ease and leisure, and whose eyes are fixed upon 'Abdu'l-Bahá for a flawless pattern of how to be; all this, that 'those who walk in darkness should come into the light' and 'those who are excluded should join the inner circle of the Kingdom'.[10]

❧

The Divine Plan, that sublime series of letters addressed by 'Abdu'l-Bahá to the Bahá'ís of North America between 26 March 1916 and 8 March 1917, constitutes one of the mighty Charters of His Father's Faith. Set forth in those fourteen Tablets, Shoghi Effendi explains, is 'the mightiest Plan ever generated through the creative power of the Most Great Name'. It is 'impelled by forces beyond our power to predict or appraise' and 'claims as the theatre for its operation territories spread over five continents and the islands of the seven seas'. Within it are held 'the seeds of the world's spiritual revival and ultimate redemption'.

In the Tablets of the Divine Plan 'Abdu'l-Bahá not only provided the broad vision necessary to carry out the responsibilities entrusted by Bahá'u'lláh to His loved ones, but He also outlined spiritual concepts and practical strategies necessary for success. In His exhortations to teach and to travel to teach; to arise personally or deputize others; to move to all parts of the world and open countries and territories, each meticulously named; to learn the relevant languages and translate and disseminate the Sacred Texts; to train the teachers of the Faith and especially youth; to teach the masses and, particularly, indigenous peoples; to be firm in the Covenant and protect the Faith; and to sow seeds and cultivate them in a process of organic growth, we find hallmarks of the entire series of Plans – each a specific stage of the Divine Plan shaped by the Head of the Faith – that will continue to unfold throughout the Formative Age.[11]

In this season, from the Day of the Covenant to the commemoration of the Ascension of 'Abdu'l-Bahá, every Bahá'í heart is stirred by remembrance of Him Who is the Mystery of God, the Centre of Bahá'u'lláh's impregnable Covenant, the Mainspring of the Oneness of Humanity, the embodiment of every Bahá'í ideal, the Most Mighty Branch of God whereunder all can find shelter. May His boundless love and tender solicitude give you reassurance and sustenance as you strive to fulfil the trust He bestowed upon you in His Testament and His Divine Plan. At night in that hallowed room in His home where He departed this life for reunion with His beloved Lord, we will testify to your fidelity to His call, evident in your tireless labours to create a refuge for humanity at this moment of increasing injustice and affliction.

Three brief years remain until the centenary of the Master's passing, when Bahá'ís the world over will gather and take account of the distance traversed over the first century of the Formative Age. May His loved ones, individually and collectively, little by little and day by day, increasingly embody His counsels: to be united in the Cause and firm in the Covenant; to avoid calumny and never speak ill of others; to see no strangers but regard all as members of one family; to set aside divergent theories and conflicting views and pursue a single purpose and common goal; to ensure that the love of Bahá'u'lláh has so mastered every organ, part, and limb as to leave no effect from the promptings of the human world; to arise with heart and soul and in one accord to teach the Cause; to march in serried lines, pressed together, each supporting the others; to cultivate good character, perseverance, strength, and determination; to know the value of this precious Faith, obey its teachings, walk in this road that is drawn straight, and show this way to the people.[12]

The close of the first century of the Formative Age is but two and a half years away. It will seal one hundred years of consecrated effort to consolidate and expand the foundation so sacrificially laid during the Faith's Heroic Age. At that time the Bahá'í community will also mark the centenary of the Ascension of 'Abdu'l-Bahá, that moment when the beloved Master was released from the confines of this world to rejoin His Father in the retreats of celestial glory. His funeral, which occurred the following day, was an event 'the like of which Palestine had never seen'. At its conclusion, His mortal remains were laid to rest within a vault of the Mausoleum of the Báb. However, it was envisaged by Shoghi Effendi that this would be a temporary arrangement. A Shrine was to be erected, of a character befitting the unique station of 'Abdu'l-Bahá, at the appropriate time.

That time has come. The Bahá'í world is being summoned to build the edifice which will forever embosom those sacred remains. It is to be constructed in the vicinity of the Riḍván Garden, on land consecrated by the footsteps of the Blessed Beauty; the Shrine of 'Abdu'l-Bahá will thus lie on the crescent traced between the Holy Shrines in 'Akká and Haifa.[13]

ᴥ

His passing took from the Bahá'ís of that era a Figure Who was the object of their ardent love and loyalty; to the faithful of this age, He remains without parallel: a perfect embodiment in word and deed of all that His Father taught, the One through Whom the Covenant of Bahá'u'lláh was 'proclaimed, championed and vindicated'. We are conscious that the coming year will also mark a century since His Will and Testament – that 'momentous', 'historic', 'immortal' Document – 'called into being, outlined the features and set in motion the processes' of the Administrative Order, 'the very pattern of that divine civilization which the almighty Law of Bahá'u'lláh is designed to establish upon earth'. This 'unique' and 'divinely-conceived' Order, this 'mighty administrative structure', had been fashioned by its Architect to perpetuate the Covenant and channel the spiritual powers of the Cause.[14]

۞

Under all conditions, the Master is your solace and support. For those who aspire to lasting change, His example guides the way – tactful and wise in His approach, penetrating in utterance, indiscriminating in fellowship, unfailing in sympathy for the downtrodden, courageous in conduct, persevering in action, imperturbable in the face of tests, unwavering in His keen sense of justice. And to all who arise to emulate Him, He offers this unfailing assurance: 'that which is confirmed is the oneness of the world of humanity. Every soul who serveth this oneness will undoubtedly be assisted and confirmed.'[15]

From the letters of Bahíyyih Khánum, the Greatest Holy Leaf

Bahíyyih Khánum, the Greatest Holy Leaf, was 'Abdu'l-Bahá's devoted and loyal sister. 'Banishing from her mind and heart every earthly attachment,' recalled Shoghi Effendi, 'renouncing the very idea of matrimony, she, standing resolutely by the side of a Brother whom she was to aid and serve so well, arose to dedicate her life to the service of her Father's glorious Cause.'[1]

Over a span of thirty years the Centre of God's Covenant rested not, nor was His human temple ever tranquil and at peace. By day, by night, He would be teaching and guiding stranger and friend alike, and protecting the Cause, and seeing to its progress, and for these things He sacrificed His life.[2]

☙

Singly and alone, He set about to reform the world, and to educate and refine its peoples. He invited all manner of beings to enter the Kingdom of God; He watered the Tree of the Faith; He guarded the celestial Lote-Tree from the tempest; He defeated the foes of the Faith, and He frustrated the hopes of the malevolent; and always vigilant, He protected God's Cause and defended His Law.

That subtle and mysterious Being, that Essence of eternal glory, underwent trials and sorrows all the days of His life. He was made the target of every calumny and malicious accusation, by foes both without and within. His lot, in all His life, was to be wronged, and be subjected to toil, to pain and grief. Under these conditions, the one and only solace of His sacred heart was to hear good news of the progress of the Faith, and the proclaiming of God's Word, and the spreading of the holy Teachings, and the unity and fervour of the friends, and the staunchness of His loved ones. This news would bring smiles to His countenance; this was the joy of His precious heart.

Meanwhile He trained a number of the faithful and reared them with the hands of His grace, and rectified their character and behaviour, and adorned them with the excellence of the favoured angels of Heaven – that they might arise today with a new spirit, and stand forth with wondrous power, and confront the forces of idle fancy, and scatter the troops upon troops of darkness with the blazing light of long endurance and high resolve; that they might shine out even as lighted candles, and moth-like, flutter so close about the lamp of the Faith as to scorch their wings.[3]

From moment to moment, at the hands of every betrayer, yet another cruel arrow was shot into His heart, and ever and again, from one or another assailant, He was calumny's target. In the dark of the night, out of the depths of His bosom, could be heard His burning sighs, and when the day broke, the wondrous music of His prayers would rise up to the denizens of the realm on high.

That Prisoner, grievously wronged, would hide His pain, and keep His wounds from view. In the depths of calamity He would smile, and even when enduring the direst of afflictions He would comfort the hearts. Although He was hemmed about with disasters, and living at the whirlwind's core of grief, He would still proclaim the Cause of God, and protect the Holy Faith, and He brought God's Word to the ears of those in East and West. He trained and nurtured friends of such a kind that whensoever their names were on His lips or spoken in His presence, His blessed face would glow and His whole being would radiate with joy. Many and many a time He would express His trust and confidence. In the gatherings held toward the close of His days, He would repeatedly tell of the apostles of Jesus. Among other things He would say that when the Spirit left this nether world and hastened away to the glorious Kingdom, He had but twelve disciples, and even of these, one was cast off; and that this small number, because they sacrificed all they had for Jesus, and immersed themselves in the radiance of that sweet and comely Being, and lost themselves in Christ, they lit the world. 'Now when I depart,' He would say, 'I have loyal loved ones that number 50,000 or more, and each one of these is a mighty fortress to guard the edifice of God, each one, for the Ark of the Faith, is strong as armour-plate. They are rooted firm as the high mountains, they are bright and rising stars, they are jewels, they are pearls.' Today, God be thanked, these qualities are radiating from the faces of the righteous, and shining upon their brows.

That blessed Being perfected His bounties for the people of Bahá, and His grace and favour were extended to those of all degrees. In the best of ways, he manifested at the end what had been shown forth at the beginning, crowning all His gifts with His Will and Testament, in which He clearly made known the obligations devolving upon every stratum of the believers, in language most consummate, comprehensive and sound, setting down with His own pen the name of Shoghi Effendi, as Guardian of the Cause and interpreter of the Holy Writ. The first of His bounties was the light He shed, the last of His gifts was that He unravelled the secrets by lifting the veil.[4]

❧

He would face the storms of tribulation with a heart full of fervour and love; He would breast the waves of calamities and oncoming ordeals with overflowing joy. With the balm of His loving-kindness, He would remedy unhealing wounds, and the medicine of His unending grace was a cure for mortal ills. Through His tenderness and care the sorrowful found comfort, and through His Words the despairing received the blissful consolation of their incomparable Lord. He would hearten the despised and the rejected with outpourings of grace.

In the pathway of Bahá'u'lláh, He made His holy breast a shield to bear adversities, made His beauteous face a target for the blows that rained upon Him from all sides. He, the Wronged One of the world, was compassed about by rebel hosts; the armies of treachery assailed Him from every direction. The disaffected were not remiss in their cruelty and aggression; never once did that arrogant crew fail to spread a calumny or to show their opposition and their malice. At every moment, they inflicted wounds upon Him, injured Him, brought fresh grief to His heart. Their sole aim was to bring down the structure of the Holy Faith and to destroy its very base and foundation. They did all in their power to split the Bahá'í community, and in their strivings to shatter the union of the believers, they neglected nothing. They joined hands with every enemy of the Faith, became boon companions of all who betrayed it. There was no mischief, no plot, no slander, no aspersion, that they would not allow themselves, no individual so vile that they would not cleave to him.

And thus, with all His own ordeals and cares, and banished from His home, He Whom the world wronged devoted Himself to counselling and nurturing the people with the utmost loving-kindness, divinely admonishing them, leading and guiding them at all times to complete and utter steadfastness in the Cause of God.

From one direction He would ward off the assaults of the nations, from another He would hold back the people of hatred from tormenting the believers. Now He would scatter the waverers' clouds of doubt, again He would demonstrate the truth of the clear and manifest Verses, and at all times and seasons He would guard the Cause of God with His very life, and protect its Law.

His fundamental purpose in enduring that continual toil and pain, and bearing those calamities, was to safeguard the divine and all-embracing Word, to shelter the tree of unity, to educate persons of capacity, to refine those who were pure in heart, and to transform the hearts of the receptive, to expound the mysteries of God and illumine the minds of the spiritual.[5]

II

ʻABDUʼL-BAHÁ IN THE TIME OF BAHÁʼUʼLLÁH

(1844 – 1921)

Írán

1844 – 1853

The birth of Bahá'u'lláh's Revelation occurred at a time when 'Abdu'l-Bahá, though a mere child, was able to perceive intuitively the glorious Mission with which His Father was invested. It seems also providential that 'Abdu'l-Bahá was born on the same day that the Báb declared His Mission to Mullá Husayn. It is significant indeed that as the Declaration of the Bab, the Herald of Bahá'u'lláh, took place on that memorable evening, so did the birth of the Person who was destined to become the recipient of His great Revelation.[1]

Adib Taherzadeh

∽

That night of 22-23 May 1844 was doubly blessed, for far to the north of Teheran Mírzá Husayn-'Alí of Núr and his beloved wife Ásíyih Khánum were expecting a third child, their two first-born sons having perished as babes . . . So it was that God's spiritual timing brought the lady Ásíyih's delivery on that very evening of the declaration of a new Prophet. There was born a son who was healthy and whole and hope fulfilled, and he was named 'Abbás, the lion.[2]

David S. Ruhe

∽

It was told of him as a little boy that he once was sent out to inspect the shepherds who had charge of his father's flocks among the Persian hills. When the review was completed he was told by his attendant it was customary to give each of the shepherds a present. He said he had nothing to give; but was told the men would expect something and something should be given them. The boy thereupon presented the shepherds with the flocks. His father hearing of this munificent gift was pleased at his son's generosity but said 'We shall have to watch 'Abbás; for next he will give away himself.'[3]

George Townshend

❦

'Abdu'l-Bahá was eight years old when Bahá'u'lláh was impris-oned in the notorious Síyáh-<u>Ch</u>ál dungeon of Ṭíhrán, following a misguided, unsuccessful attempt by two Bábís on the life of the <u>Sh</u>áh. Bahá'u'lláh's home was pillaged, His property confiscated and, overnight, His family faced persecution and poverty.

We heard each day the cries of the mob as a new victim was tortured or executed, not knowing but that it might be my father. My mother went daily to the house her aunt for news of him and generally spent the entire day there, hoping that each hour would bring some tidings. These were long and weary days for my mother, young as she was and unaccus-tomed to sorrow.

At first, on going to her aunt's, my mother would take me with her; but one day, returning unusually late, we found 'Abbás Effendi surrounded by a band of boys who had under-taken to personally molest him. He was standing in their midst as straight as an arrow – a little fellow, the youngest and smallest of the group – firmly but quietly *commanding* them not to lay their hands upon him, which, strange to say, they seemed unable to do. After that my mother thought it unsafe to leave him at home, knowing his fearless disposi-tion, and that when he went into the street, as he usually did to watch for her coming, eagerly expectant of news from his father for whom, even at that early age, he had a passionate attachment, he would be beset and tormented by the boys. So she took him with her, leaving me at home with my younger brother.[4]

Attributed to Bahíyyih Khánum

⁤⁤⁤⁤⁤⁤⁤⁤⁤ ⁤⁤⁤⁤⁤ ℰℬ

'Abdu'l-Bahá, even in early childhood, shared in the woes of His family, upon whom the most terrible troubles descended.

. . . 'Abdu'l-Bahá, then only eight years old, was brokenhearted at the ruthless treatment of His adored Father. The child suffered agonies, as a description of the tortures was related in His hearing – the cruel scourging of the feet, the long miles Bahá'u'lláh had to walk afterwards, barefooted, heavy chains cutting into the delicate flesh, the loathsome prison; the excruciating anxiety lest His very life should be taken – made a load of suffering, piteous for so young and sensitive a child to endure.[5]

All the former luxury of the family was at an end, deserted as they were by relations and friends. Homeless, utterly impoverished, engulfed in trouble, and misery, suffering from sheer want and extraordinary privations – such were the conditions under which His childhood's life was spent.[6]

Attributed to Munírih Khánum

Ba*gh*dád

1853 – 1863

After Bahá'u'lláh was released from the Síyáh-Chál – where He experienced a sublime vision announcing to Him His Divinely-ordained Mission – He and His family were exiled forever from their native land. One year after their arrival in Baghdád, Bahá'u'lláh retreated alone into the wilderness of Kurdistán, removing Himself from the plotting and bitter attacks levelled at Him by those among the exiles envious of His evident greatness. His absence of two years was particularly painful for His eldest son.

'Abdu'l-Bahá grieved over this cruel separation, but though a child of no more than ten years of age, His mien and bearing were assured and serene. His youthful shoulders had to bear responsibilities which mature men prefer to forgo. He read avidly what He could find of the Writings of the Báb. No school had ever moulded His mind, the unfoldment of which had been the loving care of Bahá'u'lláh . . .

'Abdu'l-Bahá oftentimes walked among the learned who were wise with the wisdom of age and competent with experience, and conversed with them on their themes and topics. They respected the speech of the young boy, because it was mature and enlightening, and because the speaker was modest and charming. Once a redoubtable enemy of Bahá'u'lláh remarked that had He no other proof to substantiate His exceptional powers, it were sufficient that He had reared such a son as 'Abbas Effendi.[7]

H.M. Balyuzí

ɔ

My brother was deeply attached to his father; this attachment seemed to strengthen with his growth. After our father's departure he fell into great despondency. He would go away by himself, and, when sought for, be found weeping, often falling into such paroxysms of grief that no one could console him. His chief occupation at this time was copying and committing to memory the tablets of the Báb. The childhood and youth of my brother was, in fact, in all respects unusual. He did not care for play or for amusement like other children. He would not go to school, nor would he apply himself to study. Horseback riding was the only diversion of which he was fond; in that he became proficient, being reputed to be a very skilful horseman.[8]

During the night following the next day, however, my father walked into the house. We hardly knew him; his beard and hair were long and matted – he really was a dervish in appearance. The meeting between my brother and his father was the most touching and pathetic sight I had ever seen. 'Abbás Effendi threw himself on the floor before him and kissed and embraced his feet, weeping and crying, 'Why did you leave us, why did you leave us?' while the great uncouth dervish wept over his boy. The scene carried a weight not to be expressed in words.[9]

Attributed to Bahíyyih Khánum

❧

During this time He was taken by His uncle, Mírzá Músá, to some of the meetings of the friends. There He spoke to them with a marvellous eloquence, even at that early age of eleven or twelve years. The friends wondered at His wisdom and the beauty of His person, which equalled that of His mind.

He prayed without ceasing for the return of Bahá'u'lláh. He would sometimes spend a whole night through praying a certain prayer. One day after a night so spent they found a clue! Very soon the Beloved One returned!

Now His joy was as great as His grief had been!

Many were the gatherings of the friends on the banks of the Tigris, to which the young boy was taken by His Father. These meetings, necessarily secret, were now His greatest pleasure. He drank in the teaching of divine things which were to educate the world, with an understanding of universal conceptions astounding in such a young child.[10]

Attributed to Munírih Khánum

ↁ

After a decade had passed in Baghdád, the Iranian Ambassador – alarmed at the growing influence and fame of Bahá'u'lláh – urged the Ottoman Government to summon Him to Constantinople. Ahead of His departure, Bahá'u'lláh moved to a garden on the outskirts of the city – which became known as the Garden of Riḍván – where He revealed to His family and followers His Station and His Mission.

The preparations for the journey were extremely difficult.

The Master, as He was now called, shielded His adored Father in all ways that lay in His power from undesirable intruders, from the world's insistence, and from those who merely wanted idly to see and hear something new.

He made the arrangements for the Beloved One to go to the Riḍván, there to abide until the family should have been able to make preparations for the departure.

Whilst He tarried in the Riḍván, the appointed time had arrived for the momentous proclamation.

Bahá'u'lláh confided to the eldest son, 'Abbás the Master, that He Himself was 'He Whom God shall make Manifest', heralded by the Forerunner, the Báb.

As the Master heard the soul-stirring words, and realized that His own beloved Father was he Who should educate mankind in universal conceptions, abolish prejudices, bring unity and the most Great Peace into the distracted world, establish the Kingdom of God upon this sad earth, by making religion again a healing spring for all woes of the world, He understood why the Manifestation had once again become the cause of evil men's hatred and malignant persecution.

As these things were pondered by the Master, His mind, well-endowed with a peculiar receptiveness that was inborn, and strengthened by the education given to Him by His Father, saw, as in a radiant vision, the world of the future, when the divine Message, having become known and comprehended by 'men of goodwill', would change the heart of the world, and the Kingdom where God's will shall be done *on earth* – for which we have been praying for nigh two thousand years – would be established.

Henceforth a new joy and increased devotion to His Father, Bahá'u'lláh (the Glory of God) took possession of Him. He consecrated Himself, body and soul and spirit, to the sacred work of the Bahá'í Cause, spreading abroad the new message of Love and Justice . . .[11]

Attributed to Muníríh Khánum

ల

The Báb states that the first one to believe in a Manifestation of God is the essence of the achievement of the preceding dispensation; and so, 'Abdu'l-Bahá, the first to believe with His whole being in the Mission of His Father, was the most eminent representative of the virtues called forth by the Báb. And He was also to be 'the embodiment of every Baháʼí ideal, the incarnation of every Baháʼí virtue . . .'[12]

'Abduʼl-Bahá . . . explained in brief but telling words the nature of the journey which lay ahead of them. 'Often, by day or by night we covered a distance of from twenty-five to thirty miles. No sooner would we reach a caravanserai than from sheer fatigue everyone would lie down and go to sleep: utter exhaustion having overtaken everybody they be unable even to move.' But He, Himself, often had little or no rest during these stops, for His was the duty to see that the large party, including the animals, were supplied with food and daily necessities.[13]

H.M. Balyuzí

Constantinople and Adrianople

1863 – 1868

The gruelling journey from Baghdád to Constantinople lasted three months, during which 'Abduʼl-Bahá devoted Himself tirelessly to the service of His Father and the community of exiles. Early in December 1863, the Sultán ordered the further banishment of Baháʼuʼlláh to Adrianople, on the fringes of the Ottoman Empire. As 'Abduʼl-Bahá grew into manhood, the excellence of His character became increasingly evident to all who encountered Him.

From the time when the declaration was made to him at Baghdad, 'Abbás Effendi seemed to constitute himself as the special attendant, servant, and body-guard of his father. He guarded him day and night on this journey, riding by his wagon and watching near his tent. He thus had little sleep, and, being young, became extremely weary. His horse was Arab and very fine, and so wild and spirited that no other man could mount him, but under my brother's hand as gentle and docile as a lamb. In order to get a little rest, he adopted the plan of riding swiftly a considerable distance ahead of the caravan, when, dismounting and causing his horse to lie down, he would throw himself on the ground and place his head on his horse's neck. So he would sleep until the cavalcade came up, when his horse would awake him by a kick and he would remount.[14]

During this period, as, in fact, had been the case for a number of years, 'Abbás Effendi was the chief dependence and comfort of the entire family. He had from childhood a remarkably self-sacrificing nature, habitually yielding his own wishes and giving up whatever he had to his brothers and sisters, keeping nothing for himself. He was always gentle; never became angry, and never retaliated. The life we were living afforded constantly recurring occasions for the exhibition of these qualities of his character; and his unceasing efforts did a great deal to make its conditions endurable for the other members of the family.

For the poor also he had ever been very tender-hearted, and, destitute as we were, he always contrived to find something to give to others who were in greater want.[15]

During the period of his residence at Adrianople, 'Abbás Effendi had endeared himself to every one, high and low, those of the faith and others alike. He taught much and even at that time was commonly called the 'Master'. The governor himself had become a friend of the Master's and delighted to listen to his religious discourses. It was the habit of the governor frequently to have the Master at the palace, and

when my brother could not got to the governor he sometimes came to my brother.[16]

Attributed to Bahíyyih Khánum

ᴄᴏ

'A seeker of the souls of men.' This is, indeed, a good description of both father and son. Neither the one nor the other
had much of what we call technical education, but both
understood how to cast a spell on the soul, awakening its
dormant powers. Abdul Baha had courage to frequent the
mosques and argue with the mullás; he used to be called
'the Master' *par excellence*, and the governor of Adrianople
became his friend . . .[17]

T.K. Cheyne

ᴄᴏ

It was during those five years in Roumelia that 'Abdu'l-
Bahá, the Most Great Branch, already styled by His
Father 'the Mystery of God', attained the full stature of
His unmatched and resplendent manhood. He was nine-
teen when Bahá'u'lláh and His family were ordered from
Constantinople, the seat of the Caliphate, to the remote
border of the Turkish dominions within the fringes of the
European continent. Now, twenty-four years of age, He
was greatly revered and highly esteemed not only in the
company of His Father's followers but in circles beyond.[18]

H.M. Balyuzí

'Akká

1868 – 1892

Bahá'u'lláh, along with His family and followers, arrived at their final place of banishment – the miserable, Ottoman prison city of 'Akká – on the last day of August 1868. For the next 24 years, 'Abdu'l-Bahá shielded and served His Father, eventually arranging for Bahá'u'lláh's move to properties outside of 'Akká's walls. In the meantime, the Master also cared for the exiles and the sick and impoverished inhabitants of the city, winning the love and admiration of His gaolers, city officials and the general population.

❧

At 'Akká, when nearly all the party were ill with typhoid, malaria, and dysentery, He washed the patients, nursed them, fed them, watched with them, taking no rest, until utterly exhausted, He Himself took dysentery, and for about a month remained in a dangerous condition. In 'Akká, as in Adrianople, all classes, from the Governor to the most wretched beggar, learned to love and respect Him.[19]   *J.E. Esslemont*

❧

As time went on, the Muftí of 'Akká and the Páshá, who was the Governor, became attached friends of the Master, mainly through witnessing the beauty of the life He led, in which ministering service to all was manifested before their eyes. They had begun to comprehend something of the holiness of the ideals of the exiles, and came to look upon Bahá'u'lláh with awe and respect and great honour.

The Governor, who had become friendly, would from time to time be recalled, and would be replaced by another who would take up his post in an attitude of unfriendliness to the exiles; his mind having been filled with false reports.

As these suspicions translated themselves into action, stricter rules would be made; our little freedom would be curtailed, and our lives become more and more restricted. As the days passed on, the enmity of the Governor would melt away under the warmth of the Master's invariable loving-kindness, rules would relax, and our lives become again happy, so that the friendship of the Governor made a marvellous difference to our comfort.[20]

The Master, by making all arrangements, doing all the business, seeing applicants and pilgrims, planning interviews at stated hours, protected His Father from every troublesome detail, and made it possible for Him to lead a peaceful life, with leisure in which to write His Tablets and to formulate laws and instructions for the world of the future.

The Master occupied Himself with the affairs and interests of the people of the place, all outside news being brought to Him by the Governor and the Muftí.

Every week the Master went to Bahjí, carrying all the news which would be of interest to Bahá'u'lláh.[21]

The life of the Master in 'Akká was full of work for others' good.

He would rise very early, take tea, then go forth to His self-imposed labours of love. Often He would return very late in the evening, having had no rest and no food.

He would go first to the Bírúní, a large reception room, which had been hired, on the opposite side of the street to our house. We often used to watch from our windows, the people

70

crowding there to ask for help from the Master.

. . . Some days He hardly saw His own family, so hard pressed was He by those who crowded to the Bíruní for some kind of help.

The many sick people, Bahá'í and others, were His constant care; whenever they wished to see Him, He went.

One poor old couple, who were ill in bed for a month, had twenty visits from the Master during that time.

To every sick person He sent each day a servant to ask 'Did you sleep? How are you? Do you need anything?' All their needs He supplied.

Never did He neglect anything but His own rest, His own food; the poor were always His first care.

All sweets, fruits, and cakes which had been sent to Him He would take to the Bírúní for the friends, whom He made very happy.

The Arabs called Him the 'Lord of Generosity'.

. . . For those other things the poor needed when they were ill, numberless, various, always to the Master did they turn their eyes.

. . . It would be impossible to write even a small part of the many compassionate acts of love and charity wrought by the Master; all His life was spent in ministering service to every unhappy creature who came to Him, and in being the devoted son to His Father. [22]

Attributed to Ṭúbá Khánum

❧

Many a time I was in the presence of Bahá'u'lláh when the Master was also present. Because of His presence Bahá'u'lláh would be filled with the utmost joy and gladness. One could see His blessed countenance beaming with delight and exultation so lovingly that no words can adequately describe it. Repeatedly He would laud and glorify the Master, and the mere mention of His name would suffice to evoke an indescribable feeling of ecstasy in the Person of the Blessed Beauty. No pen is capable of fully describing this.[23]

Mírzá Maḥmúd-i-Káshání

❧

It was at that time that 'Abdu'l-Bahá arrived from 'Akká. The Blessed Beauty said, 'The Master is coming, hasten to attend Him' . . . On those days Bahá'u'lláh used to sow the seeds of loyalty and servitude toward 'Him Whom God hath purposed' ['Abdu'l-Bahá] in the hearts of the believers and explained the lofty station and hidden reality of the Master to all.

Attended by everyone, 'Abdu'l-Bahá came with great humility into the presence of the Blessed Beauty. Then the Tongue of Grandeur uttered words to this effect, 'From morning until now this garden was not pleasant, but now with the presence of the Master it has become truly most delightful.'[24]

Hájí Mírzá Habíbu'lláh-i-Afnán

❧

Oh the joy of the day when Bahá'u'lláh went to the beautiful Riḍván which had been prepared for Him with such loving care by the Master, the friends, and the pilgrims!

The Master's heart was gladdened indeed to see the enjoyment of His beloved Father, resting under the big mulberry tree, by the side of the little river rippling by, the fountain which they had contrived splashing and gurgling in sounds refreshing indeed after the long years of confinement in the pestilential air of the penal fortress of 'Akká. Only those who were present there could realize in any degree what it meant to be surrounded by such profusion of flowers, their colours and their scents, after the dull walls and unfragrant odours of the prison city. [25]

Attributed to Ṭúbá Khánum

❧

During 'Abdu'l-Bahá's first years in 'Akká, He came to the attention of missionaries from the London Jews' Society.

We were received by his [Bahá'u'lláh's] son, who is apparently about 30 years of age, and has a fine intellectual countenance, with black hair and beard, and that sallow, melancholic look which distinguished nearly all Persians of the intelligent and religious class. He was dressed in a robe of white flannel, with cap of the same material, and a small white turban. Over his shoulders was thrown a brown cloth abbái . . . He had a remarkably earnest, almost solemn manner, spoke excellent Arabic fluently, and showed a minute and accurate knowledge of the Old and New Testaments, as well as an acquaintance with the history of religious thought in Europe. [26]

Thomas Chaplin

❧

We had a long interview with the son of their prophet. It was indeed strange to find an Eastern in Syria so well educated, and to hear him speak so tolerantly and intelligibly of Christ and Christianity. [27]

James Neill

73

In 1890, Professor Edward Granville Browne, an oriental-
ist from Cambridge University made his well-known visit to
Bahá'u'lláh and also encountered the Master for the first time.

Seldom have I seen one whose appearance impressed me
more. A tall strongly-built man holding himself straight as
an arrow, with white turban and raiment, long black locks
reaching almost to the shoulder, broad powerful forehead
indicating a strong intellect combined with an unswerving
will, eyes keen as a hawk's, and strongly-marked but pleasing
features – such was my first impression of 'Abbás Efendí, 'the
master' (*Áká*) as he *par excellence* is called by the Bábís. Subsequent conversation with him served only to heighten the
respect with which his appearance had from the first inspired
me. One more eloquent of speech, more ready of argu-
ment, more apt of illustration, more intimately acquainted
with the sacred books of the Jews, the Christians, and the
Muhammadans, could, I should think, scarcely be found
even amongst the eloquent, ready, and subtle race to which
he belongs. These qualities, combined with a bearing at once
majestic and genial, made me cease to wonder at the influence and esteem which he enjoyed even beyond the circle of
his father›s followers. About the greatness of this man and his
power no one who had seen him could entertain a doubt. [28]

Edward G. Browne

III

THE MINISTRY OF 'ABDU'L-BAHÁ

(1892 – 1921)

'Akká and Haifa

1892 – 1910

In the years immediately following the Ascension of Bahá'u'lláh on 29 May 1892, 'Abdu'l-Bahá was faced with the relentless attacks and the undermining of His position as Centre of the Covenant from envious and faithless family members and their supporters. In contrast, the Faith of Bahá'u'lláh was spreading to the Western World and, at the end of 1898, although He remained a prisoner in 'Akká, 'Abdu'l-Bahá was able to welcome the first Bahá'í pilgrims from the West, many of whom wrote vivid descriptions of the Master.

Suddenly the light caught a form that at first seemed a vision of mist and light. It was the Master which the candle-light had revealed to us. His white robe, and silver, flowing hair, and shining blue eyes gave the impression of a spirit, rather than of a human being. We tried to tell Him how deeply grateful we were at His receiving us. 'No,' He answered, 'you are kind to come.' This was spoken in a very careful English.

Then He smiled, and we recognized the Light which He possessed in the radiance which moved over His fine and noble face.[1]

Mary Virginia Thornburgh-Cropper

ॐ

We reached the door and stopped – before us, in the centre of the room, stood a man clad in a long raiment, with a white turban upon His head; stretching out one hand to us, while His face, which I cannot describe, was lighted by a rare, sweet smile of joy and welcome![2]

77

The Face of the Master is gloriously beautiful. His eyes read one's very soul, still they are full of divine love and fairly melt one's heart! His hair and beard are white, but soft and fine like silk. His features are finely chiselled and very classical. His forehead high and full and His mouth supremely beautiful, while His hands are small and white . . .[3]

Lua Getsinger

❧

Of that first meeting I can remember neither joy nor pain nor anything that I can name. I had been carried suddenly to too great a height; my soul had come in contact with the Divine Spirit; and this force so pure, so holy, so mighty, had overwhelmed me. He spoke to each one of us in turn of ourselves and our lives and those whom we loved, and although His words were so few and so simple they breathed the Spirit of Life to our souls.[4]

May Bolles Maxwell

❧

The Greatest Branch is all and more than anyone could ask. He is a perfect ideal of Christ and I shall never forget the look on His face as He stood in the Tomb [of Bahá'u'lláh] lighting the candles and again when He bowed His head praying just outside the room . . . He looked as if He were receiving instructions from His only superior. His face was heavenly in its sweet calm and He never shed a tear though everyone else was weeping terribly. His power is unmistakable: though a prisoner He holds the government in His own hands.[5]

In looks He is a little older and greyer than I had pictured, rather short than tall, but with a majestic bearing that at times makes Him seem like a giant. He has wonderful soft brown eyes, gray hair & beard, but very black brows, the sweetest smile in the world and a spirit shining out of His face that draws one like a magnet, and at times gives Him the expression of a martyr . . .[6]

Ella Goodall

ℰℴ

I could not put into words what I felt. Nor can words describe Our Beloved Master. Nor does one fully realize His Greatness, His love and gentleness, humility and grandeur, till they have passed beyond that Presence for the last time, and then it comes gradually, and the farther one recedes, the greater He appears.[7]

Anna Hoar

ℰℴ

The motion was almost like gliding, so smooth was it, and as he drew nearer, we noticed the mouse-coloured gown he wore with a turban to match, and there stood before us One who was the personification of all gentleness and meekness, and yet a sublime dignity rested upon him which we had never seen in others of the same faith, unusual in type as they were.[8]

With the calmness of one who can afford to await the results, and with the humility of one who knows his station in the work, both in this world and in that invisible one . . . he made no effort to convince or affect his hearers.[9]

Margaret Peeke

When the Master appeared on the threshold I was overwhelmed, for such an atmosphere of perfect Majesty and humility surrounded His whole being. He swept into the room, and, after having given us a most beautiful welcome, bade us be seated, then the flood of His words became to us as living water – I could not understand the language, but the spirit was so strong that we felt as though we knew the words even before they were given us through the clear translation of Aly Kuli Khan. At first we remained as though stunned, but soon to my great surprise, for it is something that I seldom do, I began to weep. They were not tears of sadness, oh no, they were tears of hope, and deep gratitude, tears that one might shed after having been released from a dark prison.[10]   *Laura Dreyfus Barney*

❧

The Master was busy revealing verses. His pen moved extremely rapidly across the page. Meanwhile, He was conversing with the Iranian believers in Persian, with the Mufti and Qadi in Arabic and with the Motosarraf and several of the Pashas in Turkish. All the while His pen never stopped moving. The divine spirit had enveloped the atmosphere and anyone who ventured a question was favoured with an answer until that blessed Tablet was completed and ʻAbduʼl-Bahá set the pen down.[11]

Mírzá Habíbuʼlláh Afnán

He is not a tall man, but is, nevertheless, a man of commanding presence, with a noble head splendidly set on regal shoulders, a man who would command attention respect in any assemblage.

To me, his was a personality of ineffable sweetness and charm, a reposeful dignity impossible to describe. In his face was the light of a divine love, and his smile a glimpse of the heavenly radiance. I shall never forget that smile; it came but rarely, but when it did come, lighting up a countenance habitually sad, it was beautiful to behold.[12]

William Hoar

ↄ

When the Master speaks a something is set in vibration over and above the physical words, a something which is Spirit and Life, and which bestows Spirit and Life; and it would seem that outer words are merely a means of contact, or a physical medium of connection between the soul and this Spirit of Life which is imparted to the soul . . . Perhaps the same words spoken by another would have made no impression, for his answer was a simple statement without proof. Uttered by him, however, they seemed to change the whole current of my thought, create a new consciousness in me, and supply me with the power of comprehension, so that a matter which had puzzled me for more than a year was cleared up in an instant.[13]

Hooper Harris

ↄ

As I nestled more closely against him, and as he spoke of the wondrous love of God, everything for a moment seemed clear to me, and all doubts that I may have had vanished instantly. I did not need any verbal arguments, or assurance, to convince me that divine love was the ruling and saving force of this world. I experienced it then and there, and the desire to so live as to radiate even a slight reflection of this love to others, was newly born, and, before leaving Acca, became greatly intensified.[14]

Edwin Woodcock

He was able to be to us a loving father, a companion and friend, and we could enjoy ourselves socially because we did not continually keep Him answering questions, at which time He would at once assume a different attitude and distance would come between us and one would feel His Kingship, His Greatness, the unlimited depths of His Wisdom. He is indeed as a 'well of living water springing up into everlasting life', and knowledge and wisdom come from His lips as does water from a fountain, giving life to every thirsty heart and all who will may come and take the water of life freely.[15]

(Aseyeh) Allen-Dyar

℘

At 'Abdu'l-Bahá's table, people from all walks of life, from an increasing number of countries, became the recipients of His wisdom. The notes taken of His talks by one pilgrim, Laura Dreyfus-Barney, formed the book Some Answered Questions, *a volume unique among the texts from the Central Figures of the Bahá'í Faith. 'Abdu'l-Bahá's renown also began to capture the attention of other Westerners travelling in the Holy Land.*

'I have given to you my tired moments,' were the words of 'Abdu'l-Bahá as He rose from table after answering one of my questions. As it was on this day, so it continued; between the hours of work, His fatigue would find relief in renewed activity; occasionally He was able to speak at length; but often, even though the subject might require more time, He would be called away after a few moments; again, days and even weeks would pass, in which He had no opportunity of instructing me. But I could well be patient, for I had always before me the greater lesson – the lesson of His personal life.[16]

Laura Dreyfus Barney

In this book, *Some Answered Questions*, the supreme genius of ʿAbduʾl-Bahá is overwhelmingly manifest. Men who have devoted precious years of their lives to study and research – to the building of arguments, the laying of premises, and the marshalling of facts – have never presented the fundamentals of life and belief, the basic truths of the universe around them, and the mainsprings of action, with such lucidity and coherence as are here apparent. Nor can they hope to rival, much less to match ʿAbduʾl-Baháʾs all-encompassing wisdom. And these were words spoken without previous intimation of the nature and purport of the query. Not only do His answers arrest attention and compel thought, the strength wedded to the crystal clarity of the language enchant the mind. His statements are unencumbered, His similes most apt, His reasoning is flawless. His conclusions are unhedged and emphatic, informed with authority. *Some Answered Questions* has no equal . . .[17]

H.M. Balyuzí

To ʿAbduʾl-Bahá, as a teacher and friend, came men and women from every race, religion and nation, to sit at his table like favored guests, questioning him about the social, spiritual or moral programme each had most at heart; and after a stay lasting from a few hours to many months, returning home, inspired, renewed and enlightened. The world surely never possessed such a guest-house as this.

Within its doors the rigid castes of India melted away, the racial prejudice of Jew, Christian and Muḥammadan became less than a memory; and every convention save the essential law of warm hearts and aspiring minds broke down, banned and forbidden by the unifying sympathy of the Master's house. It was like a King Arthur and the Round Table . . . but an Arthur who knighted women as well as men, and sent them away not with the sword but with the Word.[18]

Horace Holley

He is a clever, learned and respectable man, having a magnetic presence, attractive manners and a great deal of tact . . .
Abbas Effendi is a fascinating mystic, a man of most impressive presence and conversation, and his voice is musical and
mesmerizing.[19]

William Curtis

eᴧɔ

He has in the highest degree that great gift which we call
personality. His readily-given sympathy, his understanding
of human nature, his power of interesting himself in every
human soul which asks his advice and help, have made him
passionately beloved by his people. Above all, he has that
subtler quality of spirituality which is felt rather than understood by those with whom he comes into contact. He receives
the long stream of pilgrims, inquirers and pupils who come to
Akka, and now to Haifa, with unfailing gentleness, geniality,
and courtesy. He takes a personal interest in every one of the
Persians in Haifa – there are now about thirty families, some
of which were exiled with Baha U'llah, others Bahais who have
voluntarily come to Syria in order to be near the Master. He
names their children for them, helps to educate them when
they are unable to afford education for themselves, and advises
them in their material as well as their spiritual life.

It is his habit to receive the men of the community
every evening an hour after sunset, and however long and
tiring the day's work has been, he never refuses to admit
them and talk with them. It has been my privilege to assist
several times at these evening receptions. The Master's house
is simply built and simply furnished. He loves two things:
light and flowers, so that the room in which he receives his
guests has many windows, and a vase full of flowers stands

always on the table. For the rest, the walls are bare and white, the woodwork is painted white, and the chairs and divans ranged around the room are covered with an unpretentious light-coloured cotton holland material. At seven o'clock the Persians enter together, their hands folded and their heads bent, and, leaving their shoes outside in the Oriental fashion, seat themselves round the room. For each man as he comes in Abbas Effendi has a kindly greeting, a tactful remark, a personal inquiry, or sometimes a humorous sally which brings a smile to then-grave faces. Among them is often a pilgrim, a believer who has travelled from a great distance to see and learn from the Master. Abbas Effendi will draw him out; and interesting discussions follow, for the pilgrim may be a Zoroastrian from North Persia, a Parsee from India, or even a Japanese. After a moment the talk invariably turns on the spiritual life, and upon the twin *Leit-Motive* of the Master's teaching – Love and Unity.

. . . Nor is his talk entirely confined to abstractions. He is keenly interested in the political, social, and educational movements in the Western world which seem like the beginning of the fulfilment of Baha U'llah's predictions. He has discussed Esperanto with me, which may be destined to become the universal language prophesied by Baha U'llah; the efforts of Tolstoi and the Peace Conference towards the abolition of war, and the great philanthropic institutions of Europe and America. He speaks confidently of the day when Chauvinism, the wish to further the interests of one nation at the expense of another, which too often passes for legitimate patriotism, will be replaced by the endeavour to further the interests of humanity at large; of a time when the universal language will be taught in schools founded on an international basis whose educational system shall have no religious bias, no racial bias, no political bias; of an era when the attention of inventors, instead of being directed towards the construction of engines of war and destruction, will be exclusively devoted to the improvement and amelioration of the human race and the alleviation of its miseries. He discusses, too, the scientific questions of the day, and has opinions to offer which are of the most interesting nature.

. . . A Frenchman of great intelligence who has lived for many years in Haifa in an official capacity, and who often goes to Abbas Effendi's house to discuss the questions of the day with him, said to me one day with admiration, speaking of such a discussion, 'What a mind! What intuition he has!' And in the early days at Akka, when Abbas Effendi was appointed by his father to receive the visitors who came to their house – for Baha U'llah rarely admitted any to his presence except the faithful – controversialists and religionists of all kinds would come to him with the purpose of confuting him with their arguments. But Abbas Effendi was able to answer them all; and so great is the respect in which he is held, even among the fanatical Mohammedans, that ceremonial visits have been made to him by most of the principal Moslem theologians who have come to Akka or Haifa.

Another side to his character is his charity. He never makes his charities openly, or even speaks of them; but you hear of them in roundabout ways. A devout Catholic once said to me: 'Abbas Effendi helps our work among the poor every year, and' – she paused – 'if I were only permitted to tell you of the secret good that he has done!' And once in Damascus I ran across a poor Persian, who asked me to take his respectful greetings and a letter to the Master. He spoke of him with emotional affection, and then told me that during the late Adana massacres his shop had been burnt down and his father killed by the Kurds, he himself being left for dead. Abbas Effendi sent him monetary help, wrote him kindly letters which gave the unfortunate man the courage to face life again, and started him afresh. Nor, in spite of his vast correspondence, does he cease to take an interest in his protégé.

. . . I have been doubly fortunate in seeing him almost daily and in having continual long interviews with him. During these interviews, one characteristic, not, I think, particularly noticed by those who have written about him, has particularly struck me. That is, his keen sense of humour. He has the Oriental habit of illustrating his teaching with stories, and sometimes these are of a delightfully ironical and amusing nature.

. . . I have said that Abbas Effendi is fond of flowers. He is, in fact, like his father, Baha U'llah, an ardent lover of nature . . . He has a great love for Mount Carmel, and I have often met him with a few followers on the little platform, planted with rose trees, before the tomb of the Bab half-way up the mountain side; for the body of the martyred saint was secured by his followers and eventually interred on Carmel. From this little rose-garden, tended lovingly by the Persians, one has a wonderful view of the flower-covered slopes of the mountain, the little red and white town of Haifa below, and then the wide blue bay with its long crescent of sandy beach, on the further side of which Akka lies close to the water's edge within her fortified walls, white as the breast of a sea-gull.[20]

E.S. Stevens

༄

It is a noteworthy gathering. Many of these men are blind; many more are pale, emaciated, or aged . . . Most of the women are closely veiled, but enough are uncovered to cause us well to believe that, if the veils were lifted, more pain and misery would be seen. Some of them carry babes with pinched and sallow faces. There are perhaps a hundred in this gathering, and besides, many children. They are of all the races one meets in these streets – Syrians, Arabs, Ethiopians, and many others.

These people are ranged against the walls or seated on the ground, apparently in an attitude of expectation; for what do they wait? Let us wait with them.

We have not long to wait. A door opens and a man comes out. He is of middle stature, strongly built. He wears flowing light-colored robes. On his head is a light buff fez with a white cloth wound about it. He is perhaps sixty years of age. His long grey hair rests on his shoulders. His forehead is broad, full, and high, his nose slightly aquiline, his moustaches and beard, the latter full though not heavy, nearly white. His eyes are grey and blue, large, and both soft and penetrating. His bearing is simple, but there is grace, dignity, and even majesty about his movements. He passes through the crowd, and as he goes utters words of salutation. We do not understand them, but we see the benignity and the kindliness of his countenance. He stations himself at a narrow angle of the street and motions to the people to come towards him. They crowd up a little too insistently. He pushes them gently back and lets them pass him one by one. As they come they hold their hands extended. In each open palm he places some small coins. He knows them all. He caresses them with his hand on the face, on the shoulders, on the head. Some he stops and questions . . . He stops a woman with a babe and fondly strokes the child. As they pass, some kiss his hand. To all he says, 'Marhabbah, marhabbah' – [Welcome, welcome!].

So they all pass him. The children have been crowding around him with extended hands, but to them he has not given. However, at the end, as he turns to go, he throws a handful of coppers over his shoulder, for which they scramble.

During this time this friend of the poor has not been unattended. Several men wearing red fezes, and with earnest and kindly faces, followed him from the house, stood near him and aided in regulating the crowd, and now, with reverent manner and at a respectful distance, follow him away. When they address him they call him 'Master'.

This scene you may see almost any day of the year in the streets of 'Akka. There are other scenes like it, which come only at the beginning of the winter season. In the cold weather which is approaching, the poor will suffer, for, as in all cities, they are thinly clad. Some day at this season, if you are advised of the place and time, you may see the poor of 'Akka gathered at one of the shops where clothes are sold, receiving cloaks from the Master. Upon many, especially the most infirm or crippled, he himself places the garment, adjusts it with his own hands, and strokes it approvingly, as if to say, 'There! Now you will do well.' There are five or six hundred poor in 'Akka, to all of whom he gives a warm garment each year.

On feast days he visits the poor at their homes. He chats with them, inquires into their health and comfort, mentions by name those who are absent, and leaves gifts for all.

Nor is it the beggars only that he remembers. Those respectable poor who cannot beg, but must suffer in silence – those whose daily labour will not support their families – to these he sends bread secretly. His left hand knoweth not what his right hand doeth.

All the people know him and love him – the rich and the poor, the young and the old – even the babe leaping in its mother's arms. If he hears of any one sick in the city – Muslim or Christian, or of any other sect, it matters not – he is each day at their bedside, or sends a trusty messenger. If a physician is needed, and the patient poor, he brings or sends one, and also the necessary medicine. If he finds a leaking roof or a broken window menacing health, he summons a workman, and waits himself to see the breach repaired. If any one is in trouble – if a son or a brother is thrown into prison, or he is threatened at law, or falls into any difficulty too heavy for him – it is to the Master that he straightway makes appeal for counsel or for aid. Indeed, for counsel all come to him, rich as well as poor. He is the kind father of all people . . .

For more than thirty-four years this man has been a prisoner at 'Akka. But his gaolors have become his friends. The Governor of the city, the Commander of the Army Corps, respect and honor him as though he were their brother. No man's opinion or recommendation has greater weight with them. He is the beloved of all the city, high and low. And how could it be otherwise? For to this man it is the law, as it was to Jesus of Nazareth, to do good to those who injure him. Have we yet heard of any one in lands which boast the name of Christ who lived that life?

Hear how he treats his enemies. One instance of many I have heard will suffice.

When the Master came to 'Akka there lived there a certain man from Afghanistan, an austere and rigid [Muslim]. To him the Master was a heretic. He felt and nourished a great enmity towards the Master, and roused up others against him. When opportunity offered in gatherings of the people, as in the Mosque, he denounced him with bitter words.

'This man', he said to all, 'is an imposter. Why do you speak to him? Why do you have dealings with him?' And when he passed the Master on the street he was careful to hold his robe before his face that his sight might not be defiled.

Thus did the Afghan. The Master, however did thus: The Afghan was poor and lived in a mosque; he was frequently in need of food and clothing. The Master sent him both. These he accepted, but without thanks. He fell sick. The Master took him a physician, food, medicine, money. These, also, he accepted; but as he held out one hand that the physician might take his pulse, with the other he held his cloak before his face that he might not look upon the Master. For twenty-four years the Master continued his kindnesses and the Afghan persisted in his enmity. Then at last one day the Afghan came to the Master's door, and fell down, penitent and weeping, at his feet.

'Forgive me, sir!' he cried. 'For twenty-four years I have done evil to you, for twenty-four years you have done good to me. Now I know that I have been in the wrong.'

The Master bade him rise, and they became friends.

The Master is as simple as his soul is great. He claims nothing for himself – neither comfort, nor honor, nor repose. Three or four hours of sleep suffice him; all the remainder of his time and all of his strength are given to the succour of those who suffer, in spirit or in body.

'I am', he says, 'the servant of God.'

Such is 'Abbas Effendi, the Master of 'Akka.[21]

Myron Phelps

❧

The pilgrim to 'Akká is asked many questions on his return. Is this a prophet? A manifestation of divinity . . . Is it enough of Divinity to see love made perfect through suffering a life-long patience, a faith which no exile or imprisonment can dim, a love which no treachery can alter, a hope which rises a pure clear flame after being drenched with the world's indifference through a lifetime? If that is not Divinity enough for this world, what is? . . . What greater sign can you ask than the power to flood this old world with love and aspiration, with patience and courage?[22] *Jane Elizabeth Whyte*

The first sojourn in Egypt

10 August 1910 – 11 August 1911

The Young Turks Revolution in 1908 and the subsequent freeing of all political and religious prisoners of the Ottoman Empire meant that 'Abdu'l-Bahá was now a free man for the first time since he was eight years old. He immediately set about completing the construction of a mausoleum for the remains of the Báb on Mount Carmel, moving His home and family to Haifa, and planning the further proclamation of His Father's Teachings to other parts of the world. In August 1910, He left the Holy Land for the first time in 42 years, bound for Egypt. After a month's stay in Port Said, His poor health would not permit an extended journey to Europe. He remained instead in Ramleh, near Alexandria, for a full year His presence aroused intense curiosity among prominent Egyptians, the press, as well as Westerners who visited Him.

The day is not far off when the details of Abdu'l Baha's missionary journeys will be admitted to be of historical importance. How gentle and wise he was, hundreds could testify from personal knowledge . . .[23]

T.K. Cheyne

లు

Future historians will give Abdul Baha's journey the detail and the reflection it deserves; but a mere outline, in relation to the preceding study, reveals even now something of its unique importance. 'Ambassador to Humanity' was the expression used by one present at an address in Washington, and this title is perhaps as descriptive as any to hand. But how different the mission, how different the method, how different the man! If any generation could distinguish out, while still living, the nature most richly and most potently endowed with its best forces, ours has that privilege. In Abdul Baha we have a mirror focusing all that is most significant, suppressing all that is irrelevant, of our time.[24]

Horace Holley

&

The eminent Mirza Abbas Effendi, Head of the Bahai Faith in Acca, and the authority (for Bahais) throughout the world, has arrived at the Port of Alexandria . . . He is a sheikh revered throughout the world, an expert in Shariah and learned in the fluctuations and developments of Islamic history . . . he attracts spirits and souls wholly to his belief in the oneness of mankind, which in its approach corresponds to a belief in 'the unity of being' in religious belief. His teaching and guidance revolve around the elimination of prejudice, whether that is in religion, gender, nationality or the comforts of temporal life.[25]

Shaykh 'Alí Yúsuf

&

Whosoever associates with him, find him a man who has information upon all subjects of human interest; his words are eloquent and attract the hearts, and enkindle the souls. His teachings and conversation revolve around the centre of the greatest of the world's problems: To remove entirely, religious, racial and patriotic prejudices, and lay the foundation of a brotherhood and unity that will last throughout the ages and eternity.[26]

Moamid newspaper

Twice I have called upon Abbas Effendi while in Ramleh and have seen the poor and indigent gathered around his house waiting for him to come out and when he appears, they beg alms and he gives to them. This is just a short sketch of his generous qualities and I confess my inability to do it justice. His physical appearance is medium size, white hair, penetrating eyes, smiling face and wonderful countenance, courteous, and his manner, simplicity itself, disliking any ostentation and show. He is a wise man, a philosopher and his knowledge of the Turkish, Persian and Arabic is unsurpassed.

He knows the history of nations and understands the causes of their rise and fall.

He is sixty years old and on account of certain nervous ailments he has come to Egypt for a change of air. He personally reads all the articles and letters sent him from all parts of the world, and answers the most important of them in his Persian handwriting which is famous for its beauty. Many of the great men of this country and delegates from other nations have met him and he gives a personal interview to each one of them. No one has visited him without leaving him impressed by his presence and praising his qualities and wondering at his magnanimity and his astonishing mind.[27]

El Ahram newspaper

ৎ৵৹

Abdu'l-Baha in all the divine characteristics is intensely human and keenly alive to the joys and sorrows of existence. There is no one who feels more acutely the sufferings of humanity than he and no one loves his fellow-men more than he. Here, in Alexandria, he lives exactly like other men; he goes into the stores, into the mosques, into the prisons. He converses just as kindly and amiably with the humblest

man in the street as with the highest in the land. His matchless and magnetic kindness attracts all, whether ignorant or
wise, rich or poor; he is no respecter of persons and in some
instances, after a halfhour's conversation, his bitterest enemy
has become his staunchest friend. [28]

The life of Abdu'l-Baha is simple; his attitude is humble;
his needs are very few. You think that if he should come to
America you must have a house prepared and surround him
with luxuries of modern civilization. Far from it! With love,
unity, and harmony, shining like stars of heaven in your dist,
a little cottage is greater than the imperial palace of kings. All
through his life his sole purpose and aim has been to spread
the fragrances of God, to serve the Kingdom of Abha, and
to sacrifice himself for the good of the world. He has done
all these; nay, rather, his services to man cannot be measured
by any criterion. His life, like unto a tempestuous sea, is ever
in motion, casting pearls of significance and truth upon its
shore. Humanity owes to him a debt that can never be paid
with money or gratitude.[29]

Mohammed Yazdi

∾

I met Abdul Baha near Alexandria, where he was staying
with some of his followers . . . You feel at once that here is
a master of men and a marvellous spiritual personality. He
seemed to me to focus in a truly divine manner the spiritual
ideal of the coming age. When one has come in contact with
Abdul Baha's power, or rather the power behind him, one has
no doubt that this movement will vitally affect the religious
and social evolution of the whole world.[30]

Wellesley Tudor Pole

At Ramleh, Abbas Effendi might at times be seen walking about the streets. Oft times he would ride upon the electric tramway, making change and paying his fare in the most democratic fashion. His reception room was open to believers and non believers alike. Upon a visit to some unfortunates one day I asked if they knew him. 'O yes,' they responded, 'he has been in this house.' Thus in one way or another, thousands of Persians had opportunity to see Abbas Effendi; but among these how few perceived Abdu'l-Baha.

Viewed with the outer eye, he is about the medium height, with symmetrical features. His lineaments indicate meekness and gentleness, as well as power and strength. His color is about that of parchment. His hands are shapely, with the nails well manicured. His forehead is high and well rounded. His nose is slightly aquiline; his eyes light blue and penetrating; his hair is silvery, and long enough to touch the shoulders; his beard is white. His dress was the Oriental robes, graceful in their simplicity. On his head rested a light tarbush, surrounded by a white, turban. His voice is powerful, but capable of producing infinite pathos and tenderness. His carriage is erect and altogether so majestic and beautiful that it is passing strange that anyone seeing him would not be moved to say: 'This truly is the King of men!'

On the rational plane his wisdom is incomparable. During the time of my visit, persons were present from different parts of the world. But people of acquired learning are but as children to Abdu'l-Baha. They were reverent in their attitude toward him and one of them, an Oxford man, praised his wisdom with much enthusiasm. They sought his advice and found it of the highest value in application to life.

Abdu'l-Baha has the power to make his friends very happy. What music and harmony, joy and peace, may enter into the lives of those who attain this meeting! He has a balm for every wound and feeds hungry souls with the Manna of his Perfect Love. One of the friends at Cairo, a noted worker in the Cause, exclaimed, 'If I could only see Abdu'l-Baha once a week!' At Acca and Haifa were to be found those who had spent most of their lives with him. But they were all longing for his Presence. Among the letters received by him at Ramleh was one from the daughter of a king, expressing as her utmost desire a visit at the threshold of his door. This is the Power of the Spirit.[31]

Louis Gregory

෨

There was a crowd gathered in front of the Hotel Victoria. Suddenly there was a hush, a stillness, and I knew that He had come. I looked. There He was! He walked through the crowd – slowly, majestically, smiling radiantly as He greeted the bowed heads on either side. I could only get a vague impression as I could not get near Him. The sound of the wind and surf from the nearby shore drowned out His voice so I could hardly hear Him. Nevertheless, I went away happy.

A few days later, a villa was rented for the Master and His family, not far from the Hotel Victoria, in a lovely residential section that lay right next to the beautiful Mediterranean and the beaches. Like all the villas in that area, it had a garden with blossoms and flowering shrubs. It was there that 'Abdu'l-Bahá chose to receive His guests – a great variety of notables, public figures, clerics, aristocrats, writers as well as poor and despairing people.

I went there often, sometimes on the way home from school, sometimes on weekends. When I was not in school I spent most of my time in His garden. I would wait to catch a glimpse of Him as He came out for His customary walk, or conversed with pilgrims from faraway places. To hear His vibrant and melodious voice ringing in the open air, to see Him, somehow exhilarated me and gave me hope. Quite often, He came to me and smiled and talked. There was a radiance about Him, an almost unlimited kindness and love that shone from Him. Seeing Him, I was infused with a feeling of goodness. I felt humble and, at the same time, exceedingly happy.

I had many opportunities to see the Master – as we always called Him – at meetings and on festive occasions. I especially remember the first time He came to our house to address a large gathering of believers. The friends were all gathered, talking happily, waiting. Suddenly all grew quiet. From outside, before He entered the room, I could hear the voice of 'Abdu'l-Bahá, very resonant, very beautiful. Then He swept in, with His robe flowing! He was straight as an arrow. His head was thrown back. His silver-gray hair fell in waves to His shoulders. His beard was white; His eyes were keen; His forehead, broad. He wore a white turban around an ivory-colored felt cap.

He looked at everyone, smiled and welcomed all with *Khushámadíd! Khushámadíd!* (Welcome! Welcome!). I had been taught that in the presence of 'Abdu'l-Bahá, I should sit or stand with my hands crossed in front of me, and look down. I was so anxious to see Him that I found myself looking up furtively now and then. He often spoke – I was privileged to hear Him speak on many subjects. For nine months it seemed like paradise. Then He left us and sailed for Europe.[32]

'Alí M. Yazdí

୧୬

I met 'Abdu'l-Bahá first in 1909, on my way out from England and Constantinople through Syria to succeed, in Cairo, Harry Boyle as Oriental Secretary to the British Agency . . . I drove along the beach in a cab from Haifa to 'Akká and spent a very pleasant hour with the patient but unsubdued prisoner and exile. When, a few years later, he was released and visited Egypt, I had the honour of looking after him and of presenting him to Lord Kitchener, who was deeply impressed by his personality, as who could fail to be?[33]

Sir Ronald Storrs

Geneva and Thonon-les-Bains

16 August – 5 September 1911

On 11 August 1911, 'Abdu'l-Bahá left Egypt bound for Marseilles in France, to spend a fortnight resting at Thonon-les-Bains on the shore of Lake Leman and a few days in Geneva, Switzerland. There, a number of His European and American devotees were, for the first time, able to bask in His presence, away from the prison city of 'Akká.

A great white hotel. At its entrance, two oleander trees in bloom. Inside, high ceilings, white walls, glass doors, rose-coloured carpets, rose-coloured damask furniture. Beyond the green terrace with its marble balustrade, Lake Geneva. Behind the hotel, two mountains overhung with clouds. In the halls and strolling through the grounds: gay, artificial, dull-eyed people. Passing among these silently with His indescribable majesty, His strange Power and His holy sweetness, the Master – Abdu'l-Baha – unrecognized but not *unfelt*. As he passes, the dull eyes follow Him, lit up for a moment with wonder.[34]

If I could only picture to you Abdul-Baha in the West; Abdul-Baha with the power of his peace in the restless West; Abdul-Baha in the complex West with the power of his simplicity; Abdul-Baha with his noble and illumined beauty in the artificial and sceptical West; so strongly defined in his completeness against our underdevelopment!

And that illumined beauty – that dignity, not of this world – that majesty of spirit that marks him a king among men, never went unheeded; for wherever he passed eyes turned to follow, and the crowds, with involuntary reverence, stood back.

. . . One drive I shall never forget. It was a drive through scenes of rare beauty – roads winding among great hills that were as steps to the near Alps. Sitting opposite Abdul-Baha in the carriage, I saw him in a way I should like to leave to the future – were it possible for me to express it! – his powerful head vividly defined against the most sublime of backgrounds; for those near mountains of the Alps, their heads hid in rolling clouds, were his background – perfect symbol of mystery!

As an artist I should like to say to those who have not seen Abdul-Baha that his head is the strongest and most nobly sculptured that it is possible to conceive.

One more touch I must give – a few words overheard in passing two ladies:

'He has so kind, so simple an air', said one.

'Yes,' replied the other, 'and eyes of fire!'

We passed fertile hills, covered with vines and corn – or fruit trees; we passed foaming mountain torrents; we passed little villages, and always the background of these verdant scenes was the panorama of the lonely Alps, their heads wreathed with clouds. And nothing escaped his eyes. Never shall I forget his keen, sympathetic, eager, delighted observation – his tender interest in all human traces – his joy in the beautiful. He particularly seemed to enjoy the gentle hillsides – the green – the signs of verdure (think of his life spent in arid, stony Acca!) Whenever he passed a village – a human habitation – we saw his heart went out to it – though how much that heart went out these hearts could not know!

. . . We came to a great waterfall – a sparkling, snowy torrent, dashing down a black precipice. He had us stop the carriage, and walking to a spot at a little distance from us, on the very edge of the embankment, he watched for a long time in silence that immaculate outpouring. I can still see the figure of quiet power – the face of luminous purity – the Perfect Man – intent upon that manifestation of the power and purity of Nature.

. . . The simplicity of Abdul-Baha, his normality, give one the real clue to the spiritual life . . . Religion in the past took on an aspect of fear. This Abdul-Baha smiles away, teaching us the perfect repose and joy of the spirit's confidence in God as Love – the 'radiant acquiescence' in Divine Guidance.

We drove to an old inn in a cleft between two mountains, and sitting in the open porch at a rough table, had the simplest of country refreshment. Just as we were entering the inn a little group of peasant children, bunches of violets in their hands to sell, pressed around Abdul-Baha. They did not seem to see the rest of us. I can still see the dull little peasant faces raised wonderingly to that face – the outstretched hands full of violets. He took from his pocket a handful of francs and gave to them abundantly. He gives – gives – gives! His love seems never content with giving. Tirelessly he gives of his spirit and heart – like a tender father he gives of material things – little keepsakes, or, in lovely symbol, flowers.

. . . I should like to speak here of something which was of unparalleled beauty to me: His power of attraction for the children. It was moving indeed to see their upward glances when he passed or stood near them, and the looks of love which bent, as he lingeringly fondled the little heads, on those pure baby souls, so fresh from their Creator! Not that they could know, but in their innocence they felt. If only all might *remember!* [35]

Juliet Thompson

જ્ઞ

'ABDUL BAHA at Thonon, on Lake Leman!' This unexpected news, telegraphed through the courtesy of M. Dreyfus, brought my wife and me to the determination we had long agreed upon of making a pilgrimage to the Master at our earliest opportunity. With only a few days intervening before his journey to London, we set out immediately from our home in Siena, and arrived at Thonon in the afternoon of August 29. Prepared in some measure for the meeting by the noble mountain scenery through which we had passed, we approached the hotel feeling ourselves strangely aloof from the tourist world. If I could but look upon Abdul Baha from a distance I considered that I should fulfil a pilgrim's most earnest desire.

The *Hotel du Parc* lies in the midst of sweeping lawns. Groups of people were walking quietly about under the trees or seated at small tables in the open air. An orchestra played from a nearby pavilion. My wife caught sight of M. Dreyfus conversing with others, and pressed my arm. I looked up quickly. M. Dreyfus had recognized us at the same time, and as the party rose I saw among them a stately old man, robed in a cream-coloured gown, his white hair and beard shining in the sun. He displayed a beauty of stature, an inevitable harmony of attitude and dress I had never seen nor thought of in men.

Without having ever visualized the Master, I knew that this was He. My whole body underwent a shock. My heart leaped, my knees weakened, a thrill of acute, receptive feeling flowed from head to foot. I seemed to have turned into some most sensitive sense-organ, as if eyes and ears were not enough for this sublime impression. In every part of me I stood aware of Abdul Baha's presence. From sheer happiness I wanted to cry – it seemed the most suitable form of self-expression at my command. While my own personality was flowing away, even while I exhibited a state of complete humility, a new being, not my own, assumed its place. A glory, as it were, from the summits of human nature poured into me, and I was conscious of a most intense impulse to admire. In Abdul Baha I felt the awful presence of BahaUl-lah, and, as my thoughts returned to activity, I realized that I had thus drawn as near as man now may to pure spirit and pure being. This wonderful experience came to me beyond my own volition. I had entered the Master's presence and become the servant of a higher will for its own purpose. Even my memory of that temporary change of being bears strange authority over me. I know what men can become; and that single overcharged moment, shining out from the dark mountain-mass of all past time, reflects like a mirror I can turn upon all circumstances to consider their worth by an intelligence purer than my own.

After what seemed a cycle of existence, this state passed with a deep sigh, and I advanced to accept Abdul Baha's hearty welcome. During our two days' visit, we were given unusual opportunity of questioning the Master, but I soon realized that such was not the highest or most productive plane on which I could meet Him. My questions answered themselves. I yielded to a feeling of reverence which contained more than the solution of intellectual or moral problems. To look upon so wonderful a human being, to respond utterly to the charm of His presence – this brought me continual happiness. I had no fear that its effects would pass away and leave me unchanged. I was content to remain in the background. The tribute which poets have offered our human nature in its noblest manifestations came naturally to mind as I watched His gestures and listened to His stately, rhythmic speech; and every ideal environment which philosophers have dreamed to solicit and confirm those manifestations in Him seemed realized. Patriarchal, majestic, strong, yet infinitely kind, He appeared like some just king that very moment descended from his throne to mingle with a devoted people. How fortunate the nation that had such a ruler! My personal reverence, a mood unfortunately rare for a Western man, revealed to me as by an inspiration what even now could be wrought for justice and peace were reverence made a general virtue; for among us many possess the attributes of government would only the electors recognize and summon them to their rightful station.

At dinner I had further opportunity of observing Abdul Baha in his relation to our civilization. The test which the Orient passes upon the servant of a prophet is spiritual wisdom; we concern ourselves more with questions of power and effectiveness. From their alliance from wisdom made effectual, from power grown wise we must derive the future cosmopolitan virtue. Only now, while the East and West are exchanging their ideals, is this consummation becoming possible. Filled with these ideas, I followed the party of Bahais through the crowded dining-room. Abdul Baha, even more impressive walking than seated, led the way. I studied the other guests as we passed. On no face did I observe idle curiosity or amusement; on the contrary, every glance turned respectfully upon the Master, and not a few bowed their heads. Our party at this time included eighteen, of whom some were Orientals. I could not help remarking the bearing of these splendid men. A sense of well-being, of keen zest in the various activities of life without doubt the effect of their manly faith emanated from all. With this superiority, moreover, they combined a rare grace and social ease. All were natives of countries in which Bahaism has not only been a capital offence in the eyes of the law, but the object of constant popular hatred and persecution; yet not one, by the slightest trace of weariness or bitterness, showed the effects of hardship and wrong upon the soul. Toward Abdul Baha their attitude was beautifully reverent. It was the relationship of disciple to master, that association more truly educative than any relation our civilization possesses, since it educates the spirit as well as the intelligence, the heart as well as the mind. Our party took seats at two adjoining tables. The dinner was throughout cheerful and animated. Abdul Baha answered questions and made frequent observations on religion in the West. He laughed heartily from time to time indeed, the idea of asceticism or useless misery of any kind cannot attach itself to this fully-developed personality. The divine element in him does not feed at the expense of the human element, but appears rather to vitalize and enrich the human element by its own abundance, as if He had attained his spiritual development by fulfilling his social relations with the utmost ardour. Yet, as He paused in profound meditation, or raised His right hand in that compelling gesture with which He emphasises speech, I thought vividly once more of BahaUllah, whose servant he is, and could not refrain from comparing this with that other table at which a prophet broke bread. A deep awe fell upon me, and I looked with a sudden pang of compassion at my fellow-Bahais, for only a few hours before Abdul Baha had said that even in the West martyrs will be found for the Cause.

After dinner we gathered in the drawing-room. The Master's approaching visit to London was mentioned. I recoiled momentarily as I pictured Him surrounded by the terrible dehumanizing machinery of a modern city. Nevertheless, I am confident that nowhere else will BahaUllah's presence in him, as well as the principle of Bahaism, so conspicuously triumph. Precisely where our scientific industry has organized a mechanism so powerful that we have become its slaves; precisely where men have become less than things, and in so dwarfing ourselves have lost a certain spiritual insistence, a certain necessity to be, without which our slavery stands lamentably confirmed precisely there will the essential contrast between spirit and matter strike the observer most sharply. The true explanation of our unjust social arrangement does not consist in the subjection of poor to rich, but the subjection of all men alike to a pitiless mechanism; for to become rich, at least in America, implies merely a readier adaptation to the workings of the machine, a completer adjustment to the revolving wheel. But Abdul Baha rises superior to every aggregation of material particles. He is greater than railroads, than skyscrapers, than trusts; he dominates finance in its brutalist manifestation. His spiritual sufficiency, by which our human nature feels itself vindicated in its acutest agony, convinces one that the West can free itself from materialism without a social cataclysm, without civil war, without jealous and intrusive legislation, by that simplest, most ancient of revolutions, a change of heart. When by the influx of a new ideal we withdraw our obedience from the machine, its demoniac energy will frighten no more, like a whirlwind that passes into the open sea. Abdul Baha restores man to his state a little lower than the angels. Through him we recover the soul's eternal triumph-chant *I Am*.

Next day the Bahais, increased by other pilgrims from

various parts of Europe, met again at tea. On this occasion we newcomers were presented with a Bahai stone marked with BahaUllah's name. Rightly considered, such objects contain a spiritual influence quite apart from the belief of superstition a suggestive value, which, recalling the circumstances under which the objects are given and received, actually retain and set free something of the holy man's personality. Superstition errs in reckoning their power apart from the receiver's worth or his power of receptivity. At my request, Abdul Baha graciously took back the stone I had received, and returned it with a blessing for my baby girl who thus, as it were, accompanied us on our pilgrimage and shares its benefits. I had spent the morning walking about Thonon. Following so closely upon my first meeting with the Master and the unique impression this made upon me, my walk invested the commonplace of our community life with a new significance. So much that we accept as inevitable, both in people and their surroundings, is not only avoidable, but to the believer even unendurable! Yet while inwardly rebelling against the idle and vicious types, the disgusting conditions in which our cities abound, I was conscious of a new sympathy for individuals and a new series of ties by which all men are joined in one common destiny. Perhaps the most enduring advantage humanity derives from its prophets is that in their vision the broken and misapplied fragments of society are gathered into one harmony and design. What the historian ignores, what the economist gives up, the prophet both interprets and employs. The least of those who enter into a prophet's vision become thereafter for ever conscious of the invincible unity of men. Not himself only, but all men seem to undergo a new birth, a spiritual regenesis. [36]

Horace Holley

London

4 September – 3 October 1911

'Abdu'l-Bahá chose London as the scene for His first appearance before the public. A week after His arrival He addressed the congregation at the City Temple; the following week, at St John's Westminster. For a whole month, people flocked to 97 Cadogan Gardens – the home of Lady Blomfield where He was staying – to meet Him.

'Abdu'l-Bahá's first aim in His Western teaching was, as He says Himself, to create in the minds of His hearers capacity to understand and appreciate this great new Revelation. He did not wish them to be as the kings had shown themselves to be, so infected by the pride of man and the haughty scepticism of the age that they could not see the truth when it was put plainly and clearly before them. Christ, He reminded his auditors, had had the same difficulty and had spoken the parable of the sower to show it. 'Abdu'l-Bahá sought, as Christ in His day had done, to transform and spiritualize the very hearts and outlook of those to whom He spoke. Unless He could do this the exposure of one error in the minds of the people would only be followed on the next occasion by another error. No remedy was adequate except that of creating a real capacity in the human heart to see and love the truth. This and nothing less was the first and last aim of 'Abdu'l-Bahá.[37]

George Townshend

⁂

He arrived, and who shall picture Him?

A silence as of love and awe overcame us, as we looked at Him; the gracious figure, clothed in a simple white garment, over which was a light-coloured Persian 'abá; on His head He wore a low-crowned táj, round which was folded a small, fine-linen turban of purest white; His hair and short beard were of that snowy whiteness which had once been black; His eyes were large, blue-grey with long, black lashes and well-marked eyebrows; His face was a beautiful oval with warm, ivory-coloured skin, a straight, finely-modelled nose, and firm, kind mouth. These are merely outside details by which an attempt is made to convey an idea of His arresting personality.

His figure was of such perfect symmetry, and so full of dignity and grace, that the first impression was that of considerable height. He seemed an incarnation of loving understanding, of compassion and power, of wisdom and authority, of strength, and of a buoyant youthfulness, which somehow defied the burden of His years; and such years!

One saw, as in a clear vision, that He had so wrought all good and mercy that the inner grace of Him had grown greater than all outer sign, and the radiance of this inner glory shone in every glance, and word, and movement as He came with hands outstretched.

'I am very much pleased with you all. Your love has drawn me to London. I waited forty years in prison to bring the Message to you. Are you pleased to receive such a guest?'

I think our souls must have answered, for I am not conscious that anyone uttered an audible word.

The history of 'Abdu'l-Bahá's stay in our house lies in the relating of various incidents, connected with individuals, who stand out from amongst the crowd of those persons who eagerly sought His Presence.

Oh, these pilgrims, these guests, these visitors! Remembering those days, our ears are filled with the sound of their footsteps – as they came from every country in the world! Every day, all day long, a constant stream. An interminable procession!

Ministers and missionaries, Oriental scholars and occult students, practical men of affairs and mystics, Anglican-Catholics and Nonconformists, Theosophists and Hindus, Christian Scientists and doctors of medicine, Muslims, Buddhists, and Zoroastrians. There also called: politicians, Salvation Army soldiers, and other workers for human good, women suffragists, journalists, writers, poets, and healers, dressmakers and great ladies, artists and artisans, poor workless people and prosperous merchants, members of the dramatic and musical world, these all came; and none were too lowly, nor too great, to receive the sympathetic consideration of this holy Messenger, who was ever giving His life for others' good.[38]

Lady Blomfield

છ૭

In 1911 a great Persian teacher made his first appearance among us in London, though the rumour of his teaching had reached many in this country through travellers and pilgrims who had visited the small fortress town of Akka, where Abbas Effendi passed the greater part of his forty years' imprisonment and exile.

Rudyard Kipling, voicing the feeling of most of his countrymen, sang:

East is East and West is West,
And never the twain shall meet.

Abbas Effendi – or, as his followers loved to call him, Abdul Baha, signifying 'Servant of the Glory' – came to us with another song:

'East and West, North and South, all, all must join hands in one great brotherhood, unite their voices in one great prayer to the Abha Father, before the human race can rise to the divine heights and grow to the perfect stature to which the All-Father has destined it.'[39]

Thus it was that . . . the Teacher and leader of the Bahai movement was able to come and visit his followers in England. The East did come to the West, the twain did meet, holding out to each other the hand of brotherhood. Surely the dawn of a new day was heralded on that Sunday evening when the late Archdeacon of Westminster walked hand in hand with the venerable Abdul Baha up the nave of St John's Church, and invited him, not only to address the congregation, but to offer for them his prayers and blessing. For though, between the two, words and ideas were exchanged through an interpreter, both felt for each other a complete sympathy and understanding, making them feel they had reached the same standpoint though by widely divergent paths.[40]

He saw people . . . minus their trappings, whether of coronets, mitres, orders, or fine clothes; and whether the skin were white, brown, or black, he saw right to the heart, to the soul. A look of wonderful love, joy, and understanding came into his profoundly far-seeking old eyes, when he recognized in his visitor a pure heart, a soul of light; and it was as though he had found a brother or sister, someone near of kin. But when he spoke of the discord, misery, and sorrow of the world, his eyes took on an expression of unfathomable sadness, and pictures rose up before one of the ghastly scenes of death and torture those same eyes must have been forced to witness.

Still, sadness was far from the characteristic note of his face or character. He not only preached happiness, but radiated it, and, though he had learnt but a few words of English, he often repeated:

No cry – no cry – be happy – that is good.

He could wear 'the glorious morning face' enjoined by Robert Louis Stevenson, even at seven o'clock in the morning, when his zealous followers and importunate visitors not infrequently began their daily visits . . . I have often noted the happy smile . . . with which he would turn to welcome some young thing, a wide-eyed child with fixed gaze of curiosity upon his turban, or one of his hostess' young daughters who, sitting at his feet, would mischievously imitate some of the 'yearners' till he laughed like a schoolboy.

Children always received a warm welcome. They refreshed him 'like a spring of water in a dry land', as he said in his Eastern tongue. He kept pretty little presents of bead necklaces and rings and sweets ready for these small visitors, who were never shy with him, but talked away, helping him to add to his few English words, of which he made great stock. At parting he would bless them, placing his fingers on eyes, lips, and ears, with the prayer: 'God bless your eyes – may they behold only the good and the beautiful; God bless your lips – may they speak only words of love and wisdom and truth; God bless your ears – may they listen only to what is pure and lovely and of good report; may the voice of God sound always louder than the voices of the world.' His blessing recalled the prayer of the old Sarum Psalter, again showing that the East and West have met:

God be in my head and in my understanding,
God be in my eyes and in my looking,
God be in my mouth and in my speaking,
God be in my heart and in my thinking,
God be in my end and at my departing.[41]

Constance Elizabeth Maud

લૅ

This evening we have in the pulpit of the City Temple the leader of one of the most remarkable religious movements of this or any age, a movement which includes, I understand, at least three million souls. The Bahai movement, as it is called, in Hither Asia, rose on that soil just as spontaneously as Christianity rose in the middle territories adjoining, and that faith – which, by the way, is very closely akin to, I think I might say identical with, the spiritual purpose of Christianity – that movements stands for the spiritual unity of mankind; it stands for universal peace among the nations. These are good things, and the man who teaches them and commends them to three millions of followers must be a good man as well as a great . . . We, as followers of the Lord Jesus Christ, who is to us and always will be the Light of the World, view with sympathy and respect every movement of the Spirit of God in the experience of mankind, and therefore we give greeting to Abdul Baha – I do not know whether I could say in the name of the whole Christian community – that may be too much – but I think in the name of all who share the spirit of our Master, and are tyring to live their lives in that spirit.[42]

Rev. R.J. Campbell

લૅ

Whatever our views, we shall, I am sure, unite in welcoming a man who has been for forty years a prisoner for the cause of brotherhood and love.[43]

Archdeacon Wilberforce

ભ

Although of a little less than medium height, 'Abdu'l Bahá made an impression on all who met him by his dignity, friendliness, and his aura of spiritual authority. His blue-grey eyes radiated a luminosity of their own and his hands were beautiful in their grace and healing magnetism. Even his movements were infused with a kind of radiance.

His compassion for the aged, for children and the down-trodden knew no bounds. I remember once after he had visited a Salvation Army refuge near the Embankment, in London, tears came to his eyes. He could not understand how a wealthy nation like Britain could allow such poverty and loneliness in its midst. He spoke about this to Archdeacon Wilberforce of Westminster Abbey and to Dr R.J. Campbell of the City Temple and he provided a sum of money through London's Lord Mayor for the succour of the poor and derelict, then so prominent a feature of the London scene.[44]

Wellesley Tudor-Pole

ભ

Abdul Baha Abbas has a striking personality; the forty years of martyrdom spent in a Turkish prison at Acre have not quenched the noble kindliness of his nature, and in spite of the lines which indescribable hardships have left on his face, his dark eyes are alive with the fire of understanding and sympathy.[45]   *The Evening Standard newspaper*

His method of life has been, and continues to be a luminous example of the fact that, here and now, despite all the surroundings of struggle for fame and wealth and material mastery, an existence guided and guarded by the Light of the Spirit, is a possible actual thing. Those who pray for the coming of the kingdom of God on earth may see in Abbas Effendi one who dwells in that kingdom consciously, and creates an environment pulsating with the peace that passeth ordinary understanding.[46]

The Daily Chronicle newspaper

ഇ

Those who have been with 'Abdu'l-Bahá notice how, often, after speaking earnestly with people, he will suddenly turn and walk away to be alone. At such times no one follows him. On this occasion, when he finished speaking and went out through the orchard gate into the village, all were struck with his free and wonderful walk which has been described by one of our American friends as that of a shepherd or a king.

As he passed along the ragged children clustered about him by dozens, the boys saluting him as they had been taught in school, showing how instinctively they felt the greatness of his presence. Most noticeable was the silence of even the roughest men when 'Abdu'l-Bahá appeared. One poor tramp exclaimed 'He is a good man', and added, 'Ay, he's suffered!'

He took particular interest in the sick, crippled and poorly nourished children. Mothers carrying their little ones followed him, and a friend explained that this great visitor had come over the seas from the Holy Land where Jesus was born.

All day long people of every condition gathered about the gate for a chance of seeing him, and more than sixty drove or cycled to Vanners to see him, many wishing to question him on some special subject. Among them were the clergy of several denominations, a head master of a boys' public school, a member of Parliament, a doctor, a famous political writer, the vice-chancellor of a University, several journalists, a well-known poet, and a magistrate from London.

He will long be remembered as he sat in the bow window in the afternoon sunshine, his arm round a very ragged but very happy little boy, who had come to ask 'Abdu'l-Bahá for sixpence for his money box and for his invalid mother, whilst round him in the room were gathered men and women discussing Education, Socialism, the first Reform Bill, and the relation of submarines and wireless telegraphy to the new era on which man is entering.[47]

'Abdu'l-Bahá in London

❧

We who had the happiness of greeting him in London met a man of patriarchal bearing. None could approach him without veneration, but each visitor was immediately set at ease by the beautiful graciousness which marked each reception with the impress of acknowledged and realized brotherhood. Patient with all questioners, eager and apposite in reply, bent from moment to moment upon the establishment of unity, his spiritual kindliness grasped the individual and the universal alike.[48]

Eric Hammond

❧

Abdul Baha is above all things an apostle of democracy. He loves a man for the spirit within him, not for the gifts of fortune he happens to possess, and frequently he honors more those who the world esteems least. No one who saw him in England can forget his sorrow when a poor man was accidentally refused entrance to his house, nor the great pity that possessed him at sight of the poverty of an English village. He went to the postmaster, who was also the banker, and changed all his gold pieces into sixpences, so that he might comfort the hungry looking children who followed him everywhere and who treasured his gentle words and caresses even more eagerly than the sixpences.[49]

Mary Hanford Ford

&

I met the Bahi yesterday, he is a dear old man.[50]

Its more important than Cézanne, & not in the least like what you'd expect of an oriental religious now. At least, I went to conduct an inquisition & came away feeling that questions would have been an impertinence.[51]

Ezra Pound

&

Never have I beheld one more full of grace and truth, or in whom the majesty of simple devotion exhibited itself more impressively. Neither have I confronted a man who seemed more at peace with himself or with mankind.[52]

His expression is so benignant and gracious, and withal so full of sympathy and kindness, that one catches the spirit of the man long before the words have passed his lips . . .

What a force lies in the personality of Abdul Baha! Rarely, if ever, have I beheld one so imbued with truth and grace as this man. Seldom or never have I been more profoundly affected than when, in taking leave of me at our last interview, he embraced and kissed me in oriental fashion and charged me that my life should be fruitful – an influence for good – a means of aiding and uplifting others. Never perhaps before had I so well realized as then the infinity of the human soul, or the incomprehensible potency of its appeal. The personality of Abdul Baha was, and remains, a mighty mystery to me. All men are wonderful. But this man seems to include so much. And when we reflect upon his significance, he becomes more wonderful still.[53]

Richard Dimsdale Stocker

❧

Discarding preconceived ideas, a new consciousness seemed to awaken when in His presence.

Some of the minds, though as yet so finite, reached out to a recognition of the Light of the great Manifestation, now being diffused by 'Abdu'l-Bahá on all Humanity. To us He was impregnated with that Light, 'as a vesture wrapped about him, like a garment round him thrown'.

Small wonder that we mortals were overwhelmed with awe, as we drew near to the heavenly Messenger of that Immortal Spirit of Truth and Light, which had come to save the children of men from chaotic destruction.

Would Humanity awaken? Or would they continue to sleep 'unaware'?[54]

Lady Blomfield

❧

We have met together to bid farewell to 'Abdu'l-Bahá, and to thank God for his example and teaching, and for the power of his prayers to bring Light into confused thought, Hope into the place of dread, Faith where doubt was, and into troubled hearts, the Love which overmasters self-seeking and fear.

Though we all, among ourselves, in our devotional allegiance have our own individual loyalties, to all of us 'Abdu'l-Bahá brings, and has brought, a message of Unity, of sympathy and of Peace. He bids us all be real and true in what we profess to believe; and to treasure above everything the Spirit behind the form. With him we bow before the Hidden Name, before that which is of every life the Inner Life! He bids us worship in fearless loyalty to our own faith, but with ever stronger yearning after Union, Brotherhood, and Love; so turning ourselves in Spirit, and with our whole heart, that we may enter more into the mind of God, which is above class, above race, and beyond time.[55]

Professor Michael Sadler

Paris

3 October – 2 December 1911

'Abdu'l-Bahá spent nine weeks in the French capital where the first Bahá'í centre in Europe had been evolving over the previous decade. In numerous meetings – private and public – the Master explained to His hearers the social and spiritual aspects of the Bahá'í Teachings.

It was interesting in Paris to watch his audiences and observe his effect upon his hearers. In London he had been surrounded from the first with famous and prominent people, who consumed his time and lionized him. In Paris he was not so loudly heralded, and people sought him out more gradually. Every morning from 10 to 12 o'clock they gathered to meet him, and at some moment between the two hours he would seize the interval allowed by pressing private interviews and come out to meet the crowd.

There is something singularly inspiring about the presence of Abdul Baha. He so forcefully radiates faith in God and belief in mankind's power to do the square thing in all directions and make a better world that in spite of oneself pessimism disappears at his advent and is replaced by courage and the joy of life. Many persons came first to his receptions out of curiosity, but returned again, and as they reappeared their faces had lost the worn, hunted, worried look of modern life. They dropped their feeling of class consciousness, discussed the events of the day with anyone who happened to be present, even if that someone wore a shabby coat or a dark face, and broadened into vivid sympathy with the positive 'unity' of the prevailing atmosphere.

This uplift he inspires is of course Abdul Baha's peculiar charm. No one who comes into contact with him fails to experience it. All leave the interview idealists, hopeful of the future, earnestly determined to make a better world and do one's part in it.[56]

Sometimes his address was very short but always his presence was so stimulating that no one had the slightest consciousness of disappointment when he arose and left the room. Abdul-Baha is like a great magnet drawing together the noblest forces of nations and individuals. He is purely synthetic, not analytic, and his cohering power is enormous – he focalizes the temperament of every listener. The stimulus of his presence in this way is something quite indescribable; it must be experienced to be comprehended. But if one did not understand Persian or French, the electric contact with Abdul-Baha and his marvellous and poetic utterance would be sufficient to transform phlegmatic materialism into spiritual possibility.

The effect of this electric presence was that of clear and prodigious thinking which swept away like cobwebs all trivialities of sect and disunion, and pierced through to the divine harmonies which unite one to God and his neighbour. Everyone who listened to Abdul-Baha must have realized that this was no sectarian founder of a cult. This was a spiritually endowed messenger whose message touched all mankind, who came out of prison to remind men of the mighty lessons God has spoken to lift us out of barbarism and cruelty from war to peace, and that in this day we must follow even the letter of these heavenly lessons.[57]

Mary Hanford Ford

❧

Nothing in our western civilization seems to surprise him. He is erudite, and that which he has not had the occasion to see with his own eyes, he has learned in advance through study.

He is interested in all matters of art and science, in all that brings to our lives spiritual delight, concord and beauty. He integrates himself in our daily life. The masterpieces of the museum charmed him and you could have seen him on Saturday circulating with ease through the flowery sumptuousness of the chrysanthemum exposition.[58]

Excelsior newspaper

❧

The venerable face of Abdu'l-Baha, in which his young eyes sparkle, beams with intelligence and kindness. He is fatherly, affectionate, simple; he inspires trust and respect. His divine power comes no doubt from knowing how to love people and to be loved by them. He merely repeats, slowly, the great wisdom: love eachother![59]

Jean Lefranc

ↄ

And we felt a deep passion in the faintly halting voice, roughly punctuated by the guttural sounds of the Persian language, but also gently punctuated by the phrasing of his musical laughter. For the prophet is joyful and forty years in prison have left no trace. He had with him a bouquet of violets, offering one to each of his visitors; to the most resistant to his teachings and to those who had the audacity to stubbornly oppose him, the parma violets serve as his arguments, as do his hearty laugh, his beautiful and poetic arguments, and the simplicity of his Persian dress.[60]

Remy de Gourmont

ↄ

'Abdu'l-Bahá was extremely polite and wise and possessed excellent manners. He left a deep impression on those whom he met. Because he exerted much care for cleanliness and observed European customs, he was very respected. Every time that He went outside and walked in streets or parks wearing his perfectly clean 'abá and shirt, He attracted people's attention.[61]

Siyyid Hasan Taqizadeh

The precepts of Baha-Abbas are beauty itself, not to mention the charm of the images and parables: they are clear and resonant like crystal. You can see through them and maybe inside. The ear takes delight and the soul a real sweetness in it. One feels conquered at the vision of a 'Divine Jerusalem, not made with mortar, stones and word', an all-spiritual city where peace would settle between men. It is true that all the prophets predicted the same . . . But a singular seduction emanates from ʿAbduʾl-Bahá, a seduction which wraps around rather than conquers his listeners . . .[62]

La Petite république newspaper

ల

Who is this, with branch of roses in his hand, coming down the steps? A picturesque group of friends – some Iránians wearing the kola, and a few Europeans following him, little children coming up to him. They hold on to his cloak, confiding and fearless. He gives the roses to them, caressingly lifting one after another into his arms, smiling the while that glorious smile which wins all hearts. Again, we saw a cabman stop his fiacre, take off his cap and hold it in his hands, gazing amazed, with an air of reverence, whilst the majestic figure, courteously acknowledging his salutation, passed by with that walk which a friend had described as 'that of a king or of a shepherd'.

Another scene. A very poor quarter in Paris – Sunday morning – groups of men and women inclined to be rowdy. Foremost amongst them a big man brandishing a long loaf of bread in his hand, shouting, gesticulating, dancing.

Into this throng walked ʿAbduʾl-Bahá, on his way from a Mission Hall where he had been addressing a very poor congregation at the invitation of their Pastor. The boisterous man with the loaf, suddenly seeing him, stood still. He then proceeded to lay about him lustily with his staff of life, crying 'Make way, make way! He is my Father, make way.' The Master passed through the midst of the crowd, now become silent and respectfully saluting him. 'Thank you, my dear friends, thank you', he said smiling round upon them. The poor were always his especially beloved friends. He was never happier than when surrounded by them, the lowly of heart!

Who is he?
Why do the people gather round him?
Why is he here in Paris?

Shortly before Bahá'u'lláh 'returned to the shelter of Heaven', He laid a sacred charge upon his eldest son, 'Abdu'l-Bahá (literally Servant of God, the Most Glorious). This charge was that he should carry the renewed Gospel of Peace and Justice, Love and Truth, into all lands, with special insistence on the translating of all praiseworthy ideals into action. What profit is there in *agreeing* that these ideals are good? Unless they are put into practice, they are useless.

I hope to indicate, albeit too inadequately, something of that Messenger, the 'Trusted One', who came out of an Eastern prison to bring his Father's message to the bewildered nations of earth. During the Paris visit, as it had been in London, daily happenings took on the atmosphere of spiritual events. Some of these episodes I will endeavour to describe as well as I can remember them.

Every morning, according to his custom, the Master expounded the Principles of the Teaching of Bahá'u'lláh to those who gathered round him, the learned and the unlearned, eager and respectful. They were of all nationalities and creeds, from the East and from the West, including Theosophists, Agnostics, Materialists, Spiritualists, Christian Scientists, Social Reformers, Hindus, Súfís, Muslims, Buddhists, Zoro-astrians and many others. Often came workers in various Humanitarian societies, who were striving to reduce the miseries of the poor. These received special sympathy and blessing.

ʻAbduʼl-Bahá spoke in Iránian which was translated into French by Monsieur and Madame Dreyfus-Barney. My two daughters, Mary and Ellinor, our friend Miss Beatrice Platt, and I took notes of these 'Talks' from day to day. At the request of the Master, these notes were arranged and published in English. It will be seen that in these pages are gathered together the precepts of those Holy Souls who, being Individual Rays of the ONE were, in divers times and countries, incarnated here on Earth to lead the spiritual evolution of human kind.

The *words* of ʻAbduʼl-Bahá can be put on to paper, but how describe the smile, the earnest pleading, the loving-kindness, the radiant vitality, and at times the awe-inspiring authority of his spoken words? The vibrations of his voice seemed to enfold the listeners in an atmosphere of the Spirit, and to penetrate to the very core of being. We were experiencing the transforming radiance of the Sun of Truth; henceforth, material aims and unworthy ambitions shrank away into their trivial obscure retreats.

ʻAbduʼl-Bahá would often answer our questions before we asked them. Sometimes he would encourage us to put them into words.

'And now your question?' he said.

I answered, 'I am wondering about the next world,

whether I shall ask to be permitted to come back here to Earth to help?'

'Why should you wish to return here? In My Father's House are many mansions – many, many worlds! Why would you desire to come back to this particular planet?'

The visit of one man made a profound impression upon us: 'O 'Abdu'l-Bahá, I have come from the French Congo, where I have been engaged in mitigating the hardships of some of the natives. For sixteen years I have worked in that country.'

'It was a great comfort to me in the darkness of my prison to know the work which you were doing.'

Explanations were not necessary when coming to 'Abdu'l-Bahá!

One day a widow in deepest mourning came. Weeping bitterly she was unable to utter a word.

Knowing her heart's grief, 'Do not weep', said 'Abdu'l-Bahá, wiping away the tears from the piteous face. 'Do not weep! Be happy! It will be well with the boy. Bring him to see me in a few days.'

On her way out, this mother said, 'O my child! He is to go through a dangerous operation today. What can I do!'

'The Master has told you what to do. Remember his words: "Do not weep, it will be well with the boy. Be happy, and in a few days bring him to see me."'

In a few days the mother brought her boy to the Master, perfectly well.

One evening at the home of Monsieur and Madame Dreyfus-Barney, an artist was presented to 'Abdu'l-Bahá.

'Thou art very welcome. I am happy to see thee. All true art is a gift of the Holy Spirit.'

'What is the Holy Spirit?'

'It is the Sun of Truth, O Artist!'

'Where, O where, is the Sun of Truth?'

'The Sun of Truth is everywhere. It is shining on the whole world.'

'What of the dark night, when the Sun is not shining?'

'The darkness of night is past, the Sun has risen.'

'But, Master! How shall it be with the blinded eyes that cannot see the Sun's splendour?

And what of the deaf ears that cannot hear those who praise its beauty?'

'I will pray that the blind eyes may be opened, that the deaf ears may be unstopped, and that the hearts may have grace to understand.'

As 'Abdu'l-Bahá spoke, the troubled mien of the Artist gave place to a look of relief, satisfied understanding, joyous emotion.

Thus, interview followed interview. Church dignitaries of various branches of the Christian Tree came. Some earnestly desirous of finding new aspects of the Truth – 'the wisdom that buildeth up, rather than the knowledge that puffeth up'. Others there were who stopped their ears lest they should hear and understand.

One afternoon, a party of the latter type arrived. They spoke words of bigotry, of intolerance, of sheer cruelty in their bitter condemnation of all who did not accept their own particular dogma, showing themselves obsessed by 'the hate of man, disguised as love of God' – a thin disguise to the penetrating eyes of the Master! Perhaps they were dreading the revealing light of Truth which he sought to shed upon the darkness of their outworn ecclesiasticism. The new revelation was too great for their narrowed souls and fettered minds.

. . . When he referred to this visit there was a look in his eyes as if loving pity were blended with profound disapproval, as though he would cleanse the defiled temple of Humanity from the suffocating diseases of the soul! Then he uttered these words in a voice of awe-inspiring authority,

'Jesus Christ is the Lord of Compassion, and these men call themselves by His Name! *Jesus is ashamed of them!*'

He shivered as with cold, drawing his *'abá* closely about him, with a gesture as if sternly repudiating their misguided outlook.

The Japanese Ambassador to a European capital (Viscount Arawaka – Madrid) was staying at the Hôtel d'Jéna. This gentleman and his wife had been told of 'Abdu'l-Bahá's presence in Paris, and she was anxious to have the privilege of meeting him.

'I am very sad', said her Excellency. 'I must not go out this evening as my cold is severe and I leave early in the morning for Spain. If only there were a possibility of seeing him!'

This was told to the Master, who had just returned after a long, tiring day.

'Tell the lady and her husband that, as she is unable to come to me, I will call upon her.'

Accordingly, though the hour was late, through the cold and the rain he came, with his smiling courtesy, bringing joy to us all as we awaited him in the Tapestry Room.

'Abdu'l-Bahá talked with the Ambassador and his wife of conditions in Japan, of the great international importance of that country, of the vast service to mankind, of the work for the abolition of war, of the need for improving conditions of life for the worker, of the necessity of educating girls and boys equally.

The religious ideal is the soul of all plans for the good of mankind. Religion must never be used as a tool by party politicians. God's politics are mighty, man's politics are feeble.

Speaking of religion and science, the two great wings with which the bird of humankind is able to soar, he said, 'Scientific discoveries have greatly increased material civilization. There is in existence a stupendous force, as yet, happily, undiscovered by man. Let us supplicate God, the Beloved, that this force be not discovered by science until Spiritual Civilization shall dominate the human mind! In the hands of men of lower material nature, this power would be able to destroy the whole earth.'

'Abdu'l-Bahá talked of these and of many other supremely important matters for more than an hour. The friends, wondering, said, 'How is it possible that having spent all his life imprisoned in an eastern fortress, he should so well understand world problems and possess the wisdom to solve them so simply?'

Truly we were beginning to understand that the majesty of greatness, whether mental or spiritual, is always simple.

One day, I received a disquieting letter, 'It would be well to warn 'Abdu'l-Bahá that it might be dangerous for him to visit a certain country, for which I understand he proposes to set forth in the near future.'

Having regard to the sincere friendship of the writer, and knowing that sources of reliable information were available to him, this warning obviously could not be ignored.

Therefore, as requested, I laid the matter before the Master.

To my amazement, he smiled and said impressively, 'My daughter, have you not yet realized that never in my life have I been for one day out of danger, and that I should rejoice to leave this world and go to my Father?'

'Oh, Master! We do not wish that you should go from us in that manner.' I was overcome with sorrow and terror.

'Be not troubled', said 'Abdu'l-Bahá. 'These enemies have no power over my life, but that which is given them from on High. If my Beloved God so willed that my lifeblood should be sacrificed in His path, it would be a glorious day, devoutly wished for by me.'

Therefore, the friends surrounding the much-loved Master were comforted and their faith so strengthened, that when a sinister-looking man came to a group who were walking in the gardens and threateningly said, 'Are you not yet sufficiently warned? Not only is there danger for 'Abdu'l-Bahá, but also for you who are with him', the friends were unperturbed, one of them replying calmly, 'The Power that protects the Master protects also His other servants. Therefore we have no fear.'

The man departed, abashed, saying nothing more.

Two days before the close of 'Abdu'l-Bahá's visit, a woman came hurriedly into the gathering at the Avenue de Camoëns:

'Oh, how glad I am to be in time! I must tell you the amazing reason of my hurried journey from America. One day, my little girl astonished me by saying: "Mummy, if dear Lord Jesus was in the world now, what would you do?" "Darling baby, I would feel like getting on to the first train and going to Him as fast as I could." "Well, Mummy, He is in the world." I felt a great awe come over me as my tiny one spoke. "What do you mean, my precious? How do you know?" I said. "He told me Himself, so of course He is in the world." Full of wonder, I thought: Is this a sacred message which is being given to me out of the mouth of my babe? And I prayed that it might be made clear to me.

'The next day she said, insistently and as though she could not understand, "Mummy, darlin', why isn't you gone to see

Lord Jesus? He's told me two times that He is really here, in the world." "Tiny love, mummy doesn't know where He is, how could she find Him?" "We see, Mummy, we see."

'I was naturally perturbed. The same afternoon, being out for a walk with my child, she suddenly stood still and cried out, "There He is! There He is!" She was trembling with excitement and pointing at the windows of a magazine store where was a picture of 'Abdu'l-Bahá. I bought the paper, found this address, caught a boat that same night, and here I am.'

The above was written down as it was related to me. It is again the second instance of the pictured face of 'Abdu'l-Bahá arresting the beholder with a compelling force. The first incident was that of a man in deadly despair, about to take his own life; and now this innocent child!

It was of great interest to notice the effect the presence of 'Abdu'l-Bahá had upon some children. One little girl whispered, 'Look, that is Jesus when He was old.' Perhaps their unstained nature sensed the breath of holiness which was always with Him and caused them to liken Him to the Most Holy One of whom they were conscious.

One day a certain man of high degree came to 'Abdu'l-Bahá. 'I have been exiled from my country. I pray you intercede for me that I may be permitted to return.'

'You will be allowed to return.'

'Some of my land has been bought by one of the Bahá'í friends. I desire to possess that property once more.'

'It shall be given back to you and without payment.'

'Who is the young man standing behind you? May he be presented to me?'

'He is 'Aga Mírzá Jalál, son of one of the martyred brothers of Isfáhán.'

'I had no part in that crime.'

'The part you took in that event, I know. Moreover, your motive I know.'

This man, with his fellow conspirator, the 'Wolf' (so named because of his ruthless cruelty and greed) had borrowed large sums of money from the two noble and generous brothers of Isfáhán. To accuse them of being followers of Bahá'u'lláh, to bring them before a tribunal which condemned them to be executed, and to have the brothers put to death, was their plot to *avoid being required to repay the loans*.

After the death of the 'Wolf' some documents were discovered, relating to the borrowed money. This, with the addition of the interest which had accumulated, now amounted to a considerable sum. The lawyer who was in charge of the affair wrote to the son of the martyr, asking into what bank the moneys should be paid. The reply sent, with the approval of 'Abdu'l-Bahá, was that he declined to accept repayment of money which had been one reason for the shedding of his father's blood.

'Aga Mírzá Jalál was now married to a daughter of 'Abdu'l-Bahá.

Whilst these episodes were taking place, we who witnessed them seemed to be in a higher dimension where there were natural indications of the presence of the Light which in all men is latent and in 'Abdu'l-Bahá transcendent.

The constant awareness of an exhilaration, which carried us out of our everyday selves, and gave us the sense of being One with the Life-Pulse which beats through the Universe, is an experience to be treasured rather than an emotion to be described. The reader will understand that it is impossible to find fitting words for the thoughts and feelings which were with us in those Paris days.[63]

Lady Blomfield

North America

11 April – 5 December 1912

After wintering again in Egypt, 'Abdu'l-Bahá gathered His strength to sail to the United States of America, arriving in New York on 11 April 1912. For the next 239 days, He was received enthusiastically by every stratum of society. Talks were given to packed auditoria, private audiences were granted, and 'Abdu'l-Bahá's personality and talks were extensively reported in newspapers from coast to coast.

The primary purpose of 'Abdu'l-Bahá's journey to America was to officially proclaim His Station as the Centre of the Covenant, to rally the unity of the Bahá'í Community, to establish the strong foundation of love and integrity upon which the future of the Faith of Bahá'u'lláh would stand and progress. With complete disregard for His frail physical condition, the Master gave most of His time in America to the friends, to their spiritual needs, to turn their weaknesses into springboards for future greatness, to weave a web of love connections between them.[64]

Eliane Lacroix-Hopson

എ

Summoning superhuman strength, courage, and resolution, the Master sacrificed Himself to spread the Teachings of Bahá'u'lláh. Before He made this trip, He had never given a public speech or addressed audiences made up of both men and women. Yet He accustomed Himself to the ways and manners of the Western world. 'Abdu'l-Bahá spoke with great eloquence, wisdom, and brilliance. He spoke in simple language to professors, teachers, clergy, youth, and people in all walks of life. He seemed to have a mysterious power to win the love and respect of all. The Master spoke with such authority and explained profound subjects in such a clear and simple way, that no one questioned what He said. He always spoke in a kindly, loving manner. At times 'Abdu'l-Bahá was seated as He spoke. At other times He would walk back and forth or stand quietly. He seemed always to be surrounded by a lovely, celestial radiance.[65]

Friends have asked me to describe 'Abdu'l-Bahá. How can anyone describe Him? Each one of us saw Him with our own spiritual and physical eyes. It seemed that in Him we found what we most longed for. In the Master's presence I felt as though I were in another world. In those moments I seemed most conscious of His overpowering love for all mankind. From childhood 'Abdu'l-Bahá had been endowed with physical beauty, we are told. Despite His advanced age and the vicissitudes He had endured, His carriage was majestic and His posture remarkable. He seemed to me to be about five feet, nine inches tall, although His long 'abá and His white turban may have caused Him to appear taller than He was. He was strong and vibrant. He walked lightly, so that there were moments when He seemed hardly to touch the ground.[66]   *Ramona Allen Brown*

ℭ⁊

A profusion of iron grey hair bursting out at the sides of the turban and hanging long upon the neck; a large, massive head, full-domed and remarkable wide across the forehead rising like a great palisade above the eyes, which were very wide apart, their orbits large and deep, looking out from massive overhanging brows; strong Roman nose, generous ears, decisive yet kindly mouth and chin; a creamy white complexion, beard same color as his hair, worn full over the face and carefully trimmed at almost full length – this completes an insufficient word picture of this 'Wise Man Out of the East'.[67]

Wendell Phillips Dodge

❦

The dominant impression that survives in my memory of 'Abdu'l-Bahá is that of an *extraordinary nobility*: physically, in the head so massive yet so finely poised, and the modeling of the features; but spiritually, in the serenity of expression, and the suggestion of grave and responsible meditation in the deeper lines of the face. But there was also, in his complexion, carriage, and expression, an assurance of the complete *health* which is a requisite of a sane judgment. And when, as in a lighter mood, his features relaxed into the playful, the assurance was added of a sense of humor without which there is no true sense of proportion. I have never met any one concerned with the philosophies of life whose judgment might seem so reliable in matters of practical conduct.

My regret is that my meetings with him were so few and that I could not benefit by a lengthier contact with a personality combining a dignity so impressive with human traits so engaging.

I wish that he could be multiplied![68]

Herbert Putnam

❦

'Abdu'l-Bahá, upon landing in New York and being surrounded by alert and inquisitive reporters, was perfectly at home. And why not? Is there any limit to the power of spirit? Was not 'Abdu'l-Bahá's universal spirit as capable of dealing with the fast-vibrating technological Occident as it had been in dealing with the mystic and more spiritual Orient? We shall see, as this narrative continues, how He was 'all things to all men'; protean in His universality; thoroughly at home in every environment.

This majestic figure – in tarboosh, turban and flowing robes – drew the newspaper men into His aura and immediately won their favor.

'What do you think of America?' He was asked.

'I like it. Americans are optimistic. If you ask them how they are they say "All right!" If you ask them how things are going, they say, "All right!" This cheerful attitude is good.'

And so 'Abdu'l-Bahá won reporters' hearts and continued to do so throughout His stay in America. He never seemed to them, or was described by them, as a strange or exotic personality. He always received favorable and constructive notices from the press.

For eight months 'Abdu'l-Bahá travelled over the United States from coast to coast, giving addresses in churches, universities and lecture halls. Several of these addresses I was privileged to attend. As I look back on these occasions, I recall more vividly His platform presence than the contents of His addresses, which of course have all been published.

'Abdu'l-Bahá did not, as a lecturer, stand still. His movements were very dynamic. He paced back and forth on the platform as He gave forth His spiritual utterances. I felt that the general atmosphere and the effect of His words were enhanced rather than diminished by the presence of a translator. For the techniques of translation gave 'Abdu'l-Bahá a certain spiritual dignity, such as could not have been attained by a straight address in the language of His hearers.

The situation was as follows: 'Abdu'l-Bahá would make a statement of a length within the power of the translator to render; then He would stand and smile as the translation was given, or He would nod His head to affirm important points. In other words, 'Abdu'l-Bahá did not stand passive during the period of translation. He constantly illumined this translation with the dynamic power of His own spiritual personality.

And when He spoke, the Persian words – so beautiful and strong – boomed forth almost as musically as in operatic recitatives. While He spoke He was in constant and majestic motion. To hear Him was an experience unequalled in any other kind of platform delivery. It was a work of art, as well as a spiritual service. First would come this spiritual flow of thought musically expressed in a foreign tongue. Then, as the translator set forth its meaning to us, we had the added pleasure of watching 'Abdu'l-Bahá's response to the art of the translator. It was, all in all, a highly colorful and dramatic procedure.[69]

But 'Abdu'l-Bahá, for the sake of the Western world, adopted the Greek mode of presentation, carefully elaborating His theses and developing them from known and admissible premises. In no place is 'Abdu'l-Bahá ever obscure or recondite. If He wishes to present a great spiritual truth, He takes it up at an initial point where its truth will be acknowledged by all, and then develops it into a larger presentation such as can expand our very minds and souls.

And so, whatever else 'Abdu'l-Bahá was and in the future will be realized to be, it is recognizable even today that He was God's special gift to the Occident. He translated the oracular teachings of Bahá'u'lláh into a language and form easily comprehensible to the West. So that no one, having available these lucid pronouncements of 'Abdu'l-Bahá, can say that the Bahá'í Faith is hard to understand. 'Abdu'l-Bahá has set forth its Teachings with all the lucidity of daylight and the warmth of sunlight.[70]

⁊

In all my interviews with 'Abdu'l-Bahá I had an extraordinary feeling of receiving truth from a higher plane than that of the mere intellect. Man's intellect is an organ of discrimination, an instrument for analysis and attack. As we listen to other people more learned than ourselves we are pleased to get information, but we consciously reserve the right of judgment. Some of the things said to us we accept immediately; some with reservations; and some we inwardly oppose. No matter how wise or how learned the teacher, we reserve the right of our own judgment.

But with 'Abdu'l-Bahá it was different. I accepted always His statements with humility and with total conviction; not because of any assumption of authority, but because I always felt in the depths of my soul that what He said was truth. It always rang true, so to speak. Let us say, as it was said of another great leader of men, that He spoke 'with authority'.

In the course of His lectures here and abroad 'Abdu'l-Bahá discoursed on many subjects. Where did He get His wide knowledge of things and of affairs? He had had but one year of schooling at the age of seven. He had been a prisoner all His life. He had few books, no scholarly library, no encyclopedias. Yet at Schenectady, as 'Abdu'l-Bahá was being shown around the General Electric Works by Steinmetz, this 'wizard of electricity' was observed to be eagerly absorbing 'Abdu'l-Bahá's elucidation of electricity. The Rev. Moore, Unitarian clergyman who was present at the time, testified to me: 'Steinmetz's jaw seemed to drop open as he drank in 'Abdu'l-Bahá's talk.'

"'Abdu'l-Bahá, do You know everything?' Saffa Kinney is said to have asked

'No, I do not know everything. But when I need to know something, it is pictured before Me.'

And so 'Abdu'l-Bahá, on the occasion of His tour of the General Electric Works, knew more about electricity than did Steinmetz.

Shoghi Effendi has said that intuition is a power of the soul. It was this power that was always available to 'Abdu'l-Bahá, and *available in its totality*. He has spoken many times of this 'immediate knowledge' – this knowledge attained without the means of books or other humans, this strange intuitive power which to some degree is available to us all.

And often, in closing an interview after answering some abstruse question, 'Abdu'l-Bahá would say: 'Time does not permit of further answer. But meditate on this, and truth will come to you.'

And so – although 'Abdu'l-Bahá is no longer with us to answer our questions – the power of the Holy Spirit so strong in Him is still available to us to guide to fortify, to heal.[71]

Stanwood Cobb

ᘒ

A glimpse was all I succeeded in getting. The press of eager friends and curious ones was so great that it was difficult even to get inside the doors. I have only the memory of an impressive silence most unusual at such functions . . . At last I managed to press forward where I could peep over a shoulder and so got my first glimpse of 'Abdu'l-Bahá. He was seated. A cream colored fez upon His head from under which white hair flowed almost to His shoulders.

His robe, what little I could see of it, was oriental, almost white. But these were incidentals to which I could pay little attention. The impressive thing, and what I have never forgotten, was an indefinable aspect of majesty combined with an exquisite courtesy . . . Such gentleness, such love emanated from Him as I had never seen. I was not emotionally disturbed. Remember that at that time I had no conviction, almost, I might say, little or no interest in what I came later to understand by the term His 'Station' . . . What was it that these people around me had which gave to their eyes such illumination, to their hearts such gladness? What connotation did the word 'wonderful' have to them that so often it was upon their lips? I did not know, but I wanted to know as I think I had never known the want of anything before.[72]

Here I saw a man who, outwardly, like myself, lived in the world of confusion, yet, inwardly, beyond the possibility of doubt, lived and worked in that higher and real world. All His concepts, all His motives, all His actions, derived their springs from that 'World of Light'. And, which is to me a most inspiring and encouraging fact, He took it for granted that you and I, the ordinary run-of-the-mill humanity, could enter into and live and move in that world if we would.[73]

Howard Colby Ives

❧

He was sitting in the centre of the dining room near a table strewn with flowers. He wore a light pongee *'abá*. At His knees stood the Kinney children, Sanford and Howard, and His arms were around them. He was white and shining. No words could describe His ineffable peace. The people stood about in rows and circles – several hundred in the big rooms, which all open into each other. In the dining room many sat on the floor, Marjorie and I included. We made a dark background for his glory. Only our tears reflect Him, and almost everyone there was weeping just at the sight of Him. For at last we saw divinity incarnate. Divinely He turned His head from one child to the other, one group to another, I wish I could picture that turn of the head – an oh, so tender turn, with that indescribable heavenly grace caught by Leonardo da Vinci in his Christ of the Last Supper (in the study for the head) – but in ʻAbduʼl-Bahá irradiated by smiles and a lifting of those eyes filled with glory, which even Leonardo, for all his mystery, could not have painted. The very essence of compassion, the most poignant tenderness is in that turn of the head.[74]

Juliet Thompson

❧

By his bearing and by the very first few words of His address, everyone felt that this person was spiritual and divinely inspired; that His explanations were heavenly; that He was speaking from God; that He could transform the souls; that He was with God and was the herald of peace and love; that what He said was first practiced by Himself; and that He was a flame from the Kingdom which brightened and illuminated the minds and hearts of all. That august person was ʻAbduʼl-Bahá.[75]

Chairman of a meeting at the Theosophical Society, Malden,
27 August 1912

❧

This aged Persian – his face heavily lined by the sorrows and privations of a forty year imprisonment – seemed often to be gazing far beyond the crowded audience, and the aloofness of his eyes made one think that the inner vision of the Perfected Kingdom of God must be ever before him.

The Eastern figures, the sonorous phrases in a foreign language, the striking poetic similes in which the interpreter gave them forth in English, as well as the strange, indefinable impression that here indeed was one to whom things of the spirit were the only reality – all this combined to make the beholders feel as though one of the seers of old stood before them and that the ages had again rolled back to the days of Daniel.[76]

Potter A. Reade

❧

The words delivered . . . in short epigrams, took one miles and miles away from New York. Outside the window was Broadway; under the building the subway; downstairs was all the paraphernalia of a big hotel, but all these things were far less real than the picture the old teacher called up. The only things that seemed near were the mountains of Carmel, so near the Village of Nazareth, and the fields where the lilies grow more beautiful than Solomon in his glory.

The strangeness of it all, the manner of speaking, the curious language, the unfamiliar dress might will have made the listener awkward and ill at ease; but one does not feel awkward with Abdul Baha . . . It really made no difference what you did or what you said, this kind old teacher would know that you meant well.[77]

New York Times

❧

Don't laugh at Abdul Abbas. He has an idea . . . people with ideas generally are laughed at. But after the world has laughed long enough, it turns around and eats the idea very solemnly and very greedily, and digests it, and makes it part of its bone and fibre.

. . . We are not personally acquainted with Abdul Abbas, and we cannot tell how much of charlatanry may be mixed up with his doctrine. But the idea in itself is good stuff . . . he is the strange anomaly of an oriental mystic who believes in woman suffrage and in Broadway. He is worth his picture in the papers.[78]

New York City Evening Mail

ᔕ

Abdul Baha . . . was more than a personality – he was an inspiration; an idealist, whose self-devotion breathed new life into dying creeds. His gospel appealed with equal force to Christians, Moslems, and Jews; to Buddhists and Hindus, Shintoists and Parsis. His idealism was to many a manifestation of the very source of life, light, and love. He came at a time when the soul's craving for hope and faith was – seemingly – unappeased by any one of the many organized and acknowledged religions.

I first met the teacher in an up-town church. I had been sent by my paper to report the sermon. The speaker's likeness to my own father was so startling, that, immediately after the service, I entered the anteroom and told him of the remarkable resemblance. Very quietly he answered: 'I am your father and you are my son. Come and dine with me.' Another engagement prevented, but I asked if I might take breakfast with him the following morning. 'Come.' He said. I went, and after that first meeting followed others. We walked in his garden, and, as we walked, we talked. I told him of his peculiar attraction to me on account of my own outlook on life; that I came from Southern Asia and that I was a Buddhist – a Buddhist-Christian. 'So am I,' replied the teacher. 'I am also a Confucian-Christian and a Brahmin-Christian; a Jewish and a Mohammedan-Christian. I am a brother to all who love truth – truth in whatsoever garb they choose to clothe it.' . . .

No leader of men could be more simple in his tastes or more naïve in his expression of them. On the last day that I saw him he gave me his rose – he always had a freshly picked rose on his table – and kissed me on both cheeks (as was his wont). As he left me at the door he said, 'You may be waylaid on your way out. The people who are good enough to come to see me think of me and speak of me as something especially holy and set apart. But do not mind them. Think of me as your loving father and not as some divine thing to be adored.' In the reception room I was immediately surrounded by the patient watchers, who scrambled for the rose as for some sacred relic.

Those who met him carried away a nameless something that made life's pleasures brighter.[79]

Frederic Dean

સ

This man has the power of penetrating the souls of men, at least so his followers say. He understands the need of each individual soul. He is a spiritual physician. Many and beautiful are the touching incidents told of him, as he went through the East, healing the suffering, scattering kindness, clearing away prejudice, and making friends of those who formerly were his enemies. And as you sit and watch him as he speaks, noting his sad, kind eyes, his body, old before its time, his nervous hands, so full of sympathy, you cannot help but feel the personality of the teacher, and you believe, that truly he does represent hospitality, and truth, and that to be humble, to be reverent, to love all mankind are parts of him.[80]

Marion Brunot Haymaker

❧

A venerable man – like a patriarch of old – his gray beard falling upon his breast, his white locks surmounted by a white turban, his erect figure draped in the flowing garments of Persia – this is Abdul Baha Abbas Effendi – 'Servant of God', teacher of universal religion, universal peace, universal brotherhood.

When I say this is Abdul Baha, the statement refers only to the first fleeting impression of this head of the Bahai movement who is in Denver spreading the message of brotherly love of the universal religion which will be the foundation of interreligious, interracial and international brotherhood.

For when this aged man – whose presence in the dominant personality defies age – speaks, when the keen dark eyes become afire with the words he utters, the first impression of Abdul Baha becomes but a superficial one. Yesterday afternoon . . . I was thrilled for an hour by the flow of sonorous words that rolled from the lips of this man of the Orient who has a message for all this world.[81]

Alice Rohe

❧

The story of this man is rich in romance. Imprisoned for twenty years, exiled after that because he proclaimed the doctrine of brotherly love, equality of all men and the need of a recognition of the value of a spiritual life, his estate confiscated, he set out to give the message to the world at large . . .

'Abdu'l-Bahá is, first of all, a constructionist. He believes that the time of building is at hand and to this end, war among the nations must cease.[82]

Frances Belford 'Pinky' Wayne

ↁ

Abdul Baha Talks to Kate Carew of Things Spiritual and Mundane

What do you expect? What you don't expect! I found myself repeating this formula of the fortune teller, facing her pack of cards, as I entered the corridor of the Hotel Ansonia on my way to interview the Persian teacher, Abdul Baha, leader of the Bahaites.

What I expected to find was the apostle of peace, the advocate of the simple life and the universal brotherhood of man in some quiet, unobtrusive sort of place, a little apart from the madding crowd, where solitude and reflection might be his for the asking.

The Hotel Ansonia, situated at one of the traffic centres, 72[n]d street and Broadway, scarcely answers that description, does it? It was near the dinner hour. I stopped for a moment to watch the well dressed, well fed looking crowd pass to and fro. Women with pet Poms, noisy children under the guardianship of patient governesses; men, reminiscent of the 5 o'clock cocktail, bustling in from showy limousines, polite officials, overbuttoned bellboys, squirrel cage entrances whirling madly – in fact, everything moving at a high rate of speed.

I said to myself: 'Well, of all the places to find the Master.' What I didn't expect.

I might have lapsed into quite a cynical frame of mind if it hadn't been that just then I noticed how soft and squashy the carpets were, and I thought of the forty years Abdul Baha had spent in prison, and I said, 'Of course it's the carpets. They must seem awfully nice to feet that have trod prison stones. I don't blame him.'

Quite recovered, I received the news from the chirpy clerk, 'Fifth floor, Room 111', with a chirpy response, and skipped into the elevator.

On my way to the more rarefied atmosphere of the upper floors I found myself hoping that the Baha would tell me I had a lovely soul. They say he finds out the strangest things about you.

One of my friends has a rose sent to her seven years before from Akka, which, she says, still preserves the aroma of the Baha's wonderful spirit, and another, after making me promise I wouldn't tell – cross my heart and all that – stated that he had told her she was a wise woman.

Of course I wouldn't tell that, knowing her as I do.

I felt all sorts of mystic possibilities awaited me [on] the other side of the door. I stripped my mind of all its worldly debris. By a tremendous effort I shut out the seething noises of the hotel. I closed my eyes. I attained the holy calm.

At my finger's pressure on the [door]bell the door flew open with a most unholy speed.

No fumes of incense, no tinkling of bells, no prostrate figures and whispered benedictions. A ruddy faced, red haired youth with the facial line of the Orient was before me.

He was in his shirt sleeves.

I had been criticizing the lack of simplicity and when I saw it I wasn't satisfied.

Isn't that the woman of it?

Certainly there is nothing more simple than shirt sleeves!

Surprise made me speechless. He was, however, not per-turbed in the least, stood aside for me to pass and said, 'Abdul Baha and Dr Fareed are [out] driving. Will you come inside and wait?' I scented the perfume of many flowers in my long pilgrimage from the door to the salon, passing several rooms en suite, a little world by itself, an oasis in the sandstorms of glitter and glare.

Slipping into a ready chair, I looked about to find myself one of a concourse of people, all actuated by the same interest.

My editor had given me the information that there were five thousand Bahaites in America and about twenty million in the world, so why I should have expected to have the Baha all to myself I do not know, but I did.

I solaced my disappointment by studying the visitors, curious to learn what sort of people the faith drew to itself.

An enthusiastic, plump, middle-aged little person, gowned in a very worldly manner, haloed with a new spring hat, whose artificial aigrettes had the real optimistic slant, was telling the stranger seated near of a domestic distur-bance. Of course it had to do with a cook.

'I just knew if I believed hard enough,' said she, 'I could make her feel the same.'

A young woman – daughter, I judged – cast a resigned look mother's way.

Daughter was Burne Jonesy, patient to parent's aggressive personality, with the tolerance of the young-old for the old-young. Her thin, willowy frame was the expression of the gentle cynicism that comes from living with one who is over-balanced with altruistic words.

My glance then caromed with a man who had sped down the corridor ahead of me.

He had flying coattails and a black sombrero, so I classified him as from the Middle West, for in my Roget's Thesaurus those terms are synonymous.

After, several groups of foreigners, alert, silent, expectant, drew my regard. Many prosperous-looking business men and many interesting women.

There was a pretty girl on a narrow seat. You felt she must have lots of oversoul. She wore a sad, withdrawn look as of one who lives on the heights. A stout man, baldish, with a fringe of long hair on his neck, had the remaining two-thirds of the seat, lolling against her, and turning up his eyes to gaze into hers, which were, in turn, turned up. They were very much in the picture. Some suburbanites stared their way admiringly, wishing they could do it.

Suddenly there was a stir, murmurs of 'The Master!' Many stood up, a few rushed from the room, among them the Enthusiast.

From an inner apartment came now a strange medley of sounds. There was a chatter of high-pitched American voices; a beautifully modulated one, I learned afterward, was that of Dr Fareed, the interpreter and friend. Dominating all, by a peculiar weird quality, was a nasal monotone unlike any sound I had ever heard. In my retired corner I seemed to see again, as once before, at dusk, the flock of little lambkins in the park, newly born and bleating. The vision deepened and changed until in place of these were the other flocks of Scriptural days, on the slopes of Carmel, near the Galilean Sea, those watched over by the shepherds at night. The monotone ceased.

I blinked my eyes. Everybody in the room was standing, breathlessly expectant. I rose mechanically.

Abdul Baha entered.

He is scarcely above medium height, but so extraordinary in the dignity of majestic carriage that he seemed more than the average stature.

He wore, over biscuit colored velveteen trousers girdled

with white, a long, full robe of grayish wool. The Panama fez was wound with white folds.

While slowly making the round of the room his soft, penetrating, faded eyes studied us all, without seeming to do so.

One and another he termed 'My child' – and they were not all young who responded to this greeting.

He stopped longest before the young girls and boys, those 'blossoms on life's branch', as he speaks of them in Oriental imagery.

A blushing young woman introduced her escort – 'Master, we have just been married.'

Such a look of joy illumined the face that in repose looks like a sheet of parchment on which Fate has scored deep, cabalistic lines. He did not want to leave them. He held their hands a long time, then turned and blessed the young man.

My dears, if that young man ever thinks of straying from the path of loyalty, methinks the pressure of that hand will weigh heavy on his soul.

He patted several people on the cheek, an old man, an apple-cheeked youth and myself. I got a nice paternal little pat which made me feel, oh, so much more like folks.

We seated ourselves about him. A good-looking young Turk understudying Dr Fareed explained modestly: 'You know it is very difficult to translate the Master literally. I can tell you the words, but no one could possibly interpret the beautiful soul that informs them.'

Rather nice, that, I thought!

The Baha repeated a statement he had made that day to the students of Columbia University.

'The great need of this country is the spiritual philosophy, the philosophy of the language of God. Every one wants to find scientific truths, but we should seek the scientific truths of the spirit as well.

'Natural philosophy is like a very beautiful physical body, but the spiritual philosophy is the soul of that body. If this body unites with the spirit, then we have the highest perfect society.

'What God gives us in this world is for a time, our body is for a time, our millions of dollars are for a time, our houses, our automobiles, the same. But the spiritual gifts of God are forever. The greatness of this world will come to an end, but the greatness of the spiritual world is eternal.

'Read history. See how emperors and kings came and went. Nothing is left. The kingdom of the world passes; the kingdom of God will endure.'

Several questions were asked. A socialist looking person inquired:

'Do you believe in dividing property and everything?'

'You may bring all the physical powers of the earth, you may bring all the natural powers of the earth, and try by their means to make a union where all will love each other, where all will have peace – but such means will end in failure. But look how the spiritual power has brought us all together and makes us love each other. This meeting has been brought about by spiritual means. You have come because the spiritual power led you.'

'Will the East and West ever be united?'

The Baha answered immediately: 'It would be impossible by the natural forces only, but that union between the East and the West, of love between the people here and there, will come through the spiritual power. Mahomet Ali, the founder of the Bahaite faith, said that if he could spend all the cash of the universe to bring love among mankind it would result in failure, but with the spiritual power he succeeded in making the people of the East and the people of the West love each other. You coming here tonight proves this. It is a gift of God.'

Some one interrogated him concerning the mission of the theatre.

He was much agitated at this question, and the young Turk explained: 'The Master says that he went to the theatre to-day where they show how Christ was crucified ("The Terrible Meek"). He saw the acts. He wept. It is more than one thousand nine hundred years since that time. He was unable to help him. Yes, he wept, and not only he, but many others wept, too.'

I can imagine repeating his phrases to some of my clever friends, who would be sure to say: 'Why, that's as old as the hills. I don't see anything to make a fuss about in that.'

But the time honored words, even repeated by an interpreter, are so fraught with the Baha's wonderful personality that they seem never to have been uttered before. His meaning is not couched in any esoteric phrases. Again and again he has disclaimed the possession of hidden lore. Again and again he has placed the attainments of the heart and soul above those of the mind.

After a few more questions and answers the meeting is declared adjourned. Abdul Baha rises and passes into the inner room, where he gives some private hearings.

No one starts to go. He has actually made New York people forget the dinner hour.

That in itself is a victory, I think. Don't you?

From my corner I wait my turn, again absorbed watching the human current . . .

Bride and bridegroom pass with ecstatic faces. Middle West smoothes his dominant coattails. Miss Burne Jones follows at a discreet distance Enthusiastic Parent who flies about kissing everybody. I gain a damp salute on my chin.

Newspaper people go in and out, Turks, Syrians, business men, domestic and society women. Children.

It is said that the wife and daughters of Abdul Baha, brought up according to Western ideas of education, are living in Alexandria, more or less fettered by the conventionalities of that Eastern city. It is also true that in the early days of the Bahaite movement women performed prodigies of bravery and sacrifice for the faith, so I ask: 'Do you believe in woman's desire for freedom?'

He adjusts his turban – a frequent mannerism.

'The soul has no sex.'

'In a supreme moment, as in that of the Titanic disaster, should both sexes share the danger equally?'

'Women are more delicate than men. This delicacy men should take into consideration. That is their obligation. If the time ever comes when the average woman is a man's equal in physical strength there will be no need for this consideration; but not until then.'

As he says this he shakes the wonderful, full-domed head and the singsong recitation has a note of great sweetness.

I thought of his childhood, passed among such unspeakable scenes of distress – early matured into knowledge of sin and sorrow. I marvelled at his childlike simplicity, which is combined with a sort of ageless, spiritual wisdom. I asked: 'Is it possible for us ever to rid ourselves of our grown-up illusions and become, as Christ said, "as little children"?'

'Certainly. There is such a thing as innocence due to ignorance, due to weakness. It is innate in the child to be simple, but when a person becomes matured there should be such a thing as innocence of knowledge, of strength. For instance, a child, owing to certain weakness, may not lie. Even if the child wishes to tell an untruth it is incapable of doing it. This is due to his impotence: but when it becomes old and its morals receive rectitude, then through pure, conscious potency can it restrain itself from lying.'

Do we most need suffering or happiness to open to us the door of spiritual understanding?'

'Trials and suffering for the perfect man are good. For an imperfect they are a test. For example, a drunkard may, through his sin, lose all his possessions. He is cast into a great ordeal. That is his punishment. But the man who is endeavouring along the paths of virtuous achievement may meet ordeals which are really bounties for they will help him.'

'Why is a child near the spirit land?'

'Because children are so innocent. They have no stratagems. Their hearts are like spring meadows.'

'Should we train the young mind with fairy tales or something more realistic?'

'Fairy tales will not help a child. Anything without a foundation of truth lacks permanence. We should begin early to cultivate in children virtues, to teach them the realities of life.'

'Is there any way of making this life in a commercial city less crude for the young boy and girl?'

'It would be well to get them together and say "Young ladies, God has created you all human; isn't it a pity that you should pass your energy along animalistic lines? God has created you men and women in order that you may acquire his virtues, that you may progress in all the degrees, that you may be veritable angels, holy and sanctified."'

'There are so many temptations put in their way', I murmur. The Abdul Baha looks very sympathetic, but his singsong tones are relentlessly firm.

'Let them try a little of the delicacy of the spiritual world, the sweetness of its perfection and see which life is preferable. One leads man to debasement, the end of it is remorse, the end of it is scorn, the end of it is confusion. "Praise be to God you are gifted with intellect", I would say to them. "God has created you noble, why are you willing to degrade yourself? God has created you bright, radiant, how are you willing to be steeped in darkness? God has created you supreme. Why are you willing to be degraded into the abyss of despair?" Admonish them in this way and exhort them.'

I noticed a trembling of the eyelids and that the gestures of arranging his turban and stroking his beard were more nervously frequent. Dr Fareed answered to my inquiry, 'Shall I go now?'

'He has been giving of himself to every one since 7 o'clock this morning. I am a perfect physical wreck, but he is willing to go on indefinitely.'

Abdul Baha opened the half-closed eyelids to say: 'I am going to the poor in the Bowery now. I love them.'

I was invited to accompany them. The Baha met my assent with a most Chesterfieldian expression of pleasure.

Mr Mills, president of the Bahaite Society in New York, had placed his car at the disposal of Abdul Baha.

Can you picture your Aunt Kate and Abdul Baha going to it, hand in hand, through the Ansonia corridors?

Perhaps the guests didn't gurgle and gasp! Perhaps!

I did feel rather conspicuous, but I braced myself with the thought of the universal brotherhood and really got along fairly well.

When we were seated in the machine, every inch of space taken by some member of the suite, I caught myself thinking what an amusing little anecdote I might make of this happening.

Just then the Master said to me in a gentle but firm voice: 'Remember, you press people are the servants of the public. You interpret our words and acts to them. With you is a great responsibility. Please remember and treat us seriously.'

Often during the interview I had felt like saying: 'You dear old man! You fine old gentleman!' I felt more than ever like it now.

As if any one could hold up that pure white soul to ridicule.

There was another gasp of surprise at the Bowery Mission as, still hand in hand – he just wouldn't let me go – the Baha and I trotted through a lane composed of several score of the society's members. A few of the young ladies had their arms filled with flowers, which afterward filled the automobile. Some four hundred men were present, belonging to the mission.

Just before the services were concluded I saw the courier stealthily approach the platform and hand the Baha a green baize bag.

Of course, I wasn't going to let that go on without finding out all about it, and to my whispered inquiry the Baha said, smilingly: 'Some little lucky bits I am going to distribute to the men.'

What you don't expect!

I had the surprise of my life!

For what do you suppose those lucky bits were?

Silver quarters, two hundred dollars' worth of them!

Guess you didn't expect it, either.

Think of it! Some one actually coming to America and distributing money. Not here with the avowed or unavowed intention of taking it away.

It seems incredible.

Possibly I may be a little tired of mere words, dealing in them the way I do, but that demonstration of Abdul Baha's creed did more to convince me of the absolute sincerity of the man than anything else that had happened.

And it was all done so unostentatiously, so gracefully, without any fuss or fume.

The Master stood, his eyes always turned away from the

man facing him, far down the line, four or five beyond his vis-à-vis, so that when a particularly desperate looking specimen came along he was all ready for him, and, instead of one quarter, two were quietly pressed into the calloused palm.

Once a young Turk of the suite slipped in, and before the Baha recognized him got a coin. He explained that he wanted it for luck, and the Baha most benignantly patted his shoulder. When he got back to his companions they all laughed at the joke.

I imagine them a merry little family among themselves.

I had said good night on the platform, so my last view of Abdul Baha was as he stood at the head of the Bowery Mission line, a dozen or more derelicts before him, giving to each a bit of silver and a word of blessing.

And as I went out into the starlight night I murmured the phrase of an Oriental admirer who had described him as *The Breeze of God*.[83]

Kate Carew

ℰℛℴ

From 30 August to 9 September 1912, 'Abdu'l-Bahá travelled to Montreal, Canada. His devoted follower May Maxwell – who had established the first Bahá'í centres in Europe and Canada – informed the press of His visit, resulting in extensive coverage.

The strangest part of all about him is that nothing is strange. He seeks to be the embodiment of that which is most natural. Is this not turning back to religion itself? Venerable in years, he is young as a child in the purity of his outlook on life; disciplined by long years in prison, his spirit has never yet been crucified by pain. [84]

Rev. F.R. Griffen

What is it that strikes one most in this remarkable man? Is it his message . . . ? Is it his power of thought, his manner of expression, the privations he has endured? No; it is none of these. It is his great sincerity. He is a man with a mission, and he believes in it with all his soul . . .

There was a wonderful breadth and depth of feeling in that sermon. It was not the message of a fanatic or a hermit, or a man unconversant with modern thought and modern life. It was Eastern, yet it was Western . . .[85]

The Toronto Star Weekly

❧

From that hour people flocked to His presence in ever-increasing numbers – the great search of humanity for guidance, for happiness, for peace and assurance amidst the troublous conditions of the world, and none came in vain. The combined impression of His presence and His words was profound. One newspaper later pictured 'the moving scene, the crowd, 'Abdu'l-Bahá a serene majestic figure, calm, commanding, austere and wise'. His audience was held in a spell of wonder and amazement . . . even when 'Abdu'l-Bahá had finished speaking the people would not go and lingered on asking question after question, so satisfied and tranquilized by His replies that many of them followed Him later to His room. [86]

As He stood there . . . watching the milkman on his daily round – the man delivering at each door-step the morning paper – early workmen on their way to work – what were His thoughts? What was the penetration of His all-knowing, all-searching spirit in these humble lives in their unconscious journey to Him! They glanced at His mighty prophetic Figure with wonder and traces of unconscious respect, & went their way – never, never to be the same again. The light of His glance had fallen on them – the warmth & power of His Spirit had for a fraction of time surrounded them in their daily rounds, their common destiny.[87]

May Bolles Maxwell

❧

Untiringly, with divine patience and insight, 'Abdu'l-Bahá gave of His love and wisdom. Nowhere did He meet opposition, criticism or rebuff. All doors opened before Him, all hearts responded to His magic words. The believers were never far from Him all during these exalted hours. Well aware in Whose radiance they bathed, they forsook their business and homes, day after day, to drink of the spiritual water offered so freely, with such humility and sweetness.[88]

Amine De Mille

❧

There sailed from New York a few weeks ago a man who incarnated in his daily living the open mind, good will, and the unity of spirit which we liberals have made our central gospel for the past hundred years. Abdul Baha recalls the picture of our saints . . . The more we saw of him the deeper sank the impression of his pure spirituality.

Once more we realize the power of the life made flesh. A thousand words though they fall from the tongues of angels are not equal in their spiritual effect to one glimpse of the life itself incarnate in a living personality. Then there flashes on us the wealth of the meaning of the life of which we talk and dream . . .[89]

Baha'o'llah brought this great revelation to the world, but it came in Him with such sublime light that people were almost dazzled by its splendour. His splendour is so bright we can hardly look upon it. And so the next great Herald of the Kingdom takes the form of a servant, the humblest form a human being can assume. He lays aside His title; he calls himself simply, The Servant of the Glory of God.

He comes down right into the midst of men, living their life. he plants his garden; he cooks the meals for the sick people; he makes them broth in the prison; he goes up and down the country like a ministering angel of God's mercy; he is the tenderest, the simplest, the lowliest of beings in the world. When he is put in prison for teaching universal peace and universal brotherhood He counts this imprisonment the joy of his life. Abdu'l-Baha tells us how when He was one day in the streets of Acca and the chains were around his waist and his neck, the jailer, his tender-hearted jailer, said, 'Why don't you put a robe over those chains so the boys won't throw stones at you?' Abdu'l-Baha, turning to him, replied: 'These chains are my badges of honour, my badges of glory, I could not conceal them.'

Now it is this quality of service, in annihilation of self, that makes God's Holy Spirit manifest. When we visited Abdu'l-Baha in Chicago and he met us there with all the freshness and joy of this eternal morning shining through his human spirit in its brightness and its beauty, and our hearts were thrilled with the consciousness that here was one who saw God face to face, nay, that made God's love manifest right in our midst. And he said to us, 'You know it doesn't make any difference what happens to one in the physical world. I was a prisoner in a Turkish prison for forty years.' Then he told us how he slept upon the ground or upon the stone floor, how he was starved and chained and put into dungeons. 'And yet,'

He said, 'every day when I awoke in the morning I praised God that another day was before me in which I could serve Him in His prison. And every night when I lay down on the stone floor of the prison I thanked God that He had allowed me to serve His Kingdom one more day in His prison.'

Then Abdu'l-Baha, turning to us with a light in his face and a joy that was almost overwhelmingly beautiful said, 'I was in prison for forty years, and every day was a day of perfect joy.' As he said 'joy' his spirit shone so bright that in our hearts we thought we had never before known what joy and happiness meant. The people who were in the room said, 'Isn't it amazing; when we are talking here with this Servant of God, all we can think of is God; we do not even see Abdu'l-Baha.' And one woman said: 'I do not even know he is here; all I see is the Spirit of God shining in him as in a crystal or a diamond.' When she went away she did not think anything about Abdu'l-Baha the human personality; all she knew was that for one-half hour she had been in the presence of the eternal world. Like a door into the Kingdom was Abdu'l-Baha, transmitting the light of eternity. As she left his presence she said for the first time in her life she knew that God was King, and that there was no God but the God of this universe, and we could trust our lives to Him, our fortunes to Him, everything to Him because God is the Reality of realities.[90]

Albert Vail

৪১

'Abbas Effendi came and I received him with joy and reverence. Advanced years have not affected his extraordinary sagacity. He stayed about an hour and talked of diverse subjects, exceedingly useful, which indicated the wide range of his knowledge and experience. He is indeed a man of learning and one of the great personalities of the East.[91]

Prince Muhammad'-'Alí Páshá

⁊

The effect of 'Abdu'l-Bahá on those multitudes who saw and heard Him certainly promised other results. As He walked among the people, an Immortal in a less than human world, with His ineffable beauty, His scintillating power, His strange, unearthly majesty, eyes full of wonder followed Him.

The poet, Kahlil Gibran, said: 'For the first time I saw form noble enough to be the receptacle for Holy Spirit!'

An atheist went to a church to hear Him speak and later eagerly sought Him at His house. When this atheist was asked: 'Did you feel the greatness of 'Abdu'l-Bahá?' he indignantly replied: 'Would you feel the greatness of Niagara?'

Those who met Him perceived no more than their capacity could register. A society woman exclaimed: 'Such beauty – the beauty of strength! And such charm! Why, He is a perfect man of the world!' And another society woman who had talked at length with Him: 'You can hide nothing from Him! He looked into my heart and discovered all its secrets.'

A woman in sorrow, passing through a cruel experience, said: 'He took all the bitterness out of my heart.' A famous playwright, when he came from the room of 'Abdu'l-Bahá, declared: 'I have been in the presence of God!' And Lee McClung, then Treasurer of the United States, after his meeting with the Master, groping for words to describe it, said: 'I felt as if I were in the presence of a great Prophet – Isaiah – Elijah – no, that is not it. The presence of Christ – no. I felt as if I were in the presence of my Divine Father.'

The Turkish ambassador, Zia Pasha, a devout

Muhammadan, when told of the advent of Bahá'u'lláh, had scoffed at the thought of a new Prophet. But while 'Abdu'l-Bahá was in Washington Zia Pasha met Him at the Persian Embassy, invited by His Excellency Ali-Kuli Khan, and Madame Khan, and immediately arranged a dinner to be given in His honor at the Turkish Embassy. At this dinner the ambassador rose and, facing 'Abdu'l-Bahá with tears in his eyes, toasted Him as 'The Light of the age, Who has come to spread His glory and perfection among us.'[92]

Juliet Thompson

જી

His departure from New York was a remarkable sight, for Bahais had come to that city from far and near, some even from California, to bid him farewell, and when the great modern liner left her moorings the pier was black with people whose eyes were centred on the patriarchal figure with the long grey beard and snowy turban, who looked the embodiment of the Old Testament prophets and presented so remarkable a contrast to his modern surroundings. Few among the onlookers were unmoved, any women were openly weeping, and I saw men whose eyes were dim, while those of Abdul Baha's Persian followers who were left behind were unrestrained in their grief!

'Isn't it sad he is going?' said someone as the great ship slowly moved out to sea. 'Ah! But how glad for those he is going to!' was the reply from one who knew how eagerly people were waiting to welcome Abdul Baha in England and Scotland, as well as in Paris.[93]

Maude M. Holbach

England and Scotland

13 December 1912 – 21 January 1913

After an eight-day crossing of the Atlantic from New York, the ship carrying 'Abdu'l-Bahá docked into Liverpool for His second sojourn in Great Britain. This visit included meetings and audiences in Liverpool, London, Bristol, Oxford, Edinburgh, and Woking.

A closer view . . . revealed an old man, full of subdued fire, quietly resting in a luxurious alcove opposite the companion way. A mass of wrinkles upon his face, a gleam of Oriental enthusiasm in his eye, long grey hair streaming over his shoulders, there was something almost weird and bewitching about the 'Prophet of Peace' and the twentieth century 'Messiah' . . .[94]

The Liverpool Daily Post and Mercury

✑

I have heard of the wonderful journeys that he has made. I know how he never falters. He believes that he is bringing a message to the world, and we believe it too.[95]

Charlotte Despard

✑

Even the Western stranger coming into the Master's presence for the first time acknowledges an emotion akin to awe, and after a few minutes speech with him, feels the stirring of a deeper spirit of devotion than the ordinary amenities of social intercourse are calculated to arouse. For 'Abdu'l-Baha, whose mission of peace and universal brotherhood is like the coming of the four winds into the valley of dry bones, in Ezekiel's vision, is much more than a picturesque Eastern figure in the romantic setting of Western civilisation. He is a prophet. A venerable figure, of rather less than medium stature, clothed in long, flowing Persian garments, his white beard lying upon his breast, silver-grey plaited hair falling over his shoulders, dark, brooding, pitiful eyes that yet light up when a smile of singular gentleness and sweetness passes across his face, and a low, mellow voice whose tones are charged with a strange solemnity – that is the Master as the stranger sees him. But to the Bahais he is the 'Servant of God', the symbol of the unity of religions and races which it is his mission to promote. Although nearly seventy years of age, he has undertaken this tour of the Western world to proclaim his message of universal peace, and to recall the nations from their armed madness to the forgotten simplicities of the spirit. For nine months, he travelled in America, crossing the continent from coast to coast, from east to west, addressing large audiences in churches, synagogues, temples, halls, drawing-rooms, hotels, and in some of the universities. Wherever he spoke, it was at the invitation of the heads of the institution or movement which organized the meetings. He was a guest at the National Conference of Peace Societies held recently. The subject of his discourses everywhere was the same – an exposition of the teachings of Baha'o'llah, the source of the present-day Bahai faith.[96]

The Christian Commonwealth

&

When Abdul Baha first came to England, I refused all invitations to visit him. I had met those who made pilgrimages to his prison-home in Akka, and they talked so much about 'The Blessed Perfection' and 'The Manifested Splendour' that, though interested in what seemed a useful enough form of hero-worship for those to whom it appealed, I had no desire to see Abbas Effendi for myself . . .

A dear friend compelled me to accompany her to a reception of Abdul Baha . . . The submissive sweetness with which the venerable man received the homage of his followers affected me strongly. I wondered whether . . . he ever shrank from the burden of an enforced role of divinity. And an impulse seized me to see him in converse with an intellectual and spiritual peer. But when I cast about to find such a one, I realized the true greatness of the man in whose presence I found myself. I did not go forward with the rest to greet him on this first occasion. I stood at the door busy with my thoughts. And as if he knew these thoughts, as he passed out, he gave me a playful slap on the arm, as one would administer reproof to a wilful child, and his eyes danced with merriment.

Again and again I have noticed evidence of his awareness of the mental states of those around him. And I am assured that this keen intuition has been observed in his correspondence. Those whom he has never seen have been amazed to receive, from the Prophet in Akka, correct perceptions of conditions pertaining to them in America.

. . . His grey eyes are unusually expressive. In moments of excitement they become dark and deep in the piercing intensity of their gaze. I have seen them slash as if generating a kind of lightning, and then they soften and brighten and change expression with all the varying moods of his active mentality. But whether under the influence of sorrow or joy, indignation or pity, they are always surcharged with sympathy. One who knows no word of Persian can share the emotions of his soul by watching the lights and shadows in his eyes. When, as often, he closed them, then one need only follow the movements of his no less wonderful hands.[97]

Felicia Scatcherd

၄၁

It is not the words which have impressed us so much as the life. He has a right to speak, for He has spent forty years of His life in prison for the sake of the truth which was revealed to Him . . .[98]

Rev. A.B. Robb

၄၁

What struck me when 'Abdu'l-Bahá was speaking, was that He was giving expression to some wishes of our own hearts. We approve of the ideal He lays before us of education and the necessity of each one learning a trade, and His beautiful simile of the two wings on which society is to rise into a purer and clearer atmosphere, put into beautiful words what was in the minds of many of us. What impressed us most is that courage which enabled Him, during long years of imprisonment, and even in the face of death, to hold fast to His convictions.[99]

Sir Patrick Geddes

၄၁

'Abdu'l-Bahá has tremendous spiritual powers. In my opinion, He is the focal point of the spiritual, intellectual, and theological forces of the present and future centuries.[100]

David Graham Pole

Of course when I saw Him I knew who He was. Oh, you couldn't mistake Him. And that heavenly smile! It was a perpetual smile, and yet it wasn't, if you can imagine; it looked as though He smiled at everyone, and yet the smile seemed always to be there. And His eyes looked as if they were looking through you. He had the most gentle voice; I've never heard a voice like it . . . He embraced a good many people; He didn't me. He just shook hands. Several of us He just shook hands with. When 'Abdu'l-Bahá shook hands with me, He seemed to transmit something to me, and I've never been the same since.

There was an interpreter – who spoilt the whole show! It wasn't that his voice didn't suit me, it was that although 'Abdu'l-Bahá spoke in Persian, you *understood*; you knew what He was saying, somehow. One was so enamoured of His voice that one sort of *felt* what He was saying.[101]

Florence Altass

❧

To be ushered into the presence of Abdul Baha, Abbas Effendi, 'the Servant of God', is to have the curtains of time lifted back and to hold converse with a prophet of Israel. The artistic dignity of his quietly coloured Eastern gown, the white folds of his turban, and the patriarchal beard which hangs upon his bosom all contribute towards giving the immediate impression of an Eastern scholar and divine. But it is the finely moulded contour of his face, the gentle movements of his hands, and the deep expression in his eyes which make it manifest that here, indeed, is an embodiment of the prophets of old. In comparing Abdul Baha to the Biblical prophets, there is a distinction to be made. The early prophets descended upon mankind as the scourgers of iniquity and as swords of the Lord. This messenger comes as a great reconciler of all faiths, as the forerunner of universal peace. In his eyes there is suffering and love. He is a man who has looked aghast and with pity upon the turmoil of life, and has heartfelt thoughts to utter.[102]

S. Munro

ഗ

His public addresses prove that through this or that channel he had imbibed something of humanistic and even scientific culture; he was a much more complete man than St Francis of Assisi, who despised human knowledge. It is true he interpreted any facts which he gathered in the light of revealed religious truth. But he distinctly recognized the right of scientific research . . .[103]

T.K. Cheyne

ഗ

The most abiding impression I received from intimate contact with him was his immense breadth of outlook, permeated with the spirit of deep and loving kindness. Whatever the topic under discussion – ranging from religion to the weather, from sunsets to the flowers, from ethics to personal behaviour, ʿAbduʾl-Bahá always struck the universal note, the note of Oneness as between the Creator and all His creation, great or small.[104]

He was a man of great spiritual stature and prophetic vision and I shall always cherish the affection he bestowed upon me and the inspiration that his life and example have given to me ever since he first came into my life in 1908.[105]

Wellesley Tudor-Pole

Return to Paris

21 January 1913 – 12 June 1913

During His return visit to Paris, 'Abdu'l-Bahá had fewer public engagements, but a number of Bahá'ís from the East arrived to meet Him. Émigrés from Írán and the Ottoman Empire resident in the city also sought Him out. When 'Abdu'l-Bahá felt strong and well enough, He set off to Stuttgart in Germany to visit its Bahá'í community. He also made trips to Vienna and Budapest between 30 March and 1 May 1913. His presence there continued to attract attention from spiritual seekers, leaders of thought and the press.

Each morning a group assembled at his apartment, 30 rue St. Didier, where he spoke informally, sometimes answering questions, or, on request, explaining points touched on in public addresses. In this way, although there are seeming repetitions, many abstruse subjects are elucidated in these informal conferences . . . On these occasions Abdul Baha would sometimes sit by the window over-looking Paris and anon the majestic white-robed figure would pace the room as he discoursed . . .

His time in Paris was completely occupied. In the afternoons and evenings one found him surrounded by French savants and lovers of truth who sought an audience with this master of wisdom.[106]

Isobel Fraser Chamberlain

❧

He lives in an apartment almost in the shadow of the Eiffel Tower and one of the striking sights of Paris is to see him walking about in his Oriental attire through the gardens of the

Trocadero and the Champ de Mars, or visiting Notre Dame.
His life is of the simplest, his attitude humble, his needs few.
He chants at midnight and at dawn and he who would inter-
view this 'master' must be up betimes.[107]

S.S. Chamberlain

જી

Abdul Baha in my estimation is the perfect embodiment of
universal love. He is the real and ideal prophet of brotherhood
and peace. He is a perfect divine example for all of us to follow
. . . and we all love and revere Him because He is at one and
the same moment so divine and so human . . . Listen to his
words of wisdom and knowledge. Forget for an hour your own
thoughts and ideas and let your minds be filled with his ideas
of divine spirit.[108]

Charles Blech

જી

Of Abdul-Baha, the present leader of the Cause, a great
deal might be written, so full is the personality of the man.
An interview recently granted me by him in Paris left upon
my mind a profound impression. He sat in a small room,
fragrant with hyacinths. His white turban, flowing green
robes, spontaneous gestures, and above all the resonance of
his voice, called up to my mind the freshness of spring and
the impetuousness of mountain torrents. He spoke of the
spiritual value of practical things, and of the message of the
West to the East. He dwelt upon the necessity of bringing
our educational advantages within reach of all oriental races,
in the largest spirit and devoid of mental prejudices of caste
and creed . . .

Here indeed were practical precepts for the Universalism of which Abdul-Baha is the representative, and in spite of the delicate imagery of the Persian address . . . his thought was expressed with scientific force and precision. There were no abstractions, no visionary transports, but there was the alert and joyous vitality of one anxious to share his happiness and his knowledge with his fellow creatures . . . [109]

Beatrice Irwin

ↇ

He had an excellent nature. He was as simple as his aspiration was great. I liked him very much . . .

His sincerity and his aspiration for the Divine were simple and very spontaneous. One day, when I went to visit him, he was to give a lecture to his disciples. But he was sick and could not get up. Perhaps the meeting would have to be postponed. When I came near to him, he said, 'Go and take my place at today's lecture.' I was startled, unprepared as I was to hear such a request. I said to him, 'I am not a member of your sect and I know nothing about it, so how can I talk to them about anything?' But he insisted, saying, 'It does not matter. Say anything at all, it will be quite all right. Go and talk . . . Concentrate in the sitting-room and then speak.' At last he persuaded me to do it . . .

Last Monday, Abdul Baha took leave of us; in a very few days he will have left Paris, and I know many hearts which will feel a great void and will grieve.

Yet only the body is leaving us, and what is the body if not precisely that in which men are most alike, be they great or small, wise or ignorant, terrestrial or divine? Yes, you may rest assured that only his body is leaving us; his thought will remain faithfully with us, and his unchanging affection will enfold us, and his spiritual influence will always be the same, absolutely the same. Whether materially he is near or far matters little, for the divine forces elude completely the laws of the material world: they are omnipresent, always at work to satisfy every receptivity, every sincere aspiration.

So although it may be pleasant for our outer being to see his physical appearance or hear his voice, to dwell in his presence, we must truly tell ourselves that, inasmuch as it seems indispensable to us, this shows that we are still little conscious of the inner life, the true life.

Even if we do not attain to the marvellous depths of the divine life, of which only very rare individuals are constantly conscious, already in the domain of thought we escape the laws of time and space.[110]   *Mirra Alfassa*

જી

Last summer the turn came of Stuttgart, Vienna, and Budapest . . . At Vienna the Baroness von Suttner, the winner of the Nobel Peace Prize, who had been speaking in America in the Peace interest the previous year but had not then met Abdul Baha, called upon him and conferred with him upon the subject of International Peace, to promote which was their common aim.

In Budapest, where Abdul Baha met with an ovation from both scholars and social reformers, the head of the Peace Society, a high dignitary of the Church of Rome, showed his liberality by extending a warm welcome to the Oriental guest, and appearing with him on the platform at a public meeting at which a renowned Jewish professor stood on his other side, thus typifying the union of religions for which Abdul Baha pleads.[111]

Maud Holbach

Look at the son of BAHA'O'LLAH, Abdul-Baha, the Servant of God! Who can turn from his loving eyes or from the kindness of his words! He calls himself 'The Servant of God.' We recognize in him an Ambassador of God, who has come to teach us truth, light and love. O! Let us remember his words and tell them to our children and our children's children! Let us receive the blessing of Abdul-Baha – it will sanctify our lives.[112]

Consul Albert Schwarz

༄

Although I have travelled through many countries and cities of Islam, yet I have never met so lofty a character and so exalted a personage . . .[113]

Arminius Vámbéry

༄

I saw with admiration that in his facial expression peace, clean love, and perfect good intentions reflected themselves. He saw everything in such a beatific light; he found everything beautiful the outer life of the city, as well as the souls of its inhabitants. He praised the layout of our city, the traversing magnificent Danube, its good water and its good people.[114]

Róbert Nádler

༄

A great man has arrived in Budapest. He is neither an emperor, nor a prince, nor some famous writer. He is an 'apostle', the prophet of the unification of humankind, Abdul Baha, the teacher of Bahaism. For us, with minds saturated by materialism, it may look strange or even ridiculous that there is a man today who is wandering from town to town to seek salvation for his suffering fellow human beings by preaching love and human community. And still the facts provide a wonderful justification for the prophet. In America, England and on the continent, in countries where industrial production has reached the highest levels, there are millions who believe in this new manifestation and who find improvement in it.[115]

Pesti Naplo newspaper

ɔ

Abdul Beha is the child of the modern age and this is manifest in his teachings among other things. While voicing the sacred words of God, he often refers to modern ideals as well. In addition to eternal love and happiness, he wholeheartedly is a propagandist of the cause of world peace and, with more enthusiasm than even the suffragettes, he demands the right for women to vote and equality between men and women.

The novel and unselfish work of this Persian sage is worthy of respect and deserves the great sympathy by which he has been welcomed on his world tour . . .[116]

Budapest newspaper

Final years

5 December 1913 – 28 November 1921

His travels completed, 'Abdu'l-Bahá spent a further six months in Egypt before returning to the Holy Land. But the next four years of His life were fraught with danger, as the world experienced the most devastating conflict it had yet seen. He moved the

Bahá'ís out of Haifa and 'Akká and supervised the stockpiling of grain from Bahá'í-owned farms to avert a famine. 'Abdu'l-Bahá's own life was even threatened by the Turkish officials in Palestine.

Abdul Baha is now visiting Acre and living in the house of Baha'o'llah, close to the prison . . .

It is wonderful to see the venerable figure of this revered Bahai leader passing through the narrow streets of this ancient town, where he lived for forty years as a political prisoner, and to note the deep respect with which he is saluted by the Turkish officials and the officers of the garrison from the Governor downwards, who visit him constantly and listen with the deepest attention to his words. 'The master' does not teach in Syria as he did in the West, but he goes about doing good, and Mohammedans and Christians alike share his benefactions. From sunrise often until midnight he works, in spite of broken health, never sparing himself if there is a wrong to be righted or a suffering to be relieved. To Christians who regard Abdul Baha with impartial and sympathetic eyes, this wonderful selfless life cannot fail to recall that life whose tragic termination on Calvary the whole Christian world recalls to-day.[117]

Maud Holbach

ço

In his old age when he was living in Haifa he used to set aside a special hour each Friday for dispensing charity to the poor who came to ask for it; and many visitors have left pictures of the strange wild scene as the crowd of alms-seekers, many of them guileful-menacing-violent, many of them dreadful to look on, but all of them pitiable, jostled around the venerable figure of their host who walked among them distributing smiles and good cheer and warm encouragement along with the material gift that seemed to fit each case of need. It was his practice too to seek out the poor and needy in their homes, and the sight of their deprivations brought him great sadness. Returning from such a visit of charity he could hardly bring himself to partake of his own frugal supper, for thinking of their greater poverty.[118]

George Townshend

✦

One day on the sands of Galilee I met Abbas Effendi, as he is known in Palestine and Persia, or Abdul Baha, as he is better known in America. He is the recognized head of the Bahai movement, as he said he preferred to have his religion known . . . Abbas Effendi, a patriarch and prophet from Persia, is a person of tremendous magnetism. You 'feel' him when he approaches you. Irrespective of his religious teachings the wise men of the earth who have met him have considered him of the wisest who lives. And he has met the distinguished men of all nations. They have visited him in his prison home at Acre, as they visited Tolstoy at his farm in Russia . . . Wise doctors from Europe have called upon him to discuss philosophy, as it is taught in the East, and they have found that he has absorbed all the philosophies of the European continent, knows practically all about all the religions of the world, and is able to discuss each with its leaders, while to everyone who meets him he speaks, not of the error of other men's ways, but graphically and poignantly explains to every man how his religion is but a part of that great universal religion which he himself preaches and believes is soon to cover the world.

. . . Without a doubt he is the most impressive person in appearance I have ever seen. He has long white hair, a long snowy beard, his face is of a dusty whiteness and he dresses in white robes and wears a white turban. When I first met him he was walking along alone, but he was closely followed by his secretary and interpreter and three or four of his Persian followers, who like himself are exiled from their native land. No doubt I stared at him, for he had a commanding presence. His carriage was majestic and I felt instinctively that he was a person of Importance.

. . . But as I stared, he kindly saluted me and murmured a friendly greeting in Persian, which I did not understand. Instinctively, I raised my hat to him. He has a compelling personality which radiates something that commands respect and I wondered who he was.

. . . When I enquired as to his health, he assured me that he had not felt so strong for many years. Instead of undermining his constitution, his long imprisonment at Acre seems to have had the opposite effect. All of the latent energy of his young manhood seems to have been stored up for the present. He said he had no complaints to make. His life had been nothing but one succession of troubles. He had been an exile, as his father had been before him. But he spoke of these things in a soft and gentle voice.[119]

Archie Bell

ɞ

Abdul Baha is still in Syria working with that deep love and wisdom which marks all his actions when the great needs of humanity and the poor dependents on his help claim his attention. All communication has long been broken between Turkish ports and the outside world. Now and then, after innumerable difficulties, an emissary has been got through to him, taking what money is possible for the relief of his family and others. Had it not been for the great influence possessed by Abdul Baha over the Turkish leaders the Bahais would have suffered not only the loss of all their homes and loved ones, but possibly the desecration of some of their holiest spots. Abdul Baha has been the means of keeping many forces in hand and the channel for helping countless numbers of starved and terrified families. His own people are scattered in various villages for better safety, and the conditions in Syria generally are terrible.[120]

Jean Stannard

❧

During the years of the First World War, 'Abdu'l-Bahá systematically mapped out the spread of the Bahá'í Faith to the entire world in a series of letters to the Bahá'ís in North America known as the Tablets of the Divine Plan.

As war's inferno was engulfing the world, 'Abdu'l-Bahá turned His attention to the one great task remaining in His ministry, that of ensuring the proclamation to the remotest corners of the Earth of the message which had been neglected – or opposed – in Islamic and Western society alike. The instrument He devised for this purpose was the Divine Plan laid out in fourteen great Tablets, four of them addressed to the Bahá'í community of North America and ten subsidiary ones addressed to five specific segments of that community. Together with Bahá'u'lláh's Tablet of Carmel and the Master's Will and Testament, the Tablets of the Divine Plan were described by Shoghi Effendi as three of the 'Charters' of the Cause. Revealed during the darkest days of the war, in

1916 and 1917, the Divine Plan summoned the small body of American and Canadian believers to assume the role of leadership in establishing the Cause of God throughout the planet.[121]

Century of Light

✧

The world mission entrusted to the American Bahá'ís was set out in the Tablets of the Divine Plan. Designated as 'the chosen trustees and principal executors of 'Abdu'l-Bahá's Divine Plan', the American Bahá'ís were called upon to assume a preponderating role in taking the message of Bahá'u'lláh to all lthe contries of the world and for effecting the transformation in values necessary for the emergence of a world order characterized by justice, unity and peace.[122]

The Tablets of the Divine Plan were the directing and motivating force for spreading, in a strategic, systematic, and evolutionary manner the society-building values and concepts embodied in the teachings of Bahá'u'lláh. While the efforts of dedicated believers at the grassroots of a community provided the human resources for the unfoldment of this historic enterprise, 'Abdu'l-Bahá clearly foresaw the critical importance of some form of organization or administrative structure to provide leadership and sustain long-term systematic and united action.[123]

Janet Khan

✧

After the British occupied Palestine at the end of the War, 'Abdu'l-Bahá became a much-trusted advisor and confidante of the authorities. For the valuable counsel He gave, and the good influence He had upon – and the humanitarian services He rendered to – the people of the region, He received, a Knighthood. He accepted the honour as the gift of a 'just king' but never used the title. Towards the end of His life, He continued to care for the poor of Haifa and 'Akká, and Bahá'í pilgrims and other individuals from the West made special visits to meet Him.

It was a wonderful experience in the midst of the chaos of war to visit the Master at his Mount Carmel home, which even at that time remained a haven of peace and refreshment.

I well remember him, majestic yet gentle, pacing up and down the garden whilst he spoke to me about eternal realities, at a time when the whole material world was rocking on its foundations. The power of the spirit shone through his presence, giving one the feeling that a great prophet from Old Testament days had risen up in a war-stricken world, to guide and inspire all who would listen to him.[124]

Wellesley Tudor-Pole

൚

His spirit unbroken after the long years of suffering, full of enthusiasm for his teachings which he treasures above all else, respected and loved by followers and outsiders alike, Abbas Effendi spends the remainder of his life spreading his teachings in word and in writing. He works from morning till night, answers letters from countries around the world, receives visits and gives audiences.

May this friendly, idealistic old man, who has suffered so much for his ideas and ideals, have a happy twilight of his life. If there were many of these energetic personalities in the world such as Abbas Effendi and his father, what now appears to remain an illusion for many years to come and probably forever, might be possible: peace on earth and love between all peoples.[125]

Jo Goudsmit

૭〜૭

I have rarely come across a man who so completely sums up the saint, or let us say saint and philosopher combined, for the presence and image of the man are of the Middle Ages, their spirit of personal holiness, while what he says has the lucidity of the Greek, is disruptive of all religions and medi- aeval systems, is philosophic, modern, and synthetic.[126]

C.R. Ashbee

૭〜૭

Lord Allenby, after his triumphant drive through Syria, sent me to establish the Government at Haifa and throughout that district. I called upon 'Abbás Effendi on the day I arrived and was delighted to find him quite unchanged. When he came to Jerusalem he visited my house and I never failed to visit him whenever I went to Haifa. His conversation was indeed a remarkable planning, like that of an ancient prophet, far above the perplexities and pettinesses of Palestine politics, and elevating all problems into first principles.[127]

Sir Ronald Storrs

૭〜૭

There was never a more striking instance of one who desired that mankind should live in peace and goodwill and have love for others by the recognition of their inherent divine qualities.

At Haifa in 1919, I well remember seeing a white figure seated by the roadside; when he arose and walked the vision of a truly and holy saintly man impressed itself on me.[128]

Lord Lamington

❧

In 1920 I was appointed as the first High Commissioner for Palestine under the British Mandate, and took an early opportunity of paying a visit to 'Abdu'l-Bahá Effendi at his home in Haifa . . . I was impressed, as was every visitor, by 'Abdu'l-Bahá's dignity, grace and charm. Of moderate stature, his strong features and lofty expression lent to his personality an appearance of majesty. In our conversation he readily explained and discussed the principal tenets of Bahá'í, answered my inquiries and listened to my comments. I remember vividly that friendly interview of sixteen years ago, in the simple room of the villa, surrounded by gardens, on the sunny hillside of Mount Carmel.

I was glad I had paid my visit so soon, for in 1921 'Abdu'l-Bahá died. I was only able to express my respect for his creed and my regard for his person by coming from the capital to attend his funeral. A great throng had gathered together, sorrowing for his death, but rejoicing also for his life.[129]

Viscount Herbert Samuel of Carmel

❧

During the winter of 1919–1920 the writer had the great privilege of spending two and half months as the guest of 'Abdu'l-Bahá at Haifa and intimately observing His daily life. At that time, although nearly seventy-six years of age, He was still remarkably vigorous, and accomplished daily an almost incredible amount of work. Although often very weary He showed wonderful powers of recuperation, and His services were always at the disposal of those who needed them most. His unfailing patience, gentleness, kindliness and tact made His presence like a benediction. It was His custom to spend a large part of each night in prayer and meditation. From early morning until evening, except for a short siesta after lunch, He was busily engaged in reading and answering letters from many lands and in attending to the multitudinous affairs of the household and of the Cause. In the afternoon He usually had a little relaxation in the form of a walk or a drive, but even then He was usually accompanied by one or two, or a party, of pilgrims with whom He would converse on spiritual matters, or He would find opportunity by the way of seeing and ministering to some of the poor. After His return He would call the friends to the usual evening meeting in His salon. Both at lunch and supper He used to entertain a number of pilgrims and friends, and charm His guests with happy and humorous stories as well as precious talks on a great variety of subjects. 'My home is the home of laughter and mirth', He declared, and indeed it was so. He delighted in gathering together people of various races, colors, nations and religions in unity and cordial friendship around His hospitable board. He was indeed a loving father not only to the little community at Haifa, but to the Bahá'í community throughout the world.[130]

J.E. Esslemont

એ

Every evening at eight o'clock the Master holds a meeting lasting an hour or more, during which He discourses upon intricate problems concerning the Cause. The Master is seated upon the large porch in front of the house, to which ten white stone steps lead from the broad gravel path. A white stone coping borders the path on each side, providing seating space for fifty or more people who constitute the audience.

View with me that majestic Figure in white flowing garments seated before us, a white turban crowning the wonderful head with its long silvery locks lifted gently by the breeze; the beautifully moulded hands emphasising the discourse with impressive gesture. After the address a Russian refugee Bahá'í teacher chants in exquisitely modulated tones, the prayers of Bahá'u'lláh. It is impossible adequately to describe this scene. The writer became conscious of new emotions, the awakening of something so subtle, so elusive, that one could not capture it, yet so impressive that everything was cast into oblivion except the immediate present. The fragrance from the gardens on either side wafted a different scent on each breath of the night air. Roses, orange blossoms, lemon buds, tuberoses, jasmine, honeysuckle – each in turn left its definite sweetness as a fresh odour entranced one and vanished.

O that I might impress this scene upon the heart of the world! To me it is as though all eternity could not efface it; that majestic white Figure seated on the broad stone platform like a king enthroned, the setting of natural beauty so befitting His spiritual station – the gardens, the sea, the starry heavens, and the millions of gleaming points of light reflected below. Shadows deepen under the trees, while at their tops the leaves glisten and glimmer like sparkling gems. The murmur of the sea is just beyond, the waves in ever repeating undulations, coming nearer and nearer to caress the shore. The melodious chanting, the deep silences, the seated figures with bowed heads and devoted hearts.

The chant ends. In a few moments the Master rises and goes into the house. Everyone rises also and salutes in the beautiful eastern fashion, hand touching the forehead and then the heart. The spell is broken![131] *Marie Watson*

Up to the last, he continued to lead his usual active, busy life, rising early, receiving strangers in his hospitable home, instructing his disciples, attending the noonday prayer at the Mosque, dictating answers to his numerous correspondents all over the world. But gradually he was failing, a great fatigue constantly overcame him, and his family recognized afterwards that during the last few weeks he must have been trying gently to prepare them for his coming departure, but so gently that at the time they did not understand the sorrow that was drawing nearer and nearer to that serenely happy home. Within two days of his death he continued to go to the Mosque and dispense to the poor; he received the Mufti of Haifa, and in the evening attended a meeting of friends in his audience chamber. Though losing strength he constantly assured his family that he was quite well, only tired, very tired, and when on Sunday night, with his daughter by his side, he lay back and closed his eyes, they thought him asleep, so calm and serene was the passing out of his spirit.[132]

Constance Elizabeth Maud

IV

THE PASSING OF 'ABDU'L-BAHÁ

(1921)

The Passing of 'Abdu'l-Bahá

28 November 1921

The passing of 'Abdu'l-Bahá at the age of 77 came as an unexpected shock to His family and friends in the Holy Land, and the growing Bahá'í communities in numerous countries around the world. After His passing, the small number of Western pilgrims then in Haifa were allowed into the room where His body lay. At His funeral, 'the like of which Palestine had never seen',[1] some ten thousand mourners, representing every strata of society, paid homage to His saintly life of devotion to God and service to humanity. Newspapers from many different countries reported His passing with great respect.

The eyes that had always looked out with loving-kindness upon humanity, whether friends or foes, were now closed. The hands that had ever been stretched forth to give alms to the poor and the needy, the halt and the maimed, the blind, the orphan and the widow, had now finished their labour. The feet that, with untiring zeal, had gone upon the ceaseless errands of the Lord of Compassion were now at rest. The lips that had so eloquently championed the cause of the suffering sons of men, were now hushed in silence. The heart that had so powerfully throbbed with wondrous love for the children of God was now stilled. His glorious spirit had passed from the life of earth, from the persecutions of the enemies of righteousness, from the storm and stress of well nigh eighty years of indefatigable toil for the good of others.

His long martyrdom was ended![2]

Shoghi Effendi and Lady Blomfield

℘

This dire calamity, this great affliction, the passing of 'Abdu'l-Bahá, may our lives be sacrificed for His meekness, has shaken us to the very depths. Our lives lie in ruins. In our hearts, the stars of happiness have set, the lamps of joy have been put out. No more, from the rose-garden of the All-Glorious, does the nightingale warble those songs that fed the spirit in days gone by. From over the flower-beds of Heaven, the dove trills and coos no more. Now is the bright morning dark, and blazing noon is night, and the sea of woe has surged, and a storm of sorrow has overwhelmed mankind.

Alas, alas, that luminous Moon, with His ravaged breast a thicket of arrows – darts of the evil-doers' taunts, their derision, their calumnies – and His heart grieved by the malevolence of His foes and the rebellion of the violators, is now hidden behind heavy clouds, has departed from this world's horizons, and has risen upward to the realm of transcendent glory, to the all-highest Horizon.

The passing of 'Abdu'l-Bahá, may our lives be a sacrifice for His meekness, was the ultimate calamity, the most great disaster. The light has fled our hearts, and our souls are wedded to sorrow, and no power in all the world can furnish any consolation, save only the power that comes from the steadfastness of the believers and their deep-rooted faith, and their unity, and their love for one another.

Only these can lessen the pain and quiet the anguish.

Although to outward seeming the Sun of the Covenant has hidden Himself behind the clouds, and the Orb of the Testament is concealed, and on the holy horizon of glory, He has now set, and is lost to view – still His rays are shining from out His hidden place, and forever will His light shed down its splendours.

For ever and ever will He, with all that invisible grace,

and those bestowals of the spirit, lead the seeker onward, and guide the yearning, and ravish the hearts of the lovers.[3]

Bahíyyih Khánum

❧

That pure and holy, divine, benign, and benevolent Soul could never accept to see even one person sorrowful, and He did not wish that anyone should grieve. He would say, 'I cannot bear to look upon a sorrowful face.' He was the fellow-sufferer of all humanity and was loving to all on earth. When He spoke, it was usually with smiles and happiness. He would inquire after children. He desired that all should be cheerful and joyous. He would say, 'Children are the inhabitants of the Kingdom. They are always happy and cheerful.'[4]

Alas! alas! O my Master and the Guide of every helpless one! What a disaster! What an earthquake at that midnight hour, that shattered a myriad powerful bonds with but one jolt. Whereupon cries and lamentation reached the heights of heaven, and anguish, agitation, and sorrow spread throughout the world of being.[5]

Munírih Khánum

❧

At first we were as dumb and speechless, bewildered. We stood or kneeled before the bed. We gazed upon his face and could not trust our eyes. At last the bewilderment subsided and the trust asserted itself. Was it true that his eyes would open no more? Would he not open his eyes to look upon us again? Would he not open his lips to say that he was not dead? We asked the doctors [by then other physicians had been sent for] if he was dead. They said yes, the heart had ceased to beat; they said it was useless to try to revive him – it could not be done. Then, after a while, the mosquito netting over the bed was let down, and this covered from our eyes the earthly remains of our Lord. We got up and went into the adjacent room, and the door of the room out of which we came was closed.

But before this, the blood of the wounds of this blow had begun to flow, and the hurt and the pain and the moans increased with every minute. We five European pilgrims were in the room together with the holy family and the holy mother held my husband's hand and the Greatest Holy Leaf held mine. After a time we went back to the Pilgrim House, leaving the holy family alone. It was still night – no moon at all. Not long afterward the dawn broke, and at last the sun rose with great effulgence over the scene of this memorable night . . .[6]

Louise Bosch

❧

I am not worth it, that those radiant, luminous, penetrating blue eyes should have rested on me, that that kind mouth should have spoken loving, beautiful words to me – and useless my life would appear to me if the power of the experience does not give me strength to really remold my life and to lead it to a high purpose.

. . . We were permitted to see the face of the Master once more – the only ones besides the family. How beautiful it was! Such peace! Such rest! I do not believe that I shall ever in my life see again such an unspeakably beautiful face as that of 'Abdu'l-Bahá in life and in death.[7]

Johanna Hauf

❧

As I write certain memories come back to me with a strange insistence. I remember standing beside the Master in the pulpit of the City Temple, London, watching over five thousand people breathlessly absorbed in listening to 'Abdu'l-Bahá's living spiritual words, and in watching his every smile and movement.

I remember walking with him through the woods at Clifton, 1911, when he spoke of the coming of a spiritual renaissance within the Christian churches; or wandering along the Banks of the Seine at sunset, 1913, when the Master spoke of the Great War that was to come, and the Most Great Peace that would ultimately follow it.

I have sat beside him at Ramleh, Alexandria, beneath the palms, and while he spoke of the essential unity of all mankind. There were Christians, Jews, Moslems, Parsis, Hindoos and Freethinkers sitting around him on that occasion, one and all united with the same faith and aspiration. I remember walking alone with the Master on Mount Carmel's slopes, sharing his frugal meals in his Haifa house, listening to his melodious chanting within the Garden Tomb, living as one of the family within Bahá'u'lláh's house at Acre.

The Friends who read these words will bring to memory many similar scenes within their own experience and will remain ever thankful for such memories.

There is no Death. The Master lives in our midst, and the great spiritual work of human redemption goes forward unceasingly.

Despite the apparent world tribulations of the present hour, the Dawn of a new Day approaches, and it is the privilege of every man and woman alive to-day to work serenely and faithfully for the Coming of the World Peace and true human brotherhood.[8]

Wellesley Tudor Pole

The casket was carried up the mountain on the shoulders of eight men who frequently changed. Never in my life will I forget that walk. More than an hour we followed the bier which covered the human form of the beloved Master – after stormy, rainy days, radiant weather; dark blue the sea, dark blue the sky – slowly, slowly followed the crowd, reverently and shyly they followed the ruler who had gone to deep silence and rest.[9]

Johanna Hauff

⅋

There were men of all nations, of all creeds, of all walks of life, high and low, rich and poor. It seemed that never had there been such a funeral procession before. So great was the desire to help carry the casket up the mountain that some of the men were wrangling for the privilege of only touching it with their fingertips. For an hour and a half that great mass of people slowly moved along the winding road up the steep incline of Mount Carmel.[10]

John Bosch

⅋

As the vast concourse pressed round the Tabernacle of his body, waiting to be laid in its resting place, within the vault, next to that of the Báb, representatives of the various denominations, Moslems, Christians and Jews, all hearts being ablaze with fervent-love of 'Abdu'l-Bahá, some on the impulse of the moment, others prepared, raised their voices in eulogy and regret, paying their last homage of farewell to their loved one. So united were they in their acclamation of him, as the wise educator and reconciler of the human race in this perplexed and sorrowful age, that there seemed to be nothing left for the Bahá'ís to say.[11]

Shoghi Effendi and Lady Blomfield

☙

O concourse of Arabians and Persians! Whom are ye bewailing? Is it he who but yesterday was great in his life and is today in his death greater still? Shed no tears for the one that hath departed to the world of Eternity, but weep over the passing of Virtue and Wisdom, of Knowledge and Generosity. Lament for yourselves, for yours is the loss, whilst he, your lost one, is but a revered Wayfarer, stepping from your mortal world into the everlasting Home. Weep one hour for the sake of him who, for well nigh eighty years, hath wept for you! Look to your right, look to your left, look East and look West and behold, what glory and greatness have vanished! What a pillar of peace hath crumbled! What eloquent lips are hushed! Alas! In this tribulation there is no heart but aches with anguish, no eye but is filled with tears. Woe unto the poor, for lo! goodness hath departed from them, woe unto the orphans, for their loving father is no more with them! Could the life of Sir 'Abdu'l-Bahá 'Abbas have been redeemed by the sacrifices of many a precious soul, they of a certainty would gladly have offered up their lives for his life. But Fate hath otherwise ordained. Every destiny is predetermined and none can change the Divine Decree. What am I to set forth the achievements of this leader of mankind? They are too glorious to be praised, too many to recount. Suffice it to say, that he has left in every heart the most profound impression, on every tongue most wondrous praise. And he that leaveth a memory so lovely, so imperishable, he, indeed, is not dead. Be solaced then, O ye people of Baha! Endure and be patient; for no man, be he of the East or of the West, can ever comfort you, nay he himself is even in greater need of consolation.[12]

Yúsuf al-Khatíb

୧୬

I weep for the world, in that my Lord hath died; others there are who, like unto me, weep the death of their Lord . . . O bitter is the anguish caused by this heartrending calamity! It is not only our country's loss but a world affliction . . . He hath lived for well-nigh eighty years the life of the Messengers and Apostles of God. He hath educated the souls of men, hath been benevolent unto them, hath led them to the Way of Truth. Thus he raised his people to the pinnacle of glory, and great shall be his reward from God, the reward of the righteous! Hear me O people! 'Abbás is not dead, neither hath the light of Bahá been extinguished! Nay, nay! this light shall shine with everlasting splendor. The Lamp of Bahá, 'Abbás, hath lived a goodly life, hath manifested in himself the true life of the Spirit. And now he is gathered to glory, a pure angel, richly robed in benevolent deeds, noble in his precious virtues. Fellow Christians! Truly ye are bearing the mortal remains of this ever lamented one to his last resting place, yet know of a certainty that your 'Abbás will live forever in spirit amongst you, through his deeds, his words, his virtues and all the essence of his life. We say farewell to the material body of our 'Abbás, and his material body vanisheth from our gaze, but his reality, our spiritual 'Abbás, will never leave our minds, our thoughts, our hearts, our tongues.

O great revered Sleeper! Thou hast been good to us, thou hast guided us, thou hast taught us, thou hast lived amongst us greatly, with the full meaning of greatness, thou hast made us proud of thy deeds and of thy words. Thou hast raised the Orient to the summit of glory, hast shown loving kindness to the people, trained them in righteousness, and hast striven to the end, till thou hast won the crown of glory. Rest thou happily under the shadow of the mercy of the Lord thy God, and He verily, shall well reward thee.[13]

Ibrahim Nassar

മ

The calamity of the world of humanity in the loss of the benevolent Abdul-Baha cannot be compared to any other calamity, because his vacancy will never be filled by any of the people. I do not like to exaggerate in praising this great personage, because his generous hands in the path of service to humanity and his philanthropic deeds none can deny, save one whose eyes God has blinded. Abdul-Baha was great in all the stages of his life. He was genius itself, high in character and had the best reputation. He was famous in the East of the earth and in the West. He possessed this exalted station through his untiring work and he gained the highest place in the hearts through his help to the helpless, his rescue of the hopeless and his comfort to the afflicted. Abdul-Baha was a great, learned and remarkable professor. Even if his physical body has disappeared from the eyes, his immortal deeds will never disappear from the minds. Even if the physical Abdul-Baha has passed away, his name will never pass away. O thou benevolent one who art departed! Thou hast lived greatly and thou hast departed great![14]

Professor Muhammad Murad Mufti

മ

The sun of knowledge has set; the moon of virtues has disappeared; the throne of glory has crumbled, and the mountain of kindness is levelled by the departure of this benevolent one from the mortal world to the immortal realm. I do not need to explain the sublimity of the great one whom we have lost or to enumerate his great qualities, for all of you who are just are witnesses and can testify to what has been given him of personal beauty, beauty of his character, greatness of his heart, vastness of the sea of his knowledge and generosity . . . I beg your pardon if I fail in doing my duty as far as faithfulness is concerned or if I am unable to pay the generous one who has departed what he deserves of the best and highest praise, because what my tongue utters has emanated from a tender memory and broken heart. Indeed, they are wounds and not words; they are tears and not phrases . . . This is not your calamity alone. Nay, rather it is a blow to Islam, and a calamity for the whole world, of the past and the present...[15]

Professor 'Abdu'llah Mukhlis

શ

God has ordained the departure of Abdul-Baha, who is the Lord of virtues, perfections and wisdom. The people are weeping and mourning because of the separation from the one who was the eye of all time. He planted favors in his sublime rose-garden. They grew and bore sweet fruits. The creatures are the collective witnesses of his perfections and deeds that surpassed everything.[16]

Sheikh Younis Effendi el-Khatib

શ

In a century of exaggerated positivism and unrestrained materialism, it is astonishing and rare to find a philosopher of great breadth such as the late ʿAbduʾl-Bahá ʿAbbás speaking to our hearts, our feelings, and above all seeking to educate our souls by inculcating in us the most beautiful principles, recognized as the basis of all religion and of all pure morals. Through his writings, through his eloquence, through his intimate conversations, as well as through his celebrated dialogues with the most cultured – and the fervent devotees of sectarian doctrines – he knew how to persuade, he could always convince. Living examples have some special power. His life – private and public – was an example of devotion and of forgetfulness of self for the good of others . . .

His philosophy is simple, you say. But, it is great because of that very simplicity, being in conformity with human nature, which loses its beauty when it is distorted by prejudices and superstitions. ʿAbbás died in Haifa, in Palestine, in the Holy Land that has brought forth the prophets. Left sterile and abandoned for many centuries, it is coming back to life again and beginning to recover its status and original reputation. We are not the only ones to grieve for this prophet; we are not the only ones to glorify him. In Europe, in America, I say, in every land where there are men conscious of their mission in this base world, thirsty for social justice, for brotherhood, they will mourn for him also. He is dead after suffering under despotism, fanaticism, and intolerance. ʿAkká, the Turkish Bastille, served as his prison for decades. Baghdad, the Abbassid capital, was also his prison and that of his father. Persia, the ancient cradle of sweet and divine philosophy, has driven out her children, who conceived their ideas within her borders. Cannot one see in this the Will of God and a clear preference for the Holy Land, which was and will be the cradle of all generous and noble ideas? Anyone who leaves after him a past so glorious is not dead. Anyone who has written such beautiful principles has enlarged his family among all his readers and has passed on to posterity, crowned with eternity.[17]

Salomon Bouzaglo

ↈ

Most of us here have a clear picture of Sir Abdul-Baha Abbas, of his dignified figure walking thoughtfully in our streets, of his courtesy and gracious manner, of his kindness, of his love for the little children and for the flowers and of his generosity and care for the poor and suffering. So gentle was he, and so simple, that in his presence one almost forgot that he was also a great teacher, and that his writings and his conversations have been a solace and an inspiration to hundreds and thousands of people in the East and West.[18]

Sir George Stewart Symes

ↈ

When we mention Abdul-Baha, we recall sublimity of character and firmness of determination; we recall purity of the heart and the nobility of personality; we recall unexcelled intelligence and Oriental genius. Yea, when we mention Abdul Baha, we recall the excellence of morals, the exalted principles, and the noble susceptibilities. We mention him, because he loved the poor equally with the prince; we mention him because used to entertain both adults and children; we mention him because he was merciful to the orphans and gave freely to helpless and the stranger.[19]

Ahmad Effendi El-Imam

'Abdu'l-Bahá, 'the servant of his father', aimed at no less than the regeneration of the world. 'Abdu'l-Bahá visited Paris. That magnificent and good-natured old man scattered his holy words among us some ten years ago . . . Under the white turban, his eyes reflected intelligence and goodness. He was fatherly, affectionate, and simple. His power, it seemed, came from knowing how to love men, and knowing how to make himself loved by them.[20]

Le Temps newspaper

೮೨

His persistent messages as to the divine origin and unity of mankind were as impressive as the Messenger himself. He possessed singular courtesy. At his table Buddhist and Mohammedan, Hindu and Zoroastrian, Jew and Christian, sat in amity.[21]

The Morning Post

೮೨

Having once looked upon 'Abdu'l-Bahá, his personality is indelibly impressed upon the mind: the majestic venerable figure clad in the flowing aba, his head crowned with a turban white as his head and hair; the piercing deep-set eyes whose glances shake the heart; the smile the pours its sweetness over all . . .[22]

The World newspaper

೮೨

We would pay tribute to the memory of a man who wielded a vast influence for good, and who, if he was destined to see many of his ideas seemingly shattered in the world war, remained true to his convictions and to his belief in the possibility of a reign of peace and love, and who…showed the West that religion is a vital force that can never be disregarded.[23]

Times of India

ↄ

'Abdu'l-Bahá was the example of virtue, purity and perfections. He was famous in the East and in the West. His followers are counted by the thousands, throughout the world. He was the essence of dignity and kindness personified. He was very patient, merciful, affectionate and a sea of wisdom. He was in love with charity, generous and tender to the orphans and widows. He was the hope of the hopeless and the help of the helpless.[24]

Annafir newspaper

The Will and Testament of 'Abdu'l-Bahá

On 3 January 1922, the Will and Testament of 'Abdu'l-Bahá was read aloud for the first time in the house of Shoghi Effendi's aunt where he was staying, having returned from England. That the Will was in the Master's own handwriting and contained a number of His seals and signatures was clearly demonstrated to the gathering. The Guardian later wrote, 'The Charter which called into being, outlined the features and set in motion the processes of, this Administrative Order is none other than the Will and Testament of 'Abdu'l-Bahá, His greatest legacy to posterity, the brightest emanation of His mind and the mightiest instrument forged to insure the continuity of the three ages which constitute the component parts of His Father's Dispensation.'[25]

The Will and Testament of 'Abdu'l-Bahá . . . may be regarded as the offspring resulting from that mystic intercourse between Him Who had generated the forces of a God-given Faith and the One Who had been made its sole Interpreter and was recognized as its perfect Exemplar. The creative energies unleashed by the Originator of the Law of God in this age gave birth, through their impact upon the mind of Him Who had been chosen as its unerring Expounder, to that Instrument, the vast implications of which the present generation, even after the lapse of twenty-three years, is still incapable of fully apprehending. This Instrument can, if we would correctly appraise it, no more be divorced from the One Who provided the motivating impulse for its creation than from Him Who directly conceived it. The purpose of the Author of the Bahá'í Revelation had, as already observed, been so thoroughly infused into the mind of 'Abdu'l-Bahá, and His Spirit had so profoundly impregnated His being, and their aims and motives been so completely blended, that to dissociate the doctrine laid down by the former from the supreme act associated with the mission of the latter would be tantamount to a repudiation of one of the most fundamental verities of the Faith.[26]

◈

Out of the pangs of anguish which His bereaved followers have suffered, amid the heat and dust which the attacks launched by a sleepless enemy had precipitated, the Administration of Bahá'u'lláh's invincible Faith was born. The potent energies released through the ascension of the Centre of His Covenant crystallized into this supreme, this infallible Organ for the accomplishment of a Divine Purpose. The Will and Testament of 'Abdu'l-Bahá unveiled its character, reaffirmed its basis, supplemented its principles, asserted its indispensability, and enumerated its chief institutions.[27]

Shoghi Effendi

છ

This Testament was the last song of that Dove of the Rosegarden of Eternity, and He sang it on the branch of the Tree of bestowal and grace. It was His principal gift, indeed the greatest of all splendours that radiated forth from that Day-Star of bounty, out of the firmament of His bestowals. This Testament was the strong barricade built by the blessed hands of that wronged, that peerless One, to protect the garden of God's Faith. It was the mighty stronghold circling the edifice of the Law of God. This was an overflowing treasure which the Beloved freely gave, a goodly and precious legacy, left by Him to the people of Bahá. In all the world, no gift could equal this; no dazzling gem could rival such a precious pearl.[28]

The Will and Testament of 'Abdu'l-Bahá, may our souls be sacrificed for His meekness, is our guiding light about the path, it is the very bounty of the Abhá Kingdom . . . It is tidings of great joy; it is the ultimate bestowal.[29]

The Will and Testament of 'Abdu'l-Bahá is His decisive decree; it gathers the believers together; it preserves their unity; it ensures the protection of the Faith of God.[30]

What had been hidden at the beginning was made known at the end. His infinite grace became clearly manifest, and with His own mighty pen He made a perfect Covenant, naming Shoghi Effendi the Chosen Branch and Guardian of the Faith.

Thus, by God's bounty, what had been a concealed mystery and a well-guarded secret, was at last made plain.[31]

Bahíyyih Khánum

ↄ

With the passing of ʿAbduʾl-Bahá, the Apostolic Age of the Faith came to an end and the Faith entered the Formative Age. The forces of the Revelation of Baháʾuʾlláh, which streamed forth from the person of ʿAbduʾl-Bahá during His ministry, had now ceased. But ʿAbduʾl-Bahá had a plan for the believers. He did not abandon them to their own devices. He delineated in His Will and Testament the outline of a marvellous scheme to enable the believers to raise up the institutions created by Baháʾuʾlláh for the governance of society in His Dispensation. Thus the believers in the Formative Age were given the opportunity to play their part, as bidden by ʿAbduʾl-Bahá, in the building up of the institutions of the Faith which are to act as channels for carrying the spiritual energies released by Baháʾuʾlláh to every part of the planet. Central to this design was the institution of the Guardianship, which contined the essential task of preserving the purity of the water of the revelation after ʿAbduʾl-Bahá, interpreted its provisions and guided the believers in erecting the administrative order of the Faith.

Shoghi Effendi has singled out the Will and Testament of ʿAbduʾl-Bahá from among all His writings as being specially invested with divine authority capable of shaping the destiny of the Community of the Most Great name during the Formative and Golden Ages of the Faith . . .[32]

Adib Taherzadeh

ↄ

In spite of so disastrous a blow as that which struck the infant Faith when it was bereft, suddenly, of that centre of Divine guidance and authority on which it had come to rely so heavily, the fundamental principles of Bahá'u'lláh's World Order were unchanged, His Covenant inviolate. The Will and Testament of 'Abdu'l-Bahá remained the charter of the New World Order.[33]

The Will and Testament of 'Abdu'l-Bahá . . . constitutes the 'indissoluble link' between the Revelation itself and the world order which that Revelation is destined to promote.[34]

David Hofman

❦

Nothing in the Will and Testament is more striking or more important than the immensity of the power conferred by 'Abdu'l-Bahá on the Guardian, and the note of personal admiration and affection with which the appointment of Shoghi Effendi, to be the Guardian, is characterized. Bahá'u'lláh had already foreshadowed this institution, but it was left to 'Abdu'l-Bahá, the Centre of the Covenant, to define it and establish it.[35]

George Townshend

❦

Although the passing of 'Abdu'l-Bahá deprived the Bahá'í Community of the earthly presence of the Centre of Bahá'u'lláh's Covenant, the power of that Covenant became greater rather than less. Some of its hidden gems were now disclosed in the Will of 'Abdu'l-Bahá, His greatest legacy to mankind, out-weighing in importance even the multitudinous Writings in which He explained and applied the principles of His Father's Revelation.[36]

John Ferraby

☙

It is the very Charter of that Order and compels the most persistent and earnest study of all who seek to understand the destiny of mankind in this age. In the words of the Guardian of the Faith, the Will and Testament of 'Abdu'l-Bahá is 'His greatest legacy to posterity' and 'the brightest emanation of His mind'.[37]

Hasan Balyuzí

☙

When the evening of civilization approaches; when the light of custom and tradition dies; when the mind stumbles, the heart fails and the soul is enshrouded with sullen fear; when the works of shadow and darkness are done – by wars, by strife, by confusion; and the prescience of universal ruin flikes like a bat of ill omen over the uplifted heads and staring eyes; then the Divine Servant passes silently from room to room of the household of the world, lighting the lamps of hearts with the flame of spirit, whose illumination, for those who are severed from all save spirit, is as the rising of the True Dawn after the overcoming of that besetting inner twilight which the world mis-calls truth, mis-terms reality, mis-conceives as *life*.

But when the lamps of the hearts are lighted, then silently, then mysteriously, even as the Divine Servant came, so He departs; and in that departing we know Him by the glory of the illumination whose rays have penetrated the heart; or know Him not at all.

This is the first solemnity of the hush of that hour when it is realized that 'Abdu'l-Bahá, the Divine Servant, having lighted the lamps throughout the household of the East and West, departs unto that Source of Light whence He came.

The shining of the lamps of hearts lighted by the hand of the Divine Servant is the mystery whose outward manifestation stands visible in the life of the world as *Bahá'í assemblies*, lamps that shone unseen in the last flickering moments of that false illumination of the material age; lamps that shine the more brightly as material daylight ebbs from the life of men.[38]

Horace Holley

Further remembrances

Lately a great hope has come to me from one, 'Abdu'l-Bahá. I have found in His and His Father, Bahá'u'lláh's Message of Faith all my yearning for real religion satisfied . . . What I mean: these Books have strengthened me beyond belief and I am now ready to die any day full of hope. But I pray God not to take me away yet for I still have a lot of work to do.[39]

Queen Marie of Romania

જી

'Abdu'l-Bahá sorrowed with the sorrowful and the stricken and the afflicted, in deep compassion. He rejoiced with the truly joyous. Thousands thronged to His door to seek relief. Some of them sought worldly goods. But many more desired the relief which only the goods of the spirit can bestow. To them all, 'Abdu'l-Bahá gave freely and abundantly. No one found His door shut. No one was turned away. No one left His presence empty-handed. He did not merely wait for the oppressed and the bewildered and the fallen to come to Him. He went out to find them and to serve them. The learned and the wise also came to Him and drank deeply at the fount of His knowledge. Rulers and potentates, statesmen and generals, the mighty and the great came as well, and found in 'Abdu'l-Bahá a counsellor whose motives were generous and disinterested.[40]

H.M. Balyuzí

ↂ

'Abdu'l-Bahá fulfils a function different from that of any other figure in religious history. Bahá'u'lláh emphasised this fact by calling Him 'The Mystery of God,' a designation that Shoghi Effendi has said is particularly appropriate 'to One Who, though essentially human and holding a station radically and fundamentally different from that occupied by Bahá'u'lláh and His Forerunner, could still claim to be the perfect Exemplar of His Faith, to be endowed with superhuman knowledge, and to be regarded as the stainless mirror reflecting His light.'

'Abdu'l-Bahá has been endowed with a contingent infallibility that is beyond the understanding of man. All His words, His actions, His judgments and His interpretations are infallibly right, but only because Bahá'u'lláh has willed it so. 'Abdu'l-Bahá revealed nothing new; He had not the direct intercourse with God of a Divine Manifestation; nevertheless, His every act reflected the Light of God and His every word bore witness to His superhuman knowledge.[41]

John Ferraby

Endowed with a captivating charm, with an eloquence which made his conversation sought after by his most irreducible adversaries, he joined to the indomitable energy inherited from his father quite a personal gentleness, combined with that particular tact sometimes possessed by Orientals, which straightaway makes them equal to any situation. With the son of Baha'o'llah, these qualities, united to the power of self-mastery which . . . can alone render us master of others, have made of him one of the strongest and at the same time most seductive mentalities which can be imagined. His unique intelligence is capable of seizing at the first glance all the aspects of a question, and without hesitation seeing its solution; his heart attracts all the disinterested of life, who feel themselves instinctively drawn towards him.[42]

Hippolyte Dreyfus

ᴇↄ

Abdul Baha manifested to surround the earth of consciousness with a spiritual atmosphere. This atmosphere translates the Light of Truth into the Water of Life. This atmosphere is the 'Most Great Bounty', the 'Mystery of God' making our modern Revelation entirely universal, a divine Cause raised above names and forms, destined to become the very foundation of human existence in all lands.[43]

Think now of Abdul Baha not merely as the wisest being who ever walked among men – not merely as the supreme visual exemplar of the power of unity, so inexhaustible that it united both East and West, both rich and poor, both black and white, both ignorant and learned in one outpouring devotion and inspiration – think now of Abdul Baha as the manifestation of cosmic Knowledge, bringing to the earth of consciousness that surrounding atmosphere able to transform the sterile moon of thought into a fertile world of joy, of peace, of true prosperity, of constant progress, of firmly knit co-operation and service which shall truly reveal God as the Lord of all.[44]

Around the life and teachings of Abdul Baha the world's spiritual forces gather perceptibly day by day. Here at last the world has one collective centre which is truly neutral to all personal or group interests, truly responsive to all interests awake to the welfare of all. By word and by deed his miracles are daily performed; the healing of the soul's blindness, and the raising of those spiritually dead. He alone is able to reconcile divergent theories, as conflicting wills; able to unify separate traditions, as separate aims; able to interpret different truths, as different garments which the one Truth has assumed.

Time, that heals the wounds of war, though it brings a new and more grievous hurt, has never healed the inner pain of doubt by which man is tormented, a Daniel flung in the den of his own reckless will. Even this source of all hurt – the cleavage between thought and will, dream and deed – Abdul Baha removes. He is that mirror wherein every man may see reflected his own perfection, but reflected for the first time in the image of all mankind. He is that mirror wherein science and religion, economics and government, action and philosophy shine radiantly forth, in one augmented likeness and form. He is that mirror that turns equally to the East and the West; equally to man and woman; equally to here and hereafter.

Few of those whose lives have touched this life for a single hour have remained unchanged.[45]

ʿAbduʾl-Bahá's spiritual influence alone can overcome the bitterness of suspicion and the habit of hate.

ʿAbduʾl-Bahá has brought back in its fullness the ancient,

the timeless vision of brotherhood, righteousness, peace and love. 'Abdu'l-Bahá has given this vision an expression in word and deed which transcends every limitation of race, of class, of nation, and of creed. No community can claim 'Abdu'l-Bahá for their own spiritual leader, and make His inspiration the justification of separateness, as men have done with every spiritual leader of the past. In the divisions of humanity He has arisen as the true centre and point of unity, a mirror reflecting the light of one love and one teaching to every horizon. As each community, seeking relief from its own restrictions and its sufferings, turns to 'Abdu'l-Bahá for guidance, it finds all other communities illumined in the same compassionate love.[46]

Horace Holley

❧

Non-personal only in the sense of being impartially distributed, the Master's was a warm mother-love; each one felt that 'Abdu'l-Bahá's love was especially for him, just as each one appropriates his own place in the sun.[47]

Marzieh Gail

❧

He surely manifests the Christ holy spirit in his daily life, which is one of purity, simplicity, loving acts and godly counsel, and by such fruits can he best be judged. His is a life of divine servitude, and a glorious example for all who are desirous of promulgating brotherhood and peace among mankind. I have never known him to command another to do anything which he has not already fulfilled.[48]

Lua Getsinger

He showed that it is still possible, amid the whirl and rush of modern life, amid the self-love and struggle for material prosperity that everywhere prevail, to live the life of entire devotion to God and to the service of one's fellows, which Christ and Bahá'u'lláh and all the Prophets have demanded of men. Through trial and vicissitudes, calumnies, and treachery on the one hand, and through love and praise, devotion and veneration on the other, He stood like a lighthouse founded on a rock, around which wintry tempests rage and the summer ocean plays, His poise and serenity remaining ever steadfast and unshaken. He lived the life of faith, and calls on His followers to live it here and now. He raised amid a warring world the Banner of Unity and Peace, the Standard of a New Era, and He assures those who rally to its support that they shall be inspired by the Spirit of the New Day. It is the same Holy Spirit which inspired the Prophets and Saints of old, but it is a new outpouring of that Spirit, suited to the needs of the new time.[49]

J.E. Esslemont

ॐ

He had the stride and freedom of a king – or shepherd. My impression of him was that of a lion, a kingly, masterful Man of the most sweet and generous disposition. I had formed an idea of Jesus as very meek, humble, lowly, gentle, quiet, soft and sweet, and I looked for such another one. I have revised my idea of Jesus and now, as I read his Words, I see in that one of the past a Man of Authority, whose words were clear and forceful, penetrating the hearts as with a two-edged sword. I found in Abdul-Baha a man, strong, powerful, without a thought as to any act, as free and unstilted as a father with his family or a boy with playmates. Yet each movement, his walk, his greeting, his sitting down and rising up were eloquent of power, full of dignity, freedom and ability . . .

Abdul-Baha is a grand man, broad, universal in thought, standing above the world and looking down upon it in its weakness and poverty with a boundless love and an intense longing to lift it up from its wretchedness, to make it conscious of the rich bounties of God, which are so freely offered in this wonderful time, to remove the differences to bring all men, all peoples, all religions into true manhood and religion, for in reality there is but one manhood and one religion. He stands there erect, with extended arms, the Master of the Feast, calling with a loud, clear voice to all mankind: 'Come! Come! Come! Now is the time! Now is the accepted time! Come and drink of this sweet Water which is pouring in torrents upon all parts of the world!'

And, as each hungry pilgrim comes to that prison house, that banquet hall of heavenly gifts, he takes him in his arms and draws him to his breast with such sincerity and enthusiasm of love that the petty cares, thoughts and ambitions of the world vanish away, and one is at peace and in happiness because he has reached home and found love there. Father, mother, brother, all are welcoming, greeting and embracing the wanderer in that simple, natural welcome of Abdul-Baha. One wishes that the embrace might not end, it is so joyful, so comforting. Truly, I think it never does end. It opens a door of love which shall never be closed. *The home of the heart is there.*[50]

Thornton Chase

❧

One feels always an electric force about Abdu'l Baha which is both irresistible and loving. It is quite unlike that of magnetism, and has in it nothing of a hypnotic character. In fact, association with Abdul Baha has the effect of rousing the will and intelligence to a marked degree.[51]

Mary Hanford Ford

ୡୠ

The focus of the soul of this wonderful being is in the eyes. Love lingers in their depths, and tenderness quivers in flashes of sympathetic light upon the lids. If the tongue were silent the eyes would voice the Spirit's message in tremulous thrills of eloquence. When the full battery of this winsome personality is turned upon the soul, you are immersed in an ocean of love, you see that which was hitherto invisible, hear the inaudible, and attain knowledge which had seemed unknowable. As to His Power there can be no doubt. The secret of His spiritual Beauty lies in the eclipse of His personality. The Spirit of God is manifest in this perfect Temple of Servitude, this Incarnation of Love.[52]

Marjory J. Morten

ୡୠ

This power emanating from 'Abdu'l-Bahá was not expressed for the purpose of producing submission . . . Let us say, rather, that it was a privilege He gave us, of seeing a little behind the veil; of experiencing the direct effect of that Cosmic Power which in this early period of our development seems supernormal, however normal it may become to us at some distant future stage of our soul's development.

No, 'Abdu'l-Bahá never put forth any of His spiritual power to dazzle, persuade or overawe sceptics or unbelievers . . .

I have tried to describe 'Abdu'l-Baha as I saw and knew Him. But how can anyone give an adequate description of this personality that, like St Paul, was all things to all men? The Persian doctor who attended Him from 1914 till His death, when recently asked at a meeting in Milwaukee to describe 'Abdu'l-Baha, replied that this was very difficult to do; because 'Abdu'l-Baha expressed Himself differently at different times, meeting every occasion as the occasion demanded.

If one were asked to describe 'Abdu'l-Baha in a single word, that word would be: 'Protean'. This unusual adjective is derived from the name of a minor deity in Greek mythology who had the magic power to assume any form he wished. And so 'Abdu'l-Baha could be on one occasion all love; on another occasion supreme wisdom; and on other rare occasions, expressing a power that seemed cosmic.

And since love, wisdom, and power are the three principles upon which the Cosmos is run; and since 'Abdu'l-Baha was designated as our exemplar, it follows that these qualities should be developed in us all, as we grow spiritually toward the attainment of our full stature as citizens of that Kingdom of God destined to be the consumation of our planetary existence.[53]

Stanwood Cobb

ა

Those who knew 'Abdu'l-Bahá would say they could feel His overflowing love for mankind pouring from Him in great waves, and some have told how to sit beside Him in a motor-car was to feel oneself being charged by spiritual energy. What strikes many in reading His writings is that they possess a quality different from that which belongs to any human being. There is a cadence, a power in them which definitely comes from a higher world than that in which we live. It is natural, therefore, that His writings should be spoken of as Revelation. Yet He was human, not a Manifestation, and His scripture, though valid, has not the rank of the Revelation of a full Prophet. What explanation can there be of this except that the Holy Spirit is now in this Age of Truth touching men's souls with a higher degree of power than ever in the past. Our age has risen from the levels of the Kingdom of Man to the heights unapproached before of the Kingdom of God. 'Abdu'l-Bahá, the embodiment of every Bahá'í ideal, the incarnation of every Bahá'í virtue, presents man (revealed as made in the image of God) at a level higher than any we associate with man before.[54]

To live today in deed and truth the kind of life that Jesus of Nazareth lived and bade his followers lead; to love God wholeheartedly and for God's sake to love all mankind even one's slanderers and enemies; to give consistently good for evil, blessings for curses, kindness for cruelty and through a career darkened along its entire length by tragic misrepresentation and persecution to preserve one's courage, one's sweetness and calm faith in God – to do all this and yet to play the man in the world of men, sharing at home and in business the common life of humanity, administering when occasion arose affairs large and small and handling complex situations with foresight and firmness – to live in such a manner throughout a long and arduous life, and, when in the fullness of time death came, to leave to multitudes of mourners a sense of desolation and to be remembered and loved by them all as the Servant of God – to how many men is such an achievement given as it has been given in this age of ours to 'Abbás Effendi.

. . . In the story of 'Abbás Effendi the Christian comes upon something which he ardently desires and which he finds it difficult to obtain elsewhere. There awaits him here reassurance that the moral precepts of Christ are to be accepted exactly and in their entirety, that they can be lived out as fully under modern conditions as under any other, and that the highest spirituality is quite compatible with sound common sense and practical wisdom. Many of the incidents in 'Abbás Effendi's life form a commentary on the teachings of Christ and illuminate the meaning of the ancient words. Being a philosopher as well as a saint he was able to give to many a Christian enquirer explanations of the Gospel which had the authority not only of their own reasonableness and beauty but also the authority of his own true love for Christ and his life of Christlike righteousness.

Thus the beauty of Christ and of his words, obscured by so much in modern life, is through 'Abbás Effendi brought nearer to us and made real again, and a perusal of the story imparts to the Christian encouragement and light.

Christ taught that the supreme human achievement is not any particular deed nor even any particular condition of mind: but a relation to God. To be completely filled -heart-mind-soul- with love for God, such is the great ideal, the Great Commandment. In 'Abbás Effendi's character the dominant element was spirituality. Whatever was good in his life he attributed not to any separate source of virtue in himself but to the power and beneficence of God. His single aim was servitude to God. He rejoiced in being denuded of all earthly possessions and in being rich only in his love for God. He surrendered his freedom that he might become the bondservant of God; and was able at the close of his days to declare that he had spent all his strength upon the Cause of God. To him God was the centre of all existence here on earth as heretofore and hereafter. All things were in their degree mirrors of the bounty of God and outpourings of his power. Truth was the word of God. Art was the worship of

God. Life was nearness to God; Death remoteness from him. The knowledge of God was the purpose of human existence and the summit of human attainment. No learning nor education that did not lead towards this knowledge was worth pursuit. Beyond it there was no further glory, and short of it there was nothing that could be called success.

In 'Abbás Effendi this love for God was the ground and cause of an equanimity which no circumstances could shake, and of an inner happiness which no adversity affected and which in his presence brought to the sad, the lonely, or the doubting the most precious companionship and healing. He had many griefs but they were born of his sympathy and his devotion. He knew many sorrows but they were all those of a lover. Warmly emotional as he was he felt keenly the troubles of others, even of persons whom he had not actually met nor seen, and to his tender and responsive nature the loss of friends and the bereavements of which he had to face more than a few brought acute anguish. His heart was burdened always with the sense of humanity's orphanhood, and he would be so much distressed by any unkindness or discord among believers that his physical health would be affected. Yet he bore his own sufferings however numerous and great with unbroken strength. For forty years he endured in a Turkish prison rigours which would have killed most men in a twelvemonth. Through all this time he was, he said, supremely happy being close to God and in constant communion with Him. He made light of all his afflictions. Once when he was paraded through the streets in chains the soldiers who had become his friends, wished to cover up his fetters with the folds of his garment that the populace might not see and deride; but the prisoner shook off the covering and jangled aloud the bonds which he bore in the service of his Lord. When friends from foreign lands visited him in prison and seeing the cruelties to which he was subjected commiserated with him he disclaimed their sympathy, demanded their felicitations and bade them become so firm in their love for God that they too could endure calamity with a radiant acquiescence. He was not really, he said, in prison; for 'there is no prison but the prison of self' and since God's love filled his heart he was all the time in heaven.

From this engrossing love for God came the austere simplicity which marked 'Abbás Effendi's character. Christ's manner of life had been simple in the extreme. A poor man poorly clad, often in his wanderings he had no drink but the running stream, no bed but the earth, no lamp but the stars. His teaching was given in homely phrases and familiar images and the religion he revealed however difficult to follow was as plain and open as his life. His very simplicity helped to mislead his contemporaries. They could recognize the badges of greatness but not greatness itself, and they could not see the light though they knew its name. He was neither Rabbi nor S̲h̲ayk̲h̲ though he was the Messiah. He had neither throne nor sword though all things in heaven and in earth were committed into his charge.[55]

George Townshend

ல

Instead of allowing man to interpret His Writings and act upon them as he likes, Bahá'u'lláh has released the outpourings of His Revelation within the person of 'Abdu'l-Bahá who received them on behalf of all mankind. He became the recipient of the Revelation of Bahá'u'lláh and the authorized interpreter of His words. His soul embraced every virtue and power which that Revelation conferred upon Him, virtues and powers which, through the operation of the institution of the

Covenant, are to be vouchsafed progressively to humanity in the course of this Dispensation, and which are the cause of the social, the intellectual and spiritual development of man on this planet until the advent of the next Manifestation of God. 'Abdu'l-Bahá acts in this analogy as a receptacle. Before a receptacle is filled, it must first be empty. If it contains anything, even a minute quantity of any substance, that substance will pollute the pure water which is poured into it. One of the most glorious aspects of the Cause of Bahá'u'lláh is that the person of 'Abdu'l-Bahá had so surrendered His will to that of Bahá'u'lláh that He was utterly empty of self. He had nothing to express or manifest in His being except self-effacement and absolute servitude.

. . . The Person of 'Abdu'l-Bahá and His servitude to Bahá'u'lláh, His Lord, are inseparable. A true servant abides in the depth of lowliness and humility, and not in the heights of glory. The greater the measure of servitude, the lower will be the position of the individual. By virtue of His station, 'Abdu'l-Bahá occupies the lowest plane of servitude, a plane to which no other human being can ever descend. Bahá'u'lláh is the Manifestation of glory and is at the summit of majesty. 'Abdu'l-Bahá is at the opposite pole of servitude and utter selflessness. Bahá'u'lláh may be likened to the peak of a mountain, 'Abdu'l-Bahá as the lowest valley. When water pours down from the mountain top it will all accumulate in the deepest valley. In like manner, the Word of God, sent down from the Heaven of Divine Utterance, so permeated the person of 'Abdu'l-Bahá that He became a worthy carrier of the energies latent within the Revelation of Bahá'u'lláh. His whole being became the incarnation of every goodly virtue, a stainless mirror reflecting the light of glory cast upon Him by Bahá'u'lláh.

. . . 'Abdu'l-Bahá was created by God for the sole purpose of becoming the recipient of God's Revelation for this age. We shall never know His real station, because He was the 'Mystery of God', a title conferred upon Him by Bahá'u'lláh. He was the priceless gift of Bahá'u'lláh to mankind.[56]

Adib Taherzadeh

ↄ

It is because of 'Abdu'l-Bahá's exquisite ability to echo the human condition that we are helped to learn from Him what our role must be in relation to Bahá'u'lláh. The relationship between Them is frequently referred to in the Writings as that of sun and moon. All the connotations related to the Perfect Exemplar, the reflection of the light of Bahá, and the Mystery of God – descriptions of 'Abdu'l-Bahá – are couched in this metaphor. The traditional 'feminine' attributes of the moon in relation to the generative influence of the sun are also implicit in some measure, and find their culmination in Shoghi Effendi's description, in *God Passes By*, of the parental roles of these twin Figures in the genesis of the Administrative Order . . .

It would seem, with 'Abdu'l-Bahá as our Example, that the traditional concepts of passivity, inferiority and negativity associated with the moon are completely redefined in this Revelation.[57]

Bahiyyih Nakhjavani

ↄ

Now a message from God must be delivered, and there was no mankind to hear this message. Therefore, God gave the world 'Abdu'l-Bahá. 'Abdu'l-Bahá received the message of Bahá'u'lláh on behalf of the human race. He heard the voice of God; He was inspired by the spirit; He attained complete consciousness and awareness of the meaning of this message, and He pledged the human race to respond to the voice of God. My friends, to me *that* is the Covenant – that there was on this earth some one who could be a representative of an as yet uncreated race. There were only tribes, families, creeds, classes, etc., but there was no man except 'Abdu'l-Bahá, and 'Abdu'l-Bahá, as man, took to Himself the message of Bahá'u'lláh and promised God that He would bring the people into the *oneness of mankind*, and create a humanity that could be the vehicle for the laws of God. It is because 'Abdu'l-Bahá was 'Abdu'l-Bahá, and because He could be this Hearing Ear, this Answering Heart, this Consecrated Will, that an Eternal Covenant was made, and because of 'Abdu'l-Bahá, you and I are here as Bahá'ís. You and I are here as parts of the Mankind that has to be, because man is not man until he is imbued with the qualities and life of the Merciful, and there is no humanity until this one Spirit of Truth, and the guidance of the Divine Will, enters into the consciousness of all human beings to such an extent that each individual is not only drawn nearer to God, but he becomes *one* with all other men.

This process has begun. 'Abdu'l-Bahá came to this very city [Los Angeles] in pursuance of His sacred mission to create the soul and mind of man, and you who are here are the servants of the Divine Covenant. When 'Abdu'l-Bahá left this earth He laid upon the Bahá'ís the mission of fulfilling His promise to God, and He did not charge us with anything beyond the capacity of faith. He charged us with something that is impossible without faith; something that could not be attained, or something if attempted could not be carried out by division and fear, but gave to us the capacity to fulfill the promise He made to Bahá'u'lláh, and He told us the way to enter into this capacity is to *serve*.

'Abdu'l-Bahá never turned to any Bahá'í and said, 'My

son, or daughter, I want you to study fifty-eight volumes of psychology, or thirty-three volumes of history and science.' He said: 'I charge you to serve – to be active.' And with every step you take on the path of the Covenant, the qualities you need will be given you.

Faith is the basic characteristic of the Bahá'í in that it is not 'I' nor 'you' but that it is the Faith we have in God through the Covenant that will give us the capacity to do the thing that is impossible, so that the unlettered Bahá'í can be a servant of God to a degree that the greatest ecclesiastical dignitary on earth does not possess.

It seems to me that we have to continually draw back into that experience of the mysterious meeting with 'Abdu'l-Bahá and the renewal of the Covenant, because I know, perhaps as well as anyone here, the feeling of utter incapacity, of complete discouragement and bewilderment that overtakes the souls of men if for even a moment they turn away from the Covenant. We are given that which is impossible for human beings to do, but *not* that which is impossible for faith, and we will not be measured in the Kingdom in accordance with any human standard of failure or success, but I think the Master will face each one of us as we walk over the threshold on the other side of the wall, and He will just simply ask one question: 'Did you help *Me* fulfill My promise to Almighty God?'[58]

Horace Holley

છ૦

I have heard so much about 'Abdu'l-Bahá, whom people call an idealist, but I should like to call Him a realist, because no idealism, when it is strong and true, exists without the endorsement of realism. There is nothing more real than His words on truth. His words are as simple as the sunlight; again like the sunlight, they are universal . . . No Teacher, I think, is more important today than 'Abdu'l-Bahá.[59]

Yone Noguchi

ల

I shall never forget having seen 'Abdu'l-Bahá face to face.

What was He like? His bearing was majestic, and yet He was genial. He was full of contrasts: dominant, yet humble; strong, yet tender; loving and affectionate, yet He could be very stern. He was intensely human, most keenly alive to the joys and sorrows of this life. There was no one who felt more acutely than He did the sufferings of humanity.

. . . There is something I learned from 'Abdu'l-Bahá which I feel should not be forgotten. His life was not really His life alone; it was the life of every one of us. It was an example for every one of us . . . If men and women all over the world were to arise in ever-increasing numbers and make 'Abdu'l-Bahá's way of life their own, each pursuing His path with zest and confidence, what would the world be like? Would not these individuals be a new race of men?[60]

'Alí M. Yazdí

ల

BIOGRAPHICAL NOTES

Bahá'u'lláh (1817–1892)
Born Mírzá Ḥusayn-'Alí Núrí in Ṭihrán, Írán, Bahá'u'lláh ('The Glory of God') was a Manifestation of God and the Founder of the Bahá'í Faith. Bahá'u'lláh became a follower of the Báb in 1845. In 1853, Bahá'u'lláh was exiled to Baghdád for his allegiance to the Báb. Ten years later, He publicly declared Himself to be 'He whom God shall make manifest', the Messianic figure heralded by the Báb. Further exiles followed – to Constantinople, Adrianople and finally to the Ottoman prison city of 'Akká. Bahá'u'lláh revealed the equivalent of more than 100 volumes of Writings elucidating His Teachings on the unity of God, religion and humanity, and detailing the institutions and measures required to establish a global civilization. He was the Father of 'Abdu'l-Bahá.

Shoghi Effendi (1897–1957)
Shoghi Effendi Rabbání was appointed Guardian of the Bahá'í Faith in the Will and Testament of his Grandfather, 'Abdu'l-Bahá, in 1921. He was educated at Balliol College, Oxford, where he mastered the English language in order to be able to serve as 'Abdu'l-Bahá's secretary and translate the Bahá'í Writings. The Guardian was given the authority to interpret the writings of the Báb, Bahá'u'lláh and 'Abdu'l-Bahá. Shoghi Effendi spent 36 years systematically

nurturing the development, deepening the understanding, and strengthening the unity of the Bahá'í community, as it grew to reflect the diversity of the entire human race.

The Universal House of Justice (established 1963)
Ordained by Bahá'u'lláh in the Kitáb-í-Aqdas, the Universal House of Justice is the supreme governing, judicial and legislative body of the Bahá'í Faith, ordained as the agency invested with His authority to legislate on matters not covered by His Writings. In His Will and Testament, 'Abdu'l-Bahá elaborated on its functions and manner of election.

Bahíyyih Khánum (1846–1932) was the sister of 'Abdu'l-Bahá. She was distinguished for the purity of her life of service and for acting as temporary head of the Bahá'í community immediately after the passing of 'Abdu'l-Bahá and in the early days of the Guardianship.

Munírih Khánum (1848–1938) came from a distinguished Íránian Bábí family. She was married to 'Abdu'l-Bahá in 1873, outliving Him by 17 years.

Túbá Khánum (1879/80–?) was the second daughter of 'Abdu'l-Bahá. She was married to Mírzá Muhsin Afnán.

Hájí Mírzá Habíbu'lláh-i-Afnán resided in Cairo, Egypt, and made a pilgrimage and visit to 'Abdu'l-Bahá in 1897. The account of this visit was translated into English. He had previously visited the Holy Land in 1891 when he had met both Bahá'u'lláh and 'Abdu'l-Bahá.

Ahmad Effendi was a Muslim Imám who spoke at the

memorial meeting held in Haifa on the fortieth day after the passing of 'Abdu'l-Bahá.

Mirra Alfassa (1878–1973), known as 'The Mother', was a French Hindu leader. She met 'Abdu'l-Bahá on many occasions in Paris between February and June 1913. She died in Pondicherry, India, where she was head of the ashram of the Indian mystic Sri Aurobindo after his death.

Shaykh 'Álí Yúsuf (1863–1925) was an influential Egyptian politician and intellectual. He edited and founded the daily Muslim, nationalist *al-Mu'ayyad* newspaper in Cairo.

Florence Altass (1884–1982) met 'Abdu'l-Bahá in Edinburgh. She worked as a nurse in the Austrian Imperial Court and shared Bahá'í ideas with Archduke Franz-Ferdinand and his wife.

Wellesca 'Aseyeh' Allen-Dyar became a Bahá'í in 1901 and went on pilgrimage six years later. She met 'Abdu'l-Bahá again in Washington, D.C.

Charles Robert Ashbee (1863–1942) was a British architect, designer and town planner. He was the Civic Adviser to the Palestine Administration (Military, later Civil) between 1918 and 1922.

H.M. Balyúzi (1908–1980) was born in Shiraz, Iran and moved to England in 1932. He served on the National Spiritual Assembly of the Bahá'ís of the British Isles from 1933 to 1958, worked in the Persian section of the BBC, and wrote numerous scholarly articles and books. He was appointed a Hand of the Cause of God by Shoghi Effendi in 1957.

Archie Bell (1877–1943) was a correspondent for the Plain Dealer newspaper in Cleveland. While travelling in the Holy Land in 1914, he met 'Abdu'l-Bahá in Tiberias, where he was able to interview Him on two occasions.

Charles Blech (1855–1934), a French Theosophist, was president and secretary-general of the Societé Théosophique de France. He met 'Abdu'l-Bahá in Paris on 26 October 1911.

Lady Blomfield (1859–1939) was a distinguished early Bahá'í in London. After encountering the Bahá'í Teachings in 1907, she became one of its outstanding proponents. She was 'Abdu'l-Bahá's host during his visits to London and a founding supporter of the Save the Children Fund after World War I. Her book *The Chosen Highway* is a precious chronicle of the history of the Bahá'í Faith.

Louise Bosch (1870–1952) was born in Switzerland and went on pilgrimage to meet 'Abdu'l-Bahá in 1909. She and her husband John David Bosch were present when He passed away in 1921.

Salomon Bouzaglo was a progressive Jewish leader in Haifa who spoke at the funeral of 'Abdu'l-Bahá.

Florence Breed (1875–1950) was the wife of Mírzá 'Alí-Kulí Khán and mother of Marzíeh Gail. 'Abdu'l-Bahá visited their family home in Washington D.C. on 23 April 1912.

Ramona Allen Brown (1889–1975) met 'Abdu'l-Bahá in Oakland on 4 October 1912. She later settled in Majorca,

Spain, and Austria. Her *Memories of 'Abdu'l-Bahá* was published in 1980.

Edward Granville Browne (1862–1926) was born in Gloucestershire. He made an extended visit to Iran after being made a Fellow of Pembroke College, Cambridge and researched subjects that few other Western scholars had explored, many of them related to Persian history and literature. He published two translations of Bábí histories, including *A Traveller's Narrative* by 'Abdu'l-Bahá. He left vivid pen-portraits of his meetings with Bahá'u'lláh and 'Abdu'l-Bahá in 1890.

Marion Brunot Haymaker (1884–?) was an American journalist and novelist, who wrote for the *Chronicle-Telegraph*. She wrote about her meeting with 'Abdu'l-Bahá in Pittsburgh on 7 May 1912. She was president of the Pittsburgh Press Club and, later, in December 1915 presided over a talk given by the distinguished Bahá'í teacher Martha Root on the Bahá'í Faith.

Reverend R.J. Campbell (1867–1956) was an English Clergyman – originally Congregational, later Church of England – who promoted 'New Theology'. He met 'Abdu'l-Bahá at Lady Blomfield's home and invited Him to give His first ever public talk at the City Temple in London on 10 September 1911.

Kate Carew (1869–1961) was the pseudonym of Mary Williams, an American journalist and cariacaturist. She met 'Abdu'l-Bahá in New York City on 19 April 1912.

Isobel Fraser Chamberlain (1871–1939) was a Scottish Bahá'í who met 'Abdu'l-Bahá at Liverpool docks on 13 December 1912 and also spent time with Him in Paris in 1913.

Samuel Selwyn Chamberlain (1851–1916) was an American journalist who encountered 'Abdu'l-Bahá in Paris in June 1913 and interviewed Him for the *London Budget*, a Hearst newspaper, of which he was editor. He was married to Isabel Fraser Chamberlain.

Thomas Chaplin (1830–1904) was a British medical missionary at the Jerusalem Hospital of the London Jews' Society from 1860 to 1885. He was closely involved in the establishment of the Palestine Exploration Fund and was an antiquarian and archaeological authority on the Holy Land.

Thornton Chase (1847–1912), 'Disciple of 'Abdu'l-Bahá', was referred to by 'Abdu'l-Bahá as the first American Bahá'í. Chase visited 'Akká in 1907. He published several books, including a memoir of 'Abdu'l-Bahá, *In Galilee*. He passed away shortly before 'Abdu'l-Bahá's visit to California, Who made a special visit to his grave.

Thomas Kelly Cheyne (1841–1915) was a renowned English divine and Biblical critic. He was visited by 'Abdu'l-Bahá in Oxford in December 1912. Cheyne's book on the Bahá'í Faith, *The Reconciliation of Races and Religions*, was published in 1914.

Stanwood Cobb (1881–1982) was an American educator who met 'Abdu'l-Bahá in Haifa, and later in France and the United States. From 1924 to 1939, he was editor of the Bahá'í journals, *Star of the West* and *World Order*.

Helen Ellis Cole, an early American Bahá'í, visited 'Abdu'l-Bahá in the Holy Land in November 1900.

Genevieve L. Coy (1886–1963) met 'Abdu'l-Bahá in 'Akká in 1920. She moved to Írán in 1922, as director of the Tarbíyat School for girls, and in 1958, pioneered to Rhodesia (now Zimbabwe).

William Curtis (1850–1911), an American journalist specialising in South American affairs, worked with several newspapers including the *Chicago Record-Herald*. He wrote numerous books about his travels.

Amine DeMille was an American Bahá'í who wrote an account of 'Abdu'l-Bahá's stay in Canada.

Frederick Dean (1857–?) was a Buddhist and journalist who met 'Abdu'l-Bahá on several occasions in New York City. He was a reporter for *The Independent* and *The Weekly Review*.

Charlotte Despard (1844–1939) was a suffragette, writer, social worker and member of the executive committee of the Theosophical Society. She attended 'Abdu'l-Bahá's meeting at the Westminster Hotel in London on 20 December 1912.

Richard Dimsdale Stocker (1877–1935) was a writer and member of the Ethical Movement, with interests in psychology, graphology and physiognomy. After meeting 'Abdu'l-Bahá on several occasions, he wrote an article for *The Ethical World*.

Wendell Phillips Dodge (1883–1976) was an American Bahá'í, journalist, explorer and theatre producer who met

'Abdu'l-Bahá on board the SS *Cedric* in New York Harbour on 11 April 1912. He led several expeditions to the Jordan Valley and the Far East.

Hippolyte Dreyfus-Barney (d.1928), 'Disciple of 'Abdu'l-Bahá', was the first French Bahá'í, a lawyer, scholar and translator. He was introduced to the Bahá'í Faith in 1901 by May Ellis Bolles (later Maxwell). He married Laura Clifford Barney in 1911.

Laura Dreyfus-Barney (1879–1974), an American heiress, taught the Bahá'í Faith in Paris by May Ellis Bolles. During visits to the Holy Land between 1904 and 1906, she compiled copious notes of the answers to questions she posed to 'Abdu'l-Bahá, later published as *Some Answered Questions*.

John E. Esslemont (1874–1925) was a Scottish physician, named both 'Disciple of 'Abdu'l-Bahá' and 'Hand of the Cause of God' by Shoghi Effendi. 'Abdu'l-Bahá reviewed the first nine chapters of his book, *Bahá'u'lláh and the New Era,* and encouraged him to complete it. He met the Master in Haifa in November 1919, and later returned there at the request of Shoghi Effendi in 1925, shortly before his death, to serve as the Guardian's secretary.

John Ferraby (1914–1973) was born in Southsea, England. He encountered the Bahá'í Faith in 1941. Within a year, he was serving on the Local Spiritual Assembly of the Bahá'ís of London and the National Spiritual Assembly of the Bahá'ís of the British Isles. After meeting Shoghi Effendi in 1955, Ferraby was inspired to write his book, *All Things Made New*. He was named a Hand of the Cause of God in 1957.

Marzieh Gail (1908–1993) was an author and historian who met 'Abdu'l-Bahá when she was a young girl. Her essay on Him, *The Sheltering Branch*, was published in 1959.

Sir Patrick Geddes (1854–1932) was a biologist, sociologist, geographer, philanthropist and pioneering town planner. He presided over a meeting with 'Abdu'l-Bahá held at Rainy Hall in Edinburgh, Scotland. Geddes worked on a number of town planning projects in Palestine, including for Haifa and 'Akká.

Edward Getsinger (1866–1935) was, with his wife Louisa 'Lua', among the first Western pilgrims to visit 'Abdu'l-Bahá in December 1898. It was on his urging that 'Abdu'l-Bahá consented to have His voice preserved on a phonograph record.

Lua Getsinger (1871–1916), 'Disciple of 'Abdu'l-Bahá', introduced the Bahá'í Faith to Phoebe Hearst, who took the first group of pilgrims – including Lua and her husband Edward – to meet 'Abdu'l-Bahá in 'Akká. She stayed for more than a year in the Holy Land in 1902 to teach English to His household.

Kahlil Gibran (1883–1931) was a Lebanese-American poet and philosopher, best known for *The Prophet* (1923). He sketched a portrait of 'Abdu'l-Bahá in New York City in July 1912. His work, *Jesus, the Son of Man*, was inspired by the Master.

Ella Goodall Cooper (d.1951) joined the first Western pilgrimage to 'Akká in February 1899. She and her mother returned to the Holy Land together in 1908 and jointly published a book, *Daily Lessons Received at 'Akká, January 1908*. She accompanied the Master on His visits in California.

Jo Goudsmit (1873–1914) was a Dutch-Jewish immigrant to Palestine who met 'Abdu'l-Bahá in the Holy Land after the First World War, and later corresponded with him.

She wrote her impressions of Him in a letter to the *Nieuwe Rotterdamsche Courant* (Rotterdam).

Remy de Gourmont (1858–1915) was an influential French writer and critic. He met 'Abdu'l-Bahá in Paris on 20 October 1911. He was a close friend of Laura Dreyfus-Barney's sister Natalie.

Louis Gregory (1874–1951) was named posthumously as a Hand of the Cause of God. He learned of the Bahá'í Faith in 1908, visited 'Abdu'l-Bahá in Egypt, and later again in the Holy Land. In 1912, on the suggestion and encouragement of the Master, Gregory married Louise Mathews, in the first interracial marriage in the American Bahá'í community.

Rev. Frederick Robertson Griffen (1876–1966) was a Canadian Unitarian clergyman who met 'Abdu'l-Bahá in Boston in May 1912 and later in Montreal when He spoke at his church.

Julia Grundy was an early American Bahá'í who arrived in the Holy Land and stayed for 18 days in January 1905. She wrote of her experiences in *Ten Days in the Light of 'Akká*.

Eric Hammond (1852-?) was an English Bahá'í who met 'Abdu'l-Bahá in London on several occasions. He compiled the book, *'Abdu'l-Bahá in London*, and the 1909 compilation, *The Splendour of God*, for the popular 'Wisdom of the East' series.

Mary Hanford Ford (1856–1937) was a writer, lecturer, and advocate of women's suffrage.She helped form the first community of Bahá'ís in Boston. In 1910 she started writing Bahá'í books, including *The Oriental Rose*. She travelled with 'Abdu'l-Bahá during parts of his journeys in Europe and North America.

Hooper Harris (1866–1934) travelled to India to promote the Bahá'í Faith. Shoghi Effendi described Harris, on his passing, as a 'real and sincere' believer and an 'active and capable exponent of the teachings and principles of the Cause.'

Johanna Hauf was a Bahá'í from Stuttgart, Germany, who was present in Haifa when 'Abdu'l-Bahá passed away.

Anna Hoar (1863–?), wife of William Hoar, made a pilgrimage to the Holy Land in 1900.

William Hoar (1856–1922), 'Disciple of 'Abdu'l-Bahá', was visited by 'Abdu'l-Bahá at his family home in Fanwood, New Jersey, on 31 May 1912. Hoar wished 'Abdu'l-Bahá to spend a few days in the village, reasoning that the country air would be beneficial to Him. 'Abdu'l-Bahá replied, 'We have no time for amusement. We must engage ourselves in the service of the Threshold of God.'

David Hofman (1908–2003) was an author, actor, Bahá'í administrator, pioneer and teacher. He accepted the Bahá'í Faith in Canada in 1933 at the home of May Maxwell. He served on the National Spiritual Assembly of the Bahá'ís of the British Isles for 27 years before being elected to the Universal House of Justice in 1963 and serving for 25 years in the Holy Land. He was the founder of George Ronald Publisher.

Kathryn Jewett Hogensen is an American Bahá'í, author of *Lighting the Western Sky: The Hearst Pilgrimage and the Establishment of the Bahá'í Faith in the West.*

Maud Holbach (1869–?) was an English travel writer, based in Oxford. She met 'Abdu'l-Bahá in New York City and Paris.

Horace Holley (1887–1960) was born in Torrington, Connecticut. He was introduced to the Bahá'í Faith in 1909, and later served as a member and secretary of the National Spiritual Assembly of the Bahá'ís of the United States and Canada. A gifted poet and prolific essayist, he was appointed by Shoghi Effendi as a Hand of the Cause of God in 1951.

Beatrice Irwin (1877–1956) was a British-American Bahá'í of Irish origin, born in India. She met 'Abdu'l-Bahá in London and Paris in 1911 and in 1913. She was a stage lighting engineer and acted in plays on Broadway.

Howard Colby Ives (1867–1941), a Unitarian minister, met 'Abdu'l-Bahá in New York and wrote movingly about their meeting and subsequent encounters in *Portals to Freedom.*

Gertrude Käsebier (1852–1934) was a pioneering American woman photographer. She established her studio in New York City in 1897.

Mirzá Mahmúd-i-Káshání, a devoted and trusted follower of Bahá'u'lláh, was in His service in Baghdád, Adrianople and 'Akká.

Mírzá 'Alí-Kuli Khán (1879–1966) was a Persian diplomat, author and translator. He visited 'Abdu'l-Bahá in the Holy Land in 1899 and was His amanuensis for more than a year. He served as consul-general, then chief diplomatic representative and chargé d'affaires for Persia in Washington D.C., extending a befitting welcome to 'Abdu'l-Bahá in 1912.

Janet Khan, based in Brisbane, Australia, is a former member of the Research Department at the Bahá'í World Centre. She is the author of *Call to Apostleship: Reflections on the Tablets of the Divine Plan.*

Sheikh Younis Effendi el-Khatib was a renowned Muslim poet and orator who spoke at both the funeral of 'Abdu'l-Bahá and the memorial meeting held 40 days after His passing.

Eliane Lacroix-Hopson (1917–2014) was born in France and moved to the United States in 1957. She became a Bahá'í in 1962. Her book, *'Abdu'l-Bahá in New York the City of the Covenant,* was published in 1999.

James Lafayette (1853–1923) was a photographer, with studios in Dublin and London.

Lord Lamington (1860–1940), British statesman and colonial administrator, hosted 'Abdu'l-Bahá at his home in London on Christmas Day, 1912. Lamington served in Syria and Palestine, as well as Australia and India.

Jean LeFranc was a French journalist who wrote for *Le Temps.* He met 'Abdu'l-Bahá in Paris.

HRH Queen Marie of Romania (1875–1938) was the granddaughter of Queen Victoria and the first royal personage to accept the Bahá'í Faith. She wrote of the Bahá'í teachings in her syndicated newspaper articles and for *The Bahá'í World* volumes.

Constance Elizabeth Maud (1860–1929) met 'Abdu'l-Bahá at Lady Blomfield's apartment in London. Her book, *Sparks Among the Stubble* (1924), includes an entire chapter on the Master.

May Bolles Maxwell (1870–1940) 'Disciple of 'Abdu'l-Bahá', established the first Bahá'í Centre in Europe when she returned to Paris after taking part in the first Western pilgrimage to 'Akká. She was the mother of 'Amatu'l-Bahá Rúhiyyih Khánum, wife of Shoghi Effendi.

Marjory J. Morten was the co-editor of *World Order* magazine.

Prince Muhammad 'Ali Bey Pasha (1875–1955) was an Egyptian prince who visited 'Abdu'l-Bahá in New York City and Paris. They sailed together to Egypt from Marseille on 13 June 1913.

Professor 'Abdu'llah Mukhlis was Secretary of the National Mohammedan Society in Palestine. He spoke at the memorial service held on the fortieth day after the Ascension of 'Abdu'l-Bahá.

Ion S. Munro (1887–1970) was editor of the *Scots Pictorial* (Glasgow), an illustrated weekly that circulated across Scotland. 'Abdu'l-Bahá made a great impression on Munro, who interviewed Him during His stay in Edinburgh.

Prof. Muhammad Murad was a Muslim leader in Haifa who spoke at the funeral of 'Abdu'l-Bahá.

Robert Nádlér (1858–1938) was a Hungarian painter and president of the Apollo Theosophical Society in Budapest. He painted 'Abdu'l-Bahá's portrait on 13 April 1913.

Bahiyyih Nakhjavani is a writer, based in France. She is the author of several novels and non-fiction works.

Ibrahim Nassar was a celebrated Christian writer who spoke at the funeral of 'Abdu'l-Bahá.

James Neill arrived in the Holy Land in the 1870s to lead the Jerusalem Mission of the London Jews' Society. On visiting 'Akká, Neill decided to follow up Thomas Chaplin's visit to the Bahá'ís of the previous year.

Yone Noguchi (1875–1947) was an influential writer of poetry, fiction, essays and literary criticism in both English and Japanese.

Margaret Peeke, who was not a Bahá'í, was on a Mediterranean cruise and made an impromptu call on 'Abdu'l-Bahá in March 1899, after a friend asked her to visit to see if He was real.

Myron Phelps (1856–1916), a New York lawyer and religious writer, travelled to 'Akká in December 1902 with Miranda de Souza Canavarro, the first woman to convert to Buddhism in America. Phelps' book, *Life and Teachings of Abbas Effendi*, while filled with errors and personal interpretations, includes documented recollections of Bahíyyih <u>Kh</u>ánum.

David Graham Pole (1877–1952) was a Scottish lawyer who introduced 'Abdu'l-Bahá at a meeting of the Theosophical Society in Edinburgh on 9 January 1913. He was later elected Member of Parliament for South Derbyshire.

Louis McClellan Potter (1873–1912) was a sculptor who created a bronze medal with a bust of 'Abdu'l-Bahá in 1912.

Ezra Pound (1885–1972) was one of the most influential figures in modernist literature. He later recalled his encounter with 'Abdu'l-Bahá in one of his *Cantos* poems.

Herbert Putnam (1861–1955) was an American librarian who met 'Abdu'l-Bahá at the home of Agnes Parsons in Washington, D.C., on 8 November 1912.

William Henry Randall (d.1929), 'Disciple of 'Abdu'l-Bahá', visited 'Abdu'l-Bahá with his family after World War I. Randall promoted and fostered Bahá'í relations with Japan.

Potter A. Reade was an American freemason who wrote about 'Abdu'l-Bahá in the *New Age* magazine.

Rev. A.B. Robb (1872–1939) was a Scottish Presbyterian clergyman from Falkirk. He spoke the words of thanks at an Edinburgh meeting where 'Abdu'l-Bahá spoke, on 8 January 1913.

Alice Rohe (1876–1957) was an American journalist. She met 'Abdu'l-Bahá in Denver, Colorado, on 24 September 1912 and wrote an article about Him. In 1914, she moved to Rome to become the first woman to head a foreign news bureau.

David S. Ruhe (1913–2005) was a medical doctor, film-maker, painter and author. He served on the Universal House of Justice for 25 years.

Prof. Michael Sadler (1861–1943) was a prominent English educationalist, and Vice-chancellor of the University of Leeds, who presided over 'Abdu'l-Bahá's meeting at the Passmore Edwards Settlement in London on 29 September 1911. Sadler's pioneering collection of modernist art included the first works by Wassily Kandinsky owned in England.

Viscount Samuel of Carmel (1870–1963) was the British High Commissioner in Palestine from 1920–1925. He was later the leader of the Liberal Party 1931–1935.

Felicia Scatcherd (1862–1927) was an English writer, editor of the *Asiatic Review*, and an activist for Greek socialism.

Consul Albert Schwarz (1871–1931), was an active German Bahá'í. He and his wife entertained 'Abdu'l-Bahá on several occasions during His visit to Germany and took Him to the hotel and spa they owned at Bad Mergentheim.

Frances Soule-Campbell (1860–?) studied at the Philadelphia Academy of Fine Arts. She was based in Berkeley, California, where she painted portraits and miniatures. Her depiction of the Master was used as the frontispiece of the Persian edition of His talks in the West.

Theodore Spicer-Simson (1871–1959) studied at the École des Beaux-Arts in Paris and began producing medals in 1903. He was celebrated for his medals of eminent British, Irish and American figures of the day, including that of 'Abdu'l-Bahá made in 1912.

Jean Stannard (1865–1944) lived in Egypt from 1908 and later, India. In the 1920s she headed the International Bahá'í Bureau in Geneva.

David Starr Jordan (1851–1931) met 'Abdu'l-Bahá in San Fransisco on 2 October 1912 and invited Him to speak at Leland Stanford Junior University where he was President. In 1925 he won the Herman Peace Prize for the best educational plan for preserving world peace.

E.S. Stevens (1879–1972) – also known as Lady Drower – met 'Abdu'l-Bahá at Lady Blomfield's apartment on 20 December 1912, but had previously encountered Him in the Holy Land which inspired her 1911 Mills and Boon romance novel, *The Mountain of God.*

Sir Ronald Storrs (1881–1955), a British colonial administrator, was Military Governor of North Palestine in 1918, and Civil Governor of Jerusalem and Judea from 1920–1926.

Sir George Stewart Symes (1882–1962), a British soldier and colonial administrator, was the Governor of the Northern District, Palestine, based in Haifa, from 1921–1925.

Adib Taherzadeh (1921–2000) served on the National Spiritual Assembly of the Bahá'ís of the British Isles and the National Spiritual Assembly of Ireland. He was a member of the Continental Board of Counsellors of Europe from 1976 until his election to the Universal House of Justice in 1988, on which he served until his passing. His many scholarly works included *The Child of the Covenant*, an analysis of the Will and Testament of 'Abdu'l-Bahá.

André Taponier (1869–1930) was a French photographer. 'Abdu'l-Bahá was photographed at his studio several times in 1911 and again on 11 February 1913.

Hasan Taqizadeh (1878–1970) was a founder member of the Persia Committee in London. He met 'Abdu'l-Bahá in Paris. He later became Iran's ambassador to the United Kingdom.

Juliet Thompson (1873–1956), a painter, embraced the Bahá'í Faith during a stay in Paris in 1901. Her journals of her 1909 visit to the Holy Land and 'Abdu'l-Bahá's travels in the West were published as *The Diary of Juliet Thompson*.

Mary Virginia Thornburgh-Cropper (d. 1938) heard of the Bahá'í Faith from Phoebe Hearst and accompanied her on the first Western pilgrimage. Thornburgh-Cropper placed an automobile at 'Abdu'l-Bahá's disposal during His visits to London and helped arrange his intensive schedule of visitors and talks.

George Townshend (1876–1957) was a well-known Irish writer and clergyman. He recognized the Bahá'í Faith in 1921 but it was not until reaching the age of 70 that he renounced his orders and wrote a pamphlet, *The Old Churches and the New World Faith*, proclaiming his allegiance to the Bahá'í Faith. In 1951, Townshend was named a Hand of the Cause of God by Shoghi Effendi, who greatly admired Townshend's literary abilities.

Wellesley Tudor-Pole (1884–1968) was 'Abdu'l-Bahá's host at the Clifton Guest House in Bristol on two occasions in 1911 and 1913. He had met 'Abdu'l-Bahá in Egypt in 1910, and later in Paris and London. He was instrumental in the protection of 'Abdu'l-Bahá by British forces in Palestine at the end of the First World War. He wrote his memories of 'Abdu'l-Bahá in *The Writing on the Ground* (1968).

Albert Vail (1880–1966) met 'Abdu'l-Bahá in Chicago in 1912. In 1921 he was a member of the 'Bahai Temple Unity'.

Árminius Vámbéry (1832–1913) was a distinguished Jewish-Hungarian orientalist who met 'Abdu'l-Bahá on 11 April 1913. He was Professor of Oriental Languages at the University of Budapest and renowned throughout Europe.

Valentin Vaucamps invited 'Abdu'l-Bahá to his *Lumina* studio in Paris on 16 February 1913 to sit for a colour photograph using the latest technology of the time.

Marie Watson wrote an account, *My Pilgrimage to the Land of Desire*, which was published in New York in 1932.

Frances Belford 'Pinky' Wayne was a writer for the *Denver Post* who interviewed 'Abdu'l-Bahá during His visit to Denver in September 1912.

Jane Elizabeth Whyte was the wife of Reverend Alexander Whyte, Moderator of the General Assembly of the Free Church of Scotland in Edinburgh. She visited 'Akká in March 1906. 'Abdu'l-Bahá stayed with her and Reverend Whyte during His visit to Edinburgh in January 1913. She was the recipient of 'Abdu'l-Bahá's famous 'Seven Candles of Unity' Tablet.

Archdeacon Basil Wilberforce (1841–1916) was Rector of St John's Westminster and Chaplain to the House of Commons (1896–1916), and Archdeacon of Westminster (1900–1916).

Roy C. Wilhelm (1875–1951) visited 'Abdu'l-Bahá in 'Akká in 1907 with his mother. He personally received many messages from the Master and was responsible for the receipt and distribution of letters from Him addressed to Bahá'ís throughout North America. He was named posthumously as a Hand of the Cause of God by Shoghi Effendi.

Edwin Woodcock was an American Bahá'í who went on pilgrimage with his wife and mother-in-law in early 1907.

'Alí M.Yazdí (1899–1978) was a noted Bahá'í lecturer and writer who served on many national Bahá'í committees in the United States. His life is commemorated in the book, *Youth in the Vanguard* by his wife, Marion Yazdí. He wrote his memoir about 'Abdu'l-Bahá in 1975 which was published in *The Bahá'í World* Vol. XVIII.

Muhammad Yazdi (c.1850–1933) met Bahá'u'lláh in 'Akká and, with His permission, settled in Alexandria, Egypt. He established a trading company with other Bahá'ís, making Alexandria a stop for all pilgrims to 'Akká. He also opened a store in the prison city.

BIBLIOGRAPHY

'Abdu'l-Bahá. *Paris Talks*. Wilmette, Ill.: Bahá'í Publishing Trust, 2006.

— *The Promulgation of Universal Peace*. Wilmette, Ill.: Bahá'í Publishing Trust, 1982.

— *Selections from the Writings of 'Abdu'l-Bahá*. Haifa: Bahá'í World Centre, 1978.

— *Some Answered Questions*. Haifa: Bahá'í World Centre, 2014.

— *Tablets of 'Abdu'l-Bahá, Vol. 1*. New York: Bahá'í Publishing Committee, 1940.

— *The Will and Testament of 'Abdu'l-Bahá*. Wilmette, Ill.: Bahá'í Publishing Trust, 1944.

'Abdu'l-Bahá in Canada. Toronto: National Spiritual Assembly of the Bahá'ís of Canada, 1962.

'Abdu'l-Bahá in London. London, Bahá'í Publishing Trust, 1982.

Afroukhteh, Youness. *Memories of Nine Years in 'Akká*. Oxford, George Ronald, 2003.

Alfassa, Mirra. *Words of Long Ago*. India: Sri Aurobindo Ashram, 1912.

Allen Brown, Ramona. *Memories of 'Abdu'l-Bahá*. Wilmette, Ill.: Bahá'í Publishing Trust, 1980.

Armstrong-Ingram, R. Jackson. *Written in light – 'Abdu'l-Bahá and the American Bahá'í Community 1898–1921*. Los Angeles: Kalimát Press, 1998.

Bahá'í Prayers. Wilmette, Ill.: Bahá'í Publishing Trust, 2008.

The Bahá'í World Vol. IV 1930–1932. Wilmette, Ill: Bahá'í Publishing Trust, 1980.

The Bahá'í World Vol. VI 1934–1936. Wilmette, Ill: Bahá'í Publishing Trust, 1980.

The Bahá'í World Vol. XI 1946–1950. Wilmette, Ill: Bahá'í Publishing Trust, 1981.

The Bahá'í World Vol. XVIII 1979–1983. Haifa: Bahá'í World Centre, 1986.

Bahá'u'lláh. *Days of Remembrance.* Haifa: Bahá'í World Centre, 2016.

— *The Kitáb-i-Aqdas.* Haifa: Bahá'í World Centre, 1992.

— *Tablets of Bahá'u'lláh.* Haifa: Bahá'í World Centre, 1978.

Bahíyyih Khánum – *The Greatest Holy Leaf.* Haifa: Bahá'í World Centre, 1982.

Balyuzí, H.M. *'Abdu'l-Bahá – The Centre of the Covenant of Bahá'u'lláh.* Oxford: George Ronald, 1971.

— *Bahá'u'lláh, The King of Glory.* Oxford: George Ronald, 1980.

— *Eminent Bahá'ís in the time of Bahá'u'lláh.* Oxford: George Ronald, 1985.

Blomfield, Lady. *The Chosen Highway.* London: Bahá'í Publishing Trust, 1940.

Century of Light. Haifa: Bahá'í World Centre, 2001.

Chase, Thornton. *In Galilee.* Los Angeles, Kalimát Press, 1985.

Cheyne, Thomas Kelly. *The Reconciliation of Races and Religions.* London: Adam and Charles Black, 1914.

Cobb, Stanwood. *Memories of 'Abdu'l-Bahá.* Washington, D.C.: Avalon Press, 1962.

Diliberto Allen, Angelina. *John David Bosch.* Wilmette, Ill.: Bahá'í Publishing, 2019.

Egea, Amin. *The Apostle of Peace* Volume 1: 1871–1912. Oxford: George Ronald, 2017.

— *The Apostle of Peace* Volume 2: 1912–1921. Oxford: George Ronald, 2018.

Esslemont, J.E. *Bahá'u'lláh and the New Era.* Wilmette, Ill.: Bahá'í Publishing Trust, 1980.

Ferraby, John. *All Things Made New.* London: George Allen and Unwin, 1957.

Ford, Mary Hanford. *The Oriental Rose.* New York: Broadway Publishing Company, 1910.

Gail, Marzieh. *Other People Other Places*. Oxford: George Ronald, 1982.
— *The Sheltering Branch*. Oxford: George Ronald, 1959.

Hofman, David. *A Commentary on the Will and Testament of 'Abdu'l-Bahá*. Oxford: George Ronald, 1982.

Hogensen, Kathryn Jewett. *Lighting the Western Sky*. Oxford: George Ronald, 2010.

Holbach, Maud. 'The Bahai Movement; with Some Recollections of Meetings with 'Abdul Baha', *The Nineteenth Century and After*. London, Feb.1915.

Holley, Horace. *Bahá'í – The Spirit of the Age*. New York: Brentano's, 1921.
— *The Modern Social Religion*. London and Toronto: Sidgwick & Jackson, 1913.
— *Religion for Mankind*. Oxford: George Ronald, 1956.

Ives, Howard Colby. *Portals to Freedom*. Oxford: George Ronald, 1976.

Jasion, Jan. *'Abdu'l-Bahá in France 1911 & 1913*. Paris: Éditions bahá'íes France, 2016.
— *Abdu'l-Bahá in the West*. Paris: Éditions bahá'íes France, 2012.

Khan, Janet. *Call to Apostleship – Reflections on the Tablets of the Divine Plan*. Wilmette, Ill.: Bahá'í Publishing, 2016.

Maud, Constance Elizabeth. *Sparks among the Stubble*. London: Philip Allan & Co, 1924.

Maxwell, May. *An Early Pilgrimage*. Oxford: George Ronald, 1969.

Momen, Moojan. *The Bábí and Bahá'í Religions 1844–1944 – Some Contemporary Western Accounts*. Oxford: George Ronald, 1981.

Morten, Marjory. *Glimpses of 'Abdu'l-Bahá*. Pamphlet.

Munírih Khánum – Memoirs and Letters. Los Angeles: Kalimat Press, 1986.

Nakhjavani, Bahiyyih. *Response*. Oxford: George Ronald, 1981.

Nakhjavání, Violette. *The Maxwells of Montreal* Vol.1. Oxford: George Ronald Publisher, 2011.

The Passing of 'Abdu'l-Bahá. Los Angeles: Kalimát Press, 1991.

Phelps, Myron. *Life and Teachings of Abbas Effendi*, New York: G. P. Putnam's Sons, 1903.

— *The Master in 'Akká*. Los Angeles, Kalimát Press, 1985.

Pound, Omar & Spoo, Robert, ed. *Ezra Pound and Margaret Cousins – A Tragic Friendship*. Durham and London: Duke University Press, 1988.

Rabbání, Rúhíyyih. *The Priceless Pearl*. London: Bahá'í Publishing Trust, 1969.

Randall-Winckler, Bahiyyih. *William Henry Randall – Disciple of 'Abdu'l-Bahá*. Oxford: One World, 1996.

Redman, Earl. *'Abdu'l-Bahá in Their Midst*. Oxford: George Ronald, 2011.

— *Visiting 'Abdu'l-Bahá, Vol. 1 – The West Discovers the Master, 1897–1911*. Oxford, George Ronald, 2019.

Ruhe, David S. *Robe of Light: The Persian Years of the Supreme Prophet Bahá'u'lláh 1817–1853*. Oxford: George Ronald, 1994.

Shoghi Effendi. *God Passes By*. Wilmette, Ill.: Bahá'í Publishing Trust, 1944.

— *The Light of Divine Guidance* Vol. 1. Hofhein-Langenhain: Bahá'í-Verlag, 1982.

— *The World Order of Bahá'u'lláh*. Wilmette, Ill.: Bahá'í Publishing Trust, 1938.

Smith, Peter, ed. *Bahá'ís in the West*. Los Angeles, Ca.: Kalimát Press, 2004.

Spicer-Simson, Theodore. *A Collector of Characters: Reminiscences of Theodore Spicer-Simson*. Miami, FL: University of Miami Press, 1962.

Star of the West. Oxford: George Ronald, 1978.

Stevens, Ethel S. 'Abbas Effendi: His Personality, Work and Followers' *Fortnightly Review* Vol. 89, London 1911.

Stockman, Robert H. *'Abdu'l-Bahá in America*. Wilmette, Ill.: Bahá'í Publishing Trust, 2012.

Taherzadeh, Adib. *The Child of the Covenant*. Oxford: George Ronald, 2000.

— *The Covenant of Bahá'u'lláh*. Oxford: George Ronald, 1992.

— *The Revelation of Bahá'u'lláh, Vol. 1 – Baghdád 1853–1863*. Oxford, George Ronald, 1974.

Thompson, Juliet. *The Diary of Juliet Thompson*. Los Angeles, Kalimát Press: 1983.

Townshend, George. *Christ and Bahá'u'lláh*. Oxford: George Ronald, 1957.

— *The Promise of All Ages*. Oxford: George Ronald, 1961.

Tudor Pole, Wellesley. *The Writing on the Ground*. London: Neville Spearman, 1968.

Universal House of Justice. *Messages from the Universal House of Justice 1963–1986*. Wilmette, Ill.: Bahá'í Publishing Trust, 1996.

— *Messages from the Universal House of Justice 1986–2001*. Wilmette, Ill.: Bahá'í Publishing Trust, 2010.

— *Turning Point: Selected Messages of the Universal House of Justice and Supplementary Material 1996–2006*. West Palm Beach, FL.: Palabra Publications, 2006.

— *Framework for Action: Selected Messages of the Universal House of Justice and Supplementary Material 2006–2016*. West Palm Beach, FL.: Palabra Publications, 2017.

Ward, Allan L. *239 Days – 'Abdu'l-Bahá's Journey in America*. Wilmette, Ill.: Bahá'í Publishing Trust, 1979.

Watson, Marie. *My Pilgrimage to the Land of Desire*. New York: Bahá'í Publishing Committee, 1932.

World Order 7:12. Wilmette, Bahá'í Publishing Committee, 1948.

Zarqání, Mírzá Mahmud. *Mahmud's Diary*. Oxford: George Ronald, 1998.

NOTES AND REFERENCES

Introduction
1 Taherzadeh, *The Covenant of Baháʼuʼlláh*, p. 110.
2 Balyuzí, *ʼAbduʼl-Bahá*, p. 51.
3 ibid. p. 494.
4 Gail, *The Sheltering Branch*, pp. 11–12.
5 Shoghi Effendi, *The World Order of Baháʼuʼlláh*, p. 98.
6 ibid.
7 Shoghi Effendi, *Baháʼí Administration*, p. 66.
8 *Selections from the Writings of ʼAbduʼl-Bahá*, p. 78.

Part One: Testimonials

ʼAbduʼl-Bahá in the Words of Baháʼuʼlláh
1 Cited in Shoghi Effendi, *The World Order of Baháʼuʼlláh*, p. 135.
2 ibid.
3 ibid. pp. 135–6.
4 ibid. p. 136.
5 Shoghi Effendi, *God Passes By*, p. 177.
6 Baháʼuʼlláh, *Days of Remembrance*, p. 144.
7 ibid. p. 145.
8 ibid.
9 Baháʼuʼlláh, *Tablets of Baháʼuʼlláh*, pp. 227–8.
10 Baháʼuʼlláh, *The Kitáb-i-Aqdas*, p. 63.
11 ibid. p. 82.
12 Baháʼuʼlláh, *Days of Remembrance*, p. 161.
13 Ḥájí Mírzá Ḥaydar-ʼAlí, cited in Balyuzí, *ʼAbduʼl-Bahá*, pp. 26–7.
14 Baháʼuʼlláh cited in the memoirs of Mírzá Valíyuʼlláh Khán in Balyuzí, *Eminent Baháʼís in the Time of Baháʼuʼlláh*, pp. 81–2.

ʼAbduʼl-Bahá in His own Words
1 Cited in Shoghi Effendi, *The World Order of Baháʼuʼlláh*, p. 139.

2   'Abdu'l-Bahá, *Tablets of 'Abdu'l-Bahá,* p. 20.
3   ibid. pp .658–9
4   'Abdu'l-Bahá, *Paris Talks,* p. 34.
5   Cited in *Maxwell, An Early Pilgrimage,* p. 42.
6   Cited in *Afroukhteh, Memories of Nine Years in 'Akká,* pp. 186–7.
7   Cited in Shoghi Effendi, *The World Order of Bahá'u'lláh,* p.136
8   ibid. p. 138.
9   ibid. p. 133.
10   'Abdu'l-Bahá, *Selections from the Writings of 'Abdu'l-Bahá,* p. 195.
11   ibid. p. 209.
12   'Abdu'l-Bahá, *The Promulgation of Universal Peace,* p.382
13   ibid. p. 323.
14   'Abdu'l-Bahá, *Selections from the Writings of 'Abdu'l-Bahá,* pp. 225–7.
15   ibid. pp. 237–8.
16   ibid. p. 241.
17   ibid. p. 316.
18   ibid. p. 222.
19   'Abdu'l-Bahá, *The Promulgation of Universal Peace,* pp. 3–4.
20   Jasion, *'Abdu'l-Bahá in France, 1911 & 1913,* p. 313.
21   'Abdu'l-Bahá, *The Will and Testament of 'Abdu'l-Bahá,* p. 23.
22   ibid. p. 9.
23   'Abdu'l-Bahá, *The Promulgation of Universal Peace,* p. 225.
24   'Abdu'l-Bahá, *Tablets of 'Abdu'l-Bahá,* p. 715.
25   ibid. p. 216.
26   Attributed to 'Abdu'l-Bahá in Esslemont, *Bahá'u'lláh and the New Era,* p. 52.
27   Cited in Jasion, *'Abdu'l-Bahá in France,* 1911 & 1913, pp. 475–6.
28   *Star of the West,* vol. IV, No. 12, p. 208.

From the writings of Shoghi Effendi
1   Rabbání, *The Priceless Pearl,* p. 96.
2   ibid. p. 95.
3   Shoghi Effendi, *God Passes By,* pp. 239–43.
4   ibid. pp. 279–80.
5   Shoghi Effendi, *The Light of Divine Guidance,* vol.1, p. 65.
6   Shoghi Effendi, *The World Order of Bahá'u'lláh,* pp. 131–4.
7   ibid. pp. 136–9.

From the letters of the Universal House of Justice
1   Riḍván 1987, To the Bahá'ís of the World. *Messages from the Universal House of Justice 1986–2001,* p. 46.
2   Riḍván 1969, To the Bahá'ís of the World. *Messages from the Universal House of Justice 1963–1986,* p. 147.

3 7 June 1992, To the Bahá'ís of the World. *Messages from the Universal House of Justice 1986–2001*, pp. 277–8.

4 26 November 1992, To the Bahá'ís of the World. *Messages from the Universal House of Justice 1986–2001*, p. 311.

5 3 June 1982, To individual believers. *Messages from the Universal House of Justice 1986–2001*, p. 546.

6 29 December 1988, To the Followers of Bahá'u'lláh in the United States of America. *Messages from the Universal House of Justice 1986–2001*, p. 104.

7 21 March 2009, To the Bahá'ís of the World. https://www.bahai. org/library/authoritative-texts/the-universal-house-of-justice/ messages/20090321_001/1#288100650

8 Riḍván 2011, To the Bahá'ís of the World. ibid. pp. 124–5.

9 Riḍván 2012, To the Bahá'ís of the World. ibid. pp. 139–40.

10 5 December 2013, To the Bahá'ís of the World. ibid. p. 182.

11 26 March 2016, To the Bahá'ís of the world acting under the Mandate of 'Abdu'l-Bahá. ibid. pp. 237–8.

12 26 November 2018. To the Bahá'ís of the World. https://www. bahai.org/library/authoritative-texts/the-universal-house-of-justice/ messages/20181126_001/1#203887126

13 Riḍván 2019. To the Bahá'ís of the World. https://www.bahai. org/library/authoritative-texts/the-universal-house-of-justice/ messages/20190420_001/1#744198387

14 25 November 2020, To the Bahá'ís of the World. https://www. bahai.org/library/authoritative-texts/the-universal-house-of-justice/ messages/20201125_001/1#300076430

15 22 July 2020, To the Bahá'ís of the United States. https://www. bahai.org/library/authoritative-texts/the-universal-house-of-justice/ messages/20200722_001/1#870410250

From the letters of the Greatest Holy Leaf

1 Shoghi Effendi, *Bahá'í Administration*, p. 189.

2 *Bahíyyih Khánum – The Greatest Holy Leaf*, p. 130.

3 ibid. pp. 142–3.

4 ibid. pp. 145–7.

5 ibid. pp. 175–7.

Part Two: 'Abdu'l-Bahá in the Time of Bahá'u'lláh (1844–1892)

1 Taherzadeh, *The Covenant of Bahá'u'lláh*, p. 110.

2 Ruhe, *Robe of Light*, pp. 57–8.

3 Townshend, 'The Way of the Master', *The Bahá'í World*, vol. IV, p. 341.

4 Bahíyyih Khánum, cited in Phelps, *The Master in 'Akká*, p. 17.

5   Munírih Khánum, cited in Blomfield, *The Chosen Highway*, p. 80.
6   ibid. pp. 80–1.
7   Balyuzí, *'Abdu'l-Bahá*, p. 14.
8   Bahíyyih Khánum, cited in Phelps, *The Master in 'Akká*, p. 25.
9   ibid. p. 29.
10   Munírih Khánum, cited in Blomfield, *The Chosen Highway*, p. 81.
11   ibid. pp. 82–3.
12   Balyuzí, *'Abdu'l-Baha*, p. 13.
13   Balyuzí *Bahá'u'lláh, The King of Glory*, p. 179.
14   Bahíyyih Khánum, cited in Phelps, *The Master in 'Akká*, pp. 39–41.
15   ibid. p. 50.
16   ibid. p. 64.
17   Cheyne, *The Reconciliation of Races and Religions*, p. 152.
18   Balyuzí, *'Abdu'l-Bahá*, p. 21.
19   Esslemont, *Bahá'u'lláh and the New Era*, p. 53.
20   Túbá Khánum, cited in Blomfield, *The Chosen Highway*, p. 95.
21   ibid. p. 99.
22   ibid. p. 100–3.
23   *Mirzá Mahmúd-i-Káshání*, cited in Taherzadeh, *The Covenant of Bahá'u'llah*, p. 139.
24   *Hájí Mírzá Habíbu'lláh-i-Afnán* cited in ibid. pp. 139–40.
25   Túbá Khánum, cited in Blomfield, *The Chosen Highway*, p. 97.
26   Dr. Thomas Chaplin, cited in Momen, *The Bábí and Bahá'í Religions – Some Contemporary Western Accounts*, p. 211.
27   Rev. James Neil, cited in ibid. p. 213.
28   Prof. Edward G. Browne, cited in ibid. p. 228.

Part Three: The Ministry of 'Abdu'l-Bahá (1892–1921)
1   Hogensen, *Lighting the Western Sky*, p. 98.
2   ibid. p. 97.
3   ibid. p. 99.
4   ibid. pp. 97–8.
5   Redman, *Visiting 'Abdu'l-Bahá*, p. 28.
6   *Lighting the Western Sky*, p. 99.
7   *Visiting 'Abdu'l-Bahá*, p. 39.
8   ibid. p. 24.
9   ibid. p. 26.
10   ibid. pp. 44–5.
11   ibid. pp. 55–6.
12   ibid. p. 60.
13   ibid. p. 145.
14   ibid. pp. 149–50.
15   ibid. p. 170.

16 'Abdu'l-Bahá, *Some Answered Questions*, p. xix.
17 Balyuzí, *'Abdu'l-Bahá*, p. 83.
18 Holley, *The Modern Social Religion*, pp. 171–2.
19 Momen, *The Bábí and Bahá'í Religions 1844–1944 – Some Contemporary Western Accounts*, p. 320.
20 Stevens, *Fotrnightly Review*, pp. 1070–8.
21 Phelps, *Life and Teachings of Abbas Effendi*, pp. 2–10.
22 Redman, *'Abdu'l-Bahá in their Midst*, p. 291.
23 Cheyne, *The Reconciliation of Races and Religions*, p. 164.
24 Holley, *The Modern Social Religion*, p. 178.
25 Egea, *The Apostle of Peace, Volume 1: 1871–1912*, p. 60.
26 *Bahá'í News*, in *Star of the West*, vol. 1 No.14, p. 2.
27 *Bahá'í News*, in *Star of the West*, vol.1 No.19, pp. 4–5.
28 *Bahá'í News*, in *Star of the West*, vol. 1 No.17, pp. 4.
29 ibid. p. 7.
30 Egea, *The Apostle of Peace, Volume 1: 1871–1912*, pp. 78–79.
31 *Star of the West*, Vol. 2 No.10, pp. 5–6.
32 Yazdí, 'Prophet Days: Memories of 'Abdu'l-Bahá' in *The Bahá'í World*, vol. XVIII, 1979–1983, pp. 908–9.
33 Momen, *The Bábí and Bahá'í Religions 1844–1944 – Some Contemporary Western Accounts*, pp. 339–40.
34 Thompson, *The Diary of Juliet Thompson*, p. 159.
35 Thompson, 'With Abdul-Baha in Switzerland', in *Star of the West*, Vol 2 No.14, pp. 9–12.
36 Holley, *Religion for Mankind*, pp. 232–7.
37 Townshend, *Christ and Bahá'u'lláh*, p. 95.
38 Blomfield, *The Chosen Highway*, pp. 149–51.
39 Maud, *Sparks among the Stubble*, p. 83.
40 ibid. p. 86.
41 ibid. pp. 87–8.
42 Momen, *The Bábí and Bahá'í Religions 1844–1944 – Some Contemporary Western Accounts*, p. 325.
43 ibid. p. 326.
44 Tudor Pole, *The Writing on the Ground*, p. 146.
45 Egea, *The Apostle of Peace, Volume 1: 1871–1912*, pp. 101–2.
46 ibid. p. 115.
47 *'Abdu'l-Bahá in London*, pp. 89–90.
48 Egea, *The Apostle of Peace, Volume 1: 1871–1912*, pp. 153–4.
49 ibid. p. 157.
50 Pound and Spoo, ed. *Ezra Pound and Margaret Cravens – A Tragic Friendship 1910–1912*, p. 90.
51 ibid. p. 95.
52 Egea, *The Apostle of Peace, Volume 2: 1912–1921*, p. 86.

53 ibid. pp. 87–8.
54 Blomfield, *The Chosen Highway*, p. 174.
55 *'Abdu'l-Bahá in London*, p. 34.
56 Egea, *The Apostle of Peace, Volume 1: 1871–1912*, pp. 173–4.
57 Jasion, *'Abdu'l-Bahá in France 1911 & 1913*, p. 69.
58 Egea, *The Apostle of Peace, Volume 1: 1871–1912*, p. 165.
59 ibid. p. 162.
60 ibid. p. 164.
61 Jasion, *'Abdu'l-Bahá in France 1911 & 1913*, pp. 160–1.
62 ibid. pp. 179–80.
63 Blomfield, *The Bahá'í World*, vol. VI, pp. 654–8.
64 Redman, *'Abdu'l-Bahá in Their Midst*, pp. 3–4.
65 Allen Brown, *Memories of 'Abdu'l-Bahá*, pp. 39–40.
66 ibid. p.37
67 Stockman, *'Abdu'l-Bahá in America*, pp. 13–14.
68 *The Bahá'í World*, vol.VI, p. 466.
69 Cobb, *Memories of 'Abdu'l-Bahá*, pp. 11–13.
70 ibid. pp. 14.
71 ibid. pp.19–21.
72 Ives, *Portals to Freedom*, pp. 28–9.
73 ibid. p. 253.
74 Thompson, *The Diary of Juliet Thompson*, pp. 234–5.
75 Zarqání, *Mahmud's Diary*, p. 224.
76 Egea, *The Apostle of Peace, Volume 1: 1871–1912*, pp. 221–2.
77 ibid. p. 237.
78 Ward, *239 Days*, pp. 19–20.
79 Egea, *The Apostle of Peace, Volume 2: 1912–1921*, p. 445.
80 Egea, *The Apostle of Peace, Volume 1: 1871–1912*, pp. 296–7.
81 ibid. p. 478.
82 ibid. p. 485.
83 ibid. pp. 225–31.
84 *'Abdu'l-Bahá in Canada*, p. 46.
85 Ward, *239 Days*, p. 136.
86 *Abdu'l-Bahá in Canada*, pp. 52–3.
87 Nakhjavání, *The Maxwells of Montreal* Vol.1, p. 281.
88 *'Abdu'l-Bahá in Canada* p. 57.
89 Egea, *The Apostle of Peace, Volume 1: 1871–1912*, p. 566.
90 *Star of the West*, vol. XI, no. 3, pp. 47–55.
91 Balyuzí, *'Abdul-Bahá*, p. 231.
92 Thompson, 'Abdu'l-Bahá – 'The Centre of the Covenant' in *World Order* 7:12: https://bahai-library.com/thompson_abdul-baha_center_covenant
93 Egea, *The Apostle of Peace, Volume 2: 1912–1921*, p. 371.

94 Egea, *The Apostle of Peace, Volume 2: 1912–1921*, p. 5.
95 ibid. p. 24.
96 Redman, *'Abdu'l-Bahá in their Midst*, p. 285.
97 ibid. pp. 287–9.
98 ibid. p. 296.
99 Balyuzí, *'Abdu'l-Bahá*, p. 365.
100 ibid. p. 367.
101 Redman, *'Abdu'l-Bahá in their Midst*, pp. 293–4.
102 Egea, *The Apostle of Peace, Volume 2: 1912–1921*, p. 100.
103 Cheyne, *The Reconciliation of Races and Religions*, pp. 159–60.
104 Tudor Pole, *The Writing on the Ground*, p. 142.
105 ibid. p. 144.
106 Jasion, *'Abdu'l-Bahá in France 1911 & 1913*, pp. 289–90.
107 ibid. p. 666.
108 ibid. pp. 375–6.
109 Egea, *The Apostle of Peace, Volume 2: 1912–1921*, pp. 126–7.
110 Jasion, *'Abdu'l-Bahá in France 1911 & 1913*, p. 660.
111 Holbach, 'The Bahai Movment: With Some Recollections of Meetings with Abdul Baha', *The Nineteenth Century and After*, pp. 452–66.
112 *Star of the West*, vol. IV, no.9, p. 156.
113 Momen, *The Bábí and Bahá'í Religions – Some Contemporary Western Accounts*, p. 331.
114 Lederer, "Abdu'l-Bahá in Budapest' in Smith, *Bahá'ís in the West*, p. 118.
115 *The Apostle of Peace, Volume 2: 1912–1921*, pp. 133–4.
116 ibid. p. 140.
117 Egea, *The Apostle of Peace, Volume 2: 1912–1921*, p.380
118 Townshend, 'The Way of the Master', *The Bahá'í World* Vol.IV, p.341
119 Egea, *The Apostle of Peace, Volume 2: 1912–1921*, pp. 390–4.
120 ibid. pp. 409–10.
121 *Century of Light*, pp.35–36
122 Khan, *Call to Apostleship*, p. 51.
123 ibid. p. 52.
124 Tudor Pole, *The Writing on the Ground*, pp. 154–5.
125 Egea, *The Apostle of Peace, Volume 2: 1912–1921*, pp. 436.
126 Momen, *The Bábí and Bahá'í Religions – Some Contemporary Western Accounts*, p. 341.
127 ibid. p. 340.
128 Cited in Balyuzí, *'Abdu'l-Bahá*, p. 8.
129 Momen, *The Bábí and Bahá'í Religions – Some Contemporary Western Accounts*, p. 340.
130 Esslemont, *Bahá'u'lláh and the New Era*, pp. 64–5.

131 Watson, *My Pilgrimage to the Land of Desire*, pp. 4–5.
132 Maud, *Sparks among the Stubble*, p. 111.

Part Four: The Passing of 'Abdu'l-Bahá

1   Shoghi Effendi, *God Passes By*, pp. 312.
2   *The Passing of 'Abdu'l-Bahá*, p. 12.
3   *Bahíyyih Khánum – The Greatest Holy Leaf*, pp. 120–1.
4   *Munírih Khánum – Memoirs and Letters*, p. 60.
5   ibid. p. 64.
6   Balyuzí, *'Abdu'l-Bahá*, p. 463.
7   *The Passing of 'Abdu'l-Bahá*, pp. 63–4.
8   Balyuzí, *'Abdu'l-Bahá*, pp. 479–80.
9   *The Passing of 'Abdu'l-Bahá*, pp. 64–6.
10 Diliberto Allen, *John Bosch*, p. 158.
11 *The Passing of 'Abdu'l-Bahá*, pp. 17–19.
12 ibid. pp. 19–21.
13 ibid. pp. 21–3.
14 *Star of the West*, vol. 12, no.17, pp. 262–3.
15 ibid. pp. 263–4.
16 ibid. p. 264.
17 *The Passing of 'Abdu'l-Bahá*, pp. 28–9.
18 *Star of the West*, vol. 13, no.2, p. 41–2.
19 ibid. p. 44.
20 *The Passing of 'Abdu'l-Bahá*, p. 31.
21 ibid. p. 32.
22 ibid.
23 Momen, *The Bábí and Bahá'í Religions – Some Contemporary Western Accounts*, p. 349.
24 *Star of the West*, vol. 12, no. 17, p. 260.
25 Shoghi Effendi, *The World Order of Bahá'u'lláh*, p. 89.
26 Shoghi Effendi, *God Passes By*, pp. 325–6.
27 Shoghi Effendi, *The World Order of Bahá'u'lláh*, p. 89.
28 *Bahíyyih Khánum – The Greatest Holy Leaf*, p. 210.
29 ibid. p. 143.
30 ibid. p. 141.
31 ibid. pp. 177–8.
32 Taherzadeh, *The Child of the Covenant*, pp. 6–7.
33 Hofman, *A Commentary on the Will and Testament of 'Abdu'l-Bahá*, p. 2.
34 ibid. p. 3.
35 Townshend, *Christ and Bahá'u'lláh*, p. 99.
36 Ferraby, *All Things Made New*, p. 267.
37 Balyuzí, *'Abdu'l-Bahá*, p. 492.

38 Holley, *Religion for Mankind*, pp. 238–9.
39 *The Bahá'í World*, vol.6, p. 452.
40 Balyuzí, *'Abdu'l-Bahá*, pp. 3–4.
41 Ferraby, *All Things Made New*, p. 224.
42 Cited in Holley, *The Modern Social Religion*, p. 170.
43 Holley, *Bahá'í – Spirit of the Age*, p. 45.
44 ibid. p. 46.
45 ibid. pp. 70–1.
46 Holley, *Religion for Mankind*, pp. 228–9.
47 Gail, *The Sheltering Branch*, p. 23.
48 Egea, *The Apostle of Peace, Volume 1: 1871–1912*, p. 31.
49 Esslemont, *Bahá'u'lláh and the New Era*, p. 79.
50 Chase, *In Galilee*, pp. 28–55.
51 Ford, *The Oriental Rose*, pp. 158–9.
52 Morten, *Glimpses of 'Abdu'l-Baha*, pp. 11–12.
53 Cobb, *Memories of 'Abdu'l-Bahá*, pp. 8–9.
54 Townshend, *Christ and Bahá'u'lláh*, p. 96.
55 Towshend, 'The Way of the Master' in *The Bahá'í World*, vol. IV, pp. 337–9.
56 Taherzadeh, *The Covenant of Bahá'u'lláh*, p. 102–3.
57 Nakhjavani, *Response*, p. 29.
58 Holley, *Religion for Mankind*, pp. 243–5.
59 Noguchi, in *The Bahá'í World*, vol. 11, p. 457.
60 Yazdí, 'Prophet Days: Memories of 'Abdu'l-Bahá', *The Bahá'í World*, vol. XVIII, 1979–1983, pp. 910–11.

9 780853 9864